TRANSNATIONAL BUSINESS AND CORPORATE CULTURE

PROBLEMS AND OPPORTUNITIES

edited by

STUART BRUCHEY
ALLAN NEVINS PROFESSOR EMERITUS
COLUMBIA UNIVERSITY

A GARLAND SERIES

C.7.   Head of Household's Migration Decision by
       Individual's Gender   199
C.8.   Head of Household's Migration Decision by U.S.
       Immigration Status   200
C.9.   Head of Household's Migration Decision by U.S.
       Citizenship Status   201
C.10. Head of Household's Migration Decision by Presence
       of Minor-Age Children   202
C.11. Migration Decision of Male Household Heads by
       Presence of Minor-Age Children   203
C.12. Migration Decision of Female Household Heads by
       Presence of Minor-Age Children   204
C.13. Migration Decision of Single Parents and All Other
       Household Heads   205
C.14. Migration Decision of Single Mothers and All Other
       Female Household Heads   206
C.15. Migration Decision of Single Fathers and All Other
       Male Household Heads   207
C.16. Friends and Family in U.S. at Time of Interview by
       Head of Household's Most Recent U.S. Experience   208
C.17. Friends and Family in U.S. at Time of Interview by
       Head of Household's Most Recent U.S. Experience
       (Males Only)   213
C.18. Friends and Family in U.S. at Time of Interview by
       Head of Household's Most Recent U.S. Experience
       (Females Only)   218
D.1.   Standardized Parameter Estimates from Participation
       Models with Four Macroeconomic Variables   226
D.2.   Standardized Parameter Estimates from Participation
       Models with Three Macroeconomic Variables   228
G.1.   Results from First Stage of Two-Stage Least-Squares
       Earnings Regressions   244

FIGURES

6.1.   Distribution of Mexican Spells   105
6.2.   Distribution of U.S. Spells   106

MEXICAN MIGRATION TO THE UNITED STATES

THE ROLE OF MIGRATION NETWORKS AND HUMAN CAPITAL ACCUMULATION

STEVEN S. ZAHNISER

GARLAND PUBLISHING, Inc.
A MEMBER OF THE TAYLOR & FRANCIS GROUP
NEW YORK & LONDON / 1999

Library of Congress Cataloging-in-Publication Data

Zahniser, Steven.
  Mexican migration to the United States : the role of migra-
tion networks and human capital accumulation / Steven S.
Zahniser.
      p.   cm. — (Transnational business and corporate cul-
ture)
  Includes bibliographical references and index.
  ISBN 0-8153-3199-1 (alk. paper)
  1. Alien labor, Mexian—United States. 2. Immigrants—
Social networks—United States. 3. Mexicans—Social networks—
United States. 4. Mexico—Emigration and immigration.
5. United States—Emigration and immigration. I. Title. II. Series.
HD8081.M6Z34 1998
331.6'272073—dc21

JK   98-45164

Printed on acid-free, 250-year-life paper
Manufactured in the United States of America

This book is dedicated to:
my parents Robert and Edith Zahniser,
my brother David,
my partner Rose Ann M. Rentería
(who still keeps the plastic bucket at our home),
the people of San Ramon, Colima,
and my friend Roberto Luna Zamora,
who grooved to *banda*.

Contents

Tables and Figures   ix
Acknowledgments   xiii

1. Introduction   3
2. Research Issues and Literature Review   9
3. Survey Methodology   21
4. Data Profile   35
5. A Basic Participation Model   71
6. The Duration of Migration Spells   101
7. The Rewards to U.S. Experience in the Mexican Labor
   Market   125
8. Conclusion   149

Appendix
A. Survey Instrument of the Mexican Migration Project   157
B. Supplement to the Basic Questionnaire   175
C. Supplemental Tables to Chapter 4   191
D. Supplemental Tables to Chapter 5   225
E. Variables Used in Chapters 4–6 and Their Sources   233
F. Variables Used in Chapter 7 and Their Sources   239
G. Supplemental Table to Chapter 7   243

Bibliography   247
Index   251

Tables and Figures

TABLES

3.1.	Outcomes of Contacting Addresses in Sample	23
3.2.	Persons in Mexico Who Declined to be Interviewed	25
3.3.	Interviews and Refusals by Interviewer	26
3.4.	Persons in U.S. Who Declined to be Interviewed	31
4.1.	Overview of Mexican Survey Communities	37
4.2.	Migration Experience of Head of Household's Immediate Relatives	44
4.3.	Friends and Family in U.S. at Time of Interview by Head of Household's Gender	47
4.4.	Head of Household's Migration Decision by U.S. Experience of Immediate Family	52
4.5.	Head of Household's Migration Decision by U.S. Experience of Individual's Father	55
4.6.	Head of Household's Migration Decision by U.S. Experience of Individual's Mother	57
4.7.	Head of Household's Migration Decision by U.S. Experience of Individual's Siblings	59
4.8.	Head of Household's Migration Decision by U.S. Experience of Individual's Grandparents	61
4.9.	Friends and Family in U.S. at Time of Interview by Head of Household's Most Recent U.S. Experience	63
5.1.	Hypothesized Net Effects of Explanatory Variables on Head of Household's Migration Decision	76
5.2.	Results from Participation Models With Four Macroeconomic Variables	85

ix

5.3.	Results from Participation Models With Three Macroeconomic Variables	88
5.4.	Net Effects of Family Migration Experience on Repeat and First Migration	95
6.1.	Three Survival Distributions	107
6.2.	Hypothesized Signs of Parameter Estimates in Duration Models	109
6.3.	Results From Duration Models Using General Network Variables	114
6.4.	Results From Duration Models Using Relative-Specific Network Variables	118
6.5.	Net Effects of Family Migration Experience on Mexican Spells of Residence	120
7.1.	Hypothesized Net Effects of Explanatory Variables on Interview Location	128
7.2.	Hypothesized Net Effects of Explanatory Variables on Mexican Earnings	130
7.3.	Results from Probit Models Used to Generate Inverse Mills Ratios	133
7.4.	Results from Earnings Regressions for Both Genders	136
7.5.	Results from Earnings Regressions for Males Only	142
7.6.	Results from Earnings Regressions Using Two-Stage Least Squares	146
8.1.	Estimates and Projections of Mexico's Population, Median Age, and Population Growth (1950-2025)	152
8.2.	Legal Immigration to United States of Persons Born in Mexico (Fiscal Years 1981-96)	154
C.1.	U.S. Immigration Status of Head of Household	192
C.2.	Interview Location by Head of Household's U.S. Immigration Status	193
C.3.	Presence of Minor-Age Children in Household by Head of Household's Gender	194
C.4.	Number of Single-Parent Households by Head of Household's Gender	195
C.5.	Sample Statistics for LIFE26	196
C.6.	Head of Household's Most Recent Migration Experience by Individual's Gender	198

Acknowledgments

I would like to thank the many people who made this book possible. Funding came from a variety of sources, most of which have their origins in private donations. At the University of Colorado at Boulder, these sources include the Department of Economics' Campbell Dissertation Fellowship, a research grant from the Ibero-Latin American Studies Center, and from the Graduate School, a Dean's Small Grant, as well as a second grant for dissertation expenses. A postdoctoral fellowship from the Social Science Research Council's International Migration Program, funded by a grant from the Andrew W. Mellon Foundation, supported research during the 1996-97 academic year. The Mexican Migration Project also provided financial assistance, as well as access to its tremendous store of data. Finally, I would like to acknowledge the federal government's work-study and subsidized loan programs, which greatly facilitated my college education.

At the Mexican Migration Project, I would like to thank Professor Douglas Massey of the University of Pennsylvania and Professor Jorge Durand of the University of Guadalajara for allowing me to conduct my fieldwork in conjunction with their project and to utilize the project's data. Professor Massey also answered numerous questions by telephone and electronic mail as I wrote this book. I am especially indebted to four members of the project's staff. Victor Espinosa accompanied me to Mexico at the start of my fieldwork and provided me with indispensable training and advice. Kristin Espinosa sent numerous computer files and other resources to me, answered questions about the data's idiosyncrasies, and acted as an intermediary between the project and me. Following Kristin's graduation, Nolan Malone and Emilio Parrado capably assumed these responsibilities.

During my fieldwork in Mexico, I benefited from the capable assistance and companionship of Percy Ríos Alvarez, Aurora Monterrubio, and Teresa Monterrubio. Professor Durand arranged for Percy to join me in my fieldwork, and Guadalupe Castillo Tapia placed me in contact with the Monterrubio sisters. Luis Plascencia of the Tomás Rivera Center in Austin, Texas answered a pressing immigration question that someone in San Ramon asked. I also would like to thank Percy's family, as well as Ruben and Avelia Martín, for allowing me to stay overnight at their homes in Guadalajara. Similarly, I thank Jesús Sánchez for allowing me to stay at his home during my fieldwork in greater Los Angeles. Also, I would like to acknowledge two persons who must remain anonymous who allowed me to test the survey instrument on them.

During my fieldwork, I stayed at a hotel (which unfortunately must remain nameless) where I had the good fortune to meet Roberto Luna Zamora, the hotel's proprietor, his assistant, Arnoldo "No-No" Ochoa Barbosa, and Jovita, the hotel receptionist. Roberto, "No-No," and Jovita made me feel quite at ease and provided me with additional insights regarding San Ramon's history and its daily life. Roberto died suddenly in the spring of 1996, and I sorely miss his friendship. Also, the municipal government of San Ramon provided me with detailed street maps of the community, which greatly facilitated my work.

I especially would like to thank my dissertation committee, Professors Michael Greenwood, Donald Waldman, Philip Graves, Robert McNown, and Rick Rogers. As chair of my committee, Professor Greenwood swiftly worked through successive drafts of my dissertation. In one instance, he even returned a chapter before I had sat down again at my desk. Professor Greenwood initially suggested the idea of working with Professor Massey, and I am grateful for his mentorship over the past seven years. Professor Waldman provided programming assistance and suggested several different econometric approaches to my dissertation. Professors Graves, McNown, and Rogers scrutinized the final draft of my dissertation and raised critical issues about how to improve it. Outside of the committee, Professor Bárbara Robles offered feedback and provided research materials during the early stages of my project, and Professor Anna Alberini lent me several useful books.

In Colorado, I counted heavily on the friendship and support of my fellow graduate students. Hilda Guerrero proofread my supplement to the survey instrument, and Mahmood Hussain and Paul Davies provided clutch econometric advice in the days leading to my dissertation defense. After I moved from Colorado, Mahmood also re-ran several computer programs on my behalf. Raúl Barreto, Brinda Muhuhlingham, Martin Ross, Charles Rossman, Jill Van Stone, and Paul Young shared course materials and worked as study partners in advance of preliminary and comprehensive exams. This support proved crucial in my reaching the dissertation phase of my Ph.D. program.

At the University of Colorado, I benefited from the helpful computer advice of Alex Pearson, Heidi Dudek, and Susan Parker of Computer and Network Services and the work of the Norlin Library's Interlibrary Loan. Since leaving the university, I have been fortunate to have access to the computing facilities of other institutions. At the University of California at Berkeley, I am indebted to Professor Ronald Lee and Carl Mason of the Department of Demography, who provided me with a statistical computing account. At Mills College, I thank Carol Lennox, director of information technology services, and her assistant Jean Weishan for allowing me to use the school's computing facilities.

I would like to thank my parents Robert and Edith Zahniser, my brother David, and my partner Rose Ann M. Rentería for their inspiration and unswerving moral support. I am eternally grateful for Rose Ann's love and companionship, and I apologize for the excessive number of evenings spent at the computer.

Finally, I would like to express my enormous gratitude to the people of San Ramon, Colima, who graciously welcomed my fellow interviewers and me into their homes and took the time to speak with us. This work has taught me that the people of San Ramon are in many places, and I look forward to the next time that our paths cross.

Mexican Migration to the United States

CHAPTER 1

Introduction

1.1. OVERVIEW

This book evaluates the influence of migration networks and human capital accumulation on Mexican migration to the United States. Because these two factors directly affect the costs and benefits of migration, they have a tremendous impact on Mexican migration. They shape its composition, determine its size, and regulate its pace. Over the last several decades, researchers have become increasingly aware of the importance to migration of migration networks and human capital accumulation. In the United States, however, these topics are often neglected during political discourse about migration, in favor of "hot-button" issues such as the permeability of U.S. borders, immigrants' use of social services, and the competition for jobs between native- and foreign-born residents.

A migration network may be broadly defined as any socioeconomic linkage that facilitates migration between the origin and contemplated destination of a prospective migrant. Examples include:

- families with long histories of migrating between Mexico and the United States;

- migrants who help one another because they are from the same part of Mexico, even if they are strangers;

- the formation in the United States of "daughter communities," which consist of persons from the same community in Mexico; and

- individuals known as *coyotes* or *polleros* who receive money in exchange for assisting migrants to enter the United States illegally.

This definition is sufficiently loose to encompass some phenomena that are not generally thought of as migration networks, such as international money orders and electronic money transfers. However, most researchers of migration networks focus on how family and friends in the United States make migration a more attractive economic alternative, often as part of a cumulative process, and how individuals, families, and communities acquire and share migration experience. This book follows that tradition.

A number of social scientists, primarily in the fields of sociology and anthropology, have convincingly documented the existence of migration networks and completed several detailed case studies. However, the number of persons who study such networks from an economic perspective, including both economists and non-economists, is relatively small. Given the intrinsic appeal of the subject and the persistent concern of U.S. policymakers regarding illegal immigration, the topic of migration networks is still ripe for empirical research.

Human capital refers to the productive skills and abilities that people acquire during the course of their lives. These skills are learned and improved upon in a variety of settings, including the home, educational institutions, and the workplace. Since people take their human capital with them when they move from one place to another, its acquisition is extremely relevant to international migration.

Much of the existing research on human capital and migration centers on two issues. The first issue is the extent to which Mexico and other developing countries experience "brain drain" as talented citizens immigrate to countries where their work is more handsomely rewarded. The second concerns whether the earnings of foreign-born workers in the United States eventually converge on those of native-born workers with similar characteristics.

This book explores a somewhat different dimension of migration and human capital accumulation. Instead of studying the returns to human capital in the U.S. labor market, I examine the returns to U.S. migration experience (and hence human capital accumulated by migrants) in the Mexican labor market. Specifically, I compare the

Mexican earnings of migrants who have returned to Mexico to the earnings of persons who have never migrated.

1.2. THE MEXICAN MIGRATION PROJECT

The empirical foundation of this book is a unique data set that describes the migration and labor-market experiences of over 5,000 Mexicans, including both migrants and non-migrants. This data set was created by the Mexican Migration Project—an extensive, on-going survey of communities throughout western and central Mexico. Professor Jorge Durand of the University of Guadalajara and Professor Douglas Massey of the University of Pennsylvania are the project's co-directors.

I first became aware of the Mexican Migration Project in the fall of 1993, when I was a graduate student in economics at the University of Colorado at Boulder. Because of my strong interest in conducting research in Mexico, my dissertation advisor, Professor Michael Greenwood, suggested that I contact Professor Massey. Noting that the Mexican Migration Project adds one or more communities to its sample nearly every year, I asked Professor Massey if I could "piggyback" my dissertation work on top of the project. We quickly came to an agreement. In exchange for adding a new community to the sample, I could do fieldwork under the aegis of his project and utilize its data from 30 previously surveyed communities.

In December 1994 and January 1995, I traveled to San Ramon, Colima, to conduct my fieldwork.[1] San Ramon is a small town of some 7,000 inhabitants. By bus, it is some 30 minutes from Colima's state capital, also named Colima, and about two-and-a-half hours south of Guadalajara, Jalisco.

San Ramon was selected as the site of my fieldwork for several reasons. When I first approached Professor Massey, the Mexican Migration Project had not yet surveyed a community in the state of Colima. Moreover, he thought that it would be better for me to conduct my research in a small town than in a rural village, even though I had some interest in studying a farming community. Professor Massey was especially concerned about my ability to secure the trust of prospective respondents, since some might be suspicious of a researcher from the United States. In addition, I had never done survey research in Mexico, and I had only six weeks to devote to my fieldwork there before having to return to school in Colorado.

The selection of San Ramon turned out to be fortunate, as the community possesses a diverse economic base. San Ramon is a retail center for agricultural producers in the surrounding area. Some of the town's residents cultivate their own farmland, and others are employed as farm workers. A branch campus of a local college borders one side of San Ramon's central plaza. The town is also the seat of its municipality's government. Finally, because of its proximity to the state capital, San Ramon serves as an affordable bedroom community for some commuters to Colima. These varied attributes ensured that no two interviews in San Ramon were quite alike and helped make my fieldwork a rewarding experience.

With the help of three assistants, I completed 200 interviews in San Ramon. During the following summer, another interviewer and I conducted 20 more interviews in the United States with persons originally from San Ramon. These latter interviews took place in the metropolitan areas of Los Angeles, California, and Las Vegas, Nevada.

To ensure the confidentiality of the respondents, the original questionnaires from the interviews were deposited at the University of Guadalajara, where the staff of the Mexican Migration Project recorded the data in several computer files. At the insistence of one of the project's sponsors, the original questionnaires were recently destroyed as an additional safeguard of the respondents' privacy.

In the spring of 1995, I began my preliminary analysis of the data collected from the 30 previously surveyed communities. The information collected during my fieldwork was added to the computer files during the course of 1995. In early 1996, I proceeded to work on the final analysis for my dissertation. Additional data work for this book was performed in 1997 and 1998.

1.3. ECONOMETRIC ANALYSIS

The central part of this book contains three sets of econometric models that intensively use data from the Mexican Migration Project. Each set explores a different question regarding migration networks and human capital accumulation. The three questions are:

1. Who participates in Mexican migration to the United States?

2. What determines the length of time that an individual resides on one side of the U.S.-Mexican border before moving to the other?

3. How much is U.S. migration experience worth in the Mexican labor market?

All three sets of econometric models focus on the head of household, and a full range of this individual's characteristics are taken into account.

The question of who participates in Mexican migration to the United States is one of continuing interest to researchers, and a substantial body of work already has been done on the subject. The existing evidence indicates that Mexicans who have access to a migration network are far more likely to participate in international migration. To re-examine this issue, I use a series of logit models to gauge the influence of migration networks and other factors on the migration decision. The results from these models are compared to previous research and provide a benchmark for the book's other econometric models.

Migration networks may also affect how long the household head lives on one side of the border before moving to the other. If networks actually encourage participation in migration, then they should also shorten the time that a person lives in Mexico before migrating to the United States, either as a first-time migrant or as a repeat migrant. However, the direction in which networks influence how much time a migrant spends in the United States before returning to Mexico is not immediately apparent. Networks may encourage longer spells of U.S. residence or repeated shorter ones, or they may have no appreciable effect whatsoever.

A group of two-state duration models addresses the second question outlined above. The two states in the models correspond to residence in the United States and residence in Mexico. While logit models and other limited dependent variable models constitute an established approach to the study of the migration decision, the application of duration models to migration is relatively new. My duration models thus generate fresh empirical results and provide an opportunity to think critically about the methodology of such models.

In the third group of models, the logarithm of the household head's monthly earnings in Mexico is regressed on a vector of explanatory variables that include total U.S. migration experience. The main purpose of these models is to determine the return to such experience in the Mexican labor market. Since the potential Mexican earnings of migrants still in the United States may differ from the actual earnings of comparable persons in Mexico, the earnings regressions include a correction for possible selection bias.

1.4. ORGANIZATION OF THE BOOK

The book is organized as follows. Chapter 2 reviews some of the existing literature on migration networks, considers the meaning of migration networks within an economic context, and discusses several issues regarding their measurement. Chapter 3 describes the survey methodology of my fieldwork and provides a brief account of my experiences in San Ramon and in the Los Angeles and Las Vegas areas. Chapter 4 profiles the data used in the econometric models, emphasizing the relation of migration networks to other factors central to the migration decision. Chapters 5, 6, and 7 contain respectively the logit, duration, and earnings models identified above. Finally, Chapter 8 summarizes the book's important findings and discusses their implications for U.S. policymakers.

NOTES

1. To ensure the safety and privacy of the respondents, the pseudonym "San Ramon" is used in place of the town's true name.

CHAPTER 2
Research Issues and Literature Review

2.1. INTRODUCTION

This chapter reviews some of the previous research about migration networks and considers several issues related to their study.[1] The chapter is organized as follows. Section 2.2 outlines the economic functions served by migration networks and how they may influence the decision making of Mexican households. Section 2.3 examines some of the existing literature about migration networks. An emphasis is placed on econometric studies that estimate the effects of networks on migration decisions. Section 2.4 contemplates some methodological issues related to the study of migration networks. This section is distinct from Chapter 3, which describes the survey methodology of my fieldwork, in that it focuses on general research themes rather than the details of survey research. Finally, Section 2.5 identifies several topics regarding migration networks that warrant further study.

2.2. THE ECONOMIC FUNCTIONS OF MIGRATION NETWORKS

In Chapter 1, a migration network was defined to be any socioeconomic link between the origin and destination of a prospective migrant that facilitates migration between the two points. There are many types of migration networks in addition to those identified in Chapter 1. Social clubs consisting of *paisanos*, persons who come from the same community in Mexico, and remittances, the money sent by migrants to their families in Mexico, are two more examples. However, this book concentrates on two aspects of migration networks: (1) persons in the United States who assist the migration of their friends and relatives; and (2) family members and friends with previous U.S. migration experience. In econometric studies, the presence of these networks is typically indicated using one or more dummy variables.

Migration networks facilitate migration by serving a number of economic functions.[2] First, networks lower the costs of migration. Friends and family often provide the migrant with an initial place to stay in the United States for little to no cost. Some migrants even become housemates of their U.S. contacts or rent rooms from them. Friends and relatives may share transportation costs between Mexico and the United States, making crossing the border the primary obstacle for the undocumented migrant. Also, friends and family members may do small favors for the migrant, such as providing rides and lending money. For a migrant with limited resources, these favors can be extremely important.

Persons who have previously migrated to the United States may share their knowledge of the migratory process with others, enabling subsequent migrants to enter the United States in the most cost-effective manner possible. This transfer of information may make migrants more astute in dealing with *coyotes* and more skilled in avoiding apprehension and deportation by the U.S. Immigration and Naturalization Service (INS). Migrants may also learn about available community resources and social services in the United States.

Second, migration networks may reduce the risks associated with migration.[3] In addition to lowering the probability of being deported, networks may limit the risks of being unemployed in the United States and of receiving less than one's reservation wage. They may also make dealing with *coyotes* less risky. For instance, an undocumented migrant who enters the United States with a *coyote*'s assistance may divide the payments to the *coyote* into thirds—one third payable up front, one third payable upon crossing the border, and one third payable by the migrant's family once he or she is delivered to them. Living with friends or relatives while in the United States may also increase the migrant's personal safety, in comparison to living alone or with strangers in unfamiliar surroundings.

Third, migration networks may provide the migrant with valuable job contacts. These contacts may increase the probability that the migrant finds work in the United States, decrease the search time, and even boost the wage received. In fact, networks help some migrants to secure employment in the United States prior to their departure from Mexico. In my fieldwork, I interviewed a man whose brother owns an engine repair shop in the Los Angeles area. The respondent arranged in advance for two of his sons to migrate to California and to work in his brother's shop. Sometimes a single employer in the United States will act as a springboard for an entire stream of migrants emanating from a single community. Massey, et al. (1987) give the example of a restaurant in the San Francisco area that historically has served this function for migrants from a small town in the state of Jalisco.

Such job contacts, however, are not essential, as a large number of migrants find work simply by looking themselves. Consider the heads of household interviewed by the Mexican Migration Project who have U.S. migration experience. Of those individuals, 22.76 percent obtained their most recent U.S. job by conducting their own search. By survey community, this proportion ranges from 10.31 to 41.18 percent. For San Ramon, 17.95 percent of the migrant heads of household found their most recent U.S. job in this manner.[4]

Fourth, migration networks may make life in the United States more appealing to the migrant. Often researchers note that migration networks reduce the "psychic costs" of migrating to the United States. Alternatively, in the spirit of Graves and Linneman (1979) and Graves and Knapp (1984), one may view the presence of friends, family, and *paisanos* in the migrant's destination as a positive amenity of that place. These amenities can be as simple as sitting around with *paisanos* and drinking beer and as elaborate as immigrant associations and other social organizations organized along the line of *paisanaje*.[5]

My fieldwork in the Los Angeles area yielded an unusual example of such an amenity. There I interviewed a migrant who lives next door to another migrant from the state of Colima. In stark contrast to the freeway that borders his house, the neighbor raises rabbits, geese, hens, and gamecocks in his backyard, just as he would do in Mexico and much to the delight of his friend from San Ramon. Occasionally the two neighbors get together with other persons from Mexico and stage clandestine cock fights, although they are reluctant to divulge the precise location.

2.3. PREVIOUS RESEARCH

2.3.1. Origins of the Concept

The concept of migration networks fittingly has an extensive system of roots that extend deep into several academic disciplines. Over the years, researchers have studied migration networks from a variety of perspectives, often using different terms to refer to the phenomenon. Within sociology, for instance, Massey, et al. (1987) emphasize the work of Tilly and Brown (1967) on the "auspices of migration" and that of MacDonald and MacDonald (1974) and Graves and Graves (1974) on "migration chains."

In economics, Nelson (1959) posits the existence of a "relative and friends multiplier" that influences the level of migration from one state to another in the United States. As providers of information and as an attribute of some prospective destinations, relatives and friends affect the importance of other variables explaining internal migration, such as income and unemployment levels in the origin and destination, distance between pairs of states, and their industrial similarity. Greenwood (1969, 1970) conducts early work about the role of "migrant stock" in internal U.S. migration. He defines migrant stock to be the number of persons born in one U.S. state who live in another, but this concept is easily transferred to the context of international migration.

More recently, in anthropology, Hirabayashi (1993) identifies the migrant associations of Zapotec Indians in Mexico City as a form of "cultural capital." Migrants use this cultural capital to confront the demands of life both in their home communities and in Mexico City. To different extents, the associations also socialize migrants and non-migrants about life in Mexico outside the Zapotec communities.

This diverse body of literature has drawn attention to migration networks from many quarters, to the point that networks are now an established subject in the study of international migration. In recent years, the Mexican Migration Project has played an auspicious role in the further study of migration networks. The project has provided the empirical base for the extensive qualitative and quantitative study of migration to the United States from western and central Mexico.[6] In addition, the project's data have been the foundation of several Ph.D. dissertations,[7] introducing a new generation of scholars to the study of international migration between Mexico and the United States in general and of migration networks in particular.

2.3.2. Econometric Studies

Practically all of the econometric studies about migration networks and Mexican migration to the United States focus on the influence of networks on the migration decision. These studies indicate that migration networks exercise a strongly positive and statistically significant effect on the probability of migrating. One of the first prominent studies on this topic is Taylor (1984). He employs a multinomial logit model to study the prospective migrant's choice among four competing alternatives: (1) attending school in Mexico, (2) remaining in the village, (3) migrating within Mexico, and (4) migrating to the United States. Using data for 1982 from two villages in the state of Michoacán, Taylor examines this decision for each member of the household.

Sprouse (1991) uses the same general type of model to examine the choice of each household member among the alternatives of migrating to the United States, migrating within Mexico, and remaining in one's village to work. His data are from four *ejidos* in the state of San Luís Potosí for 1990.[8] In addition, Sprouse runs a simple probit model to examine the decision between migrating to the United States and remaining in Mexico.

In recent years, the competing option of migrating within Mexico has attracted little attention from researchers, at least in the English-language literature that I have reviewed. Why this has been the case is not immediately apparent. It may be that the topic of internal migration in Mexico is not sufficiently novel for contemporary researchers. Or persistent economic problems in Mexico over the past 15 years may have made internal migration a less viable option than in years past.[9] During my fieldwork in San Ramon, I encountered few individuals who had recently migrated within Mexico, outside of those persons who perform farm labor or construction work in nearby communities within the state of Colima. Another possibility is that the people drawn to other parts of Mexico have moved there for good. Locating such people and then interviewing them as part of an extensive survey project would be a formidable task.

Two closely related works about the migration decision are García España and Massey (1987) and García España (1992). Except for a few differences in model specifications and the data used, the two works contain essentially the same empirical evidence. Both feature a pair of logit models: one examining the probability that any member of the household migrated to the United States during the 1979-81 period, and another focusing on the individual probability of migrating during the 1980-82 period. The former model relies on data collected in September and October 1981 by the Mexican Social Security Institute (*Instituto Mexicano de Seguridad Social*—IMSS), and the latter utilizes data from the Mexican Migration Project.

Because of the strong empirical evidence of the importance of migration networks, scholars of Mexico-U.S. migration now routinely include network variables in their research about topics other than migration networks. In a study of the migration spells of undocumented Mexican migrants, Kossoudji (1992) finds that the INS's policy of apprehending and deporting undocumented migrants has the unintended and counterproductive effects of shortening the Mexican spells and lengthening the U.S. spells of migrants who are not apprehended. She includes a variable denoting the presence of migration networks and finds that they extend the U.S. spells of migrants who eventually leave the United States voluntarily.

In an innovative study, Taylor (1987) estimates the expected income gains from migration and incorporates them in a structural probit model of the migration decision of household members. Migration networks form one factor that Taylor uses to estimate the size of Mexico-U.S. remittances. Curiously, networks slightly reduce the size of these remittances, a result that Taylor attributes to a hypothesized negative relationship between remittances and the number of family members in the United States.

Stark and Taylor (1989) study whether feelings of relative deprivation in Mexican sending communities motivate Mexico-U.S. migration.[10] The econometric techniques used are similar to those in Taylor (1987), except that a term estimating the relative deprivation of the household in the absence of a household member's migration is included. Stark and Taylor also find that migration networks reduce the size of remittances and increase the probability that the individual migrates to the United States.

2.4. METHODOLOGICAL ISSUES

2.4.1. How Does One Measure a Migration Network?

Perhaps the most central issue regarding the empirical study of migration networks is how exactly does one measure a migration network. In the econometric literature about migration networks, researchers typically employ a dummy variable that indicates whether an individual has friends or relatives who live in the United States or who at least have previous U.S. migration experience. This approach is straightforward but has several shortcomings. First, as I will examine below, migration networks can vary greatly in terms of their quality, and the mere presence of a Mexican migrant in the United States does not mean that the migrant would help family members or friends if they crossed the border, too. One thing that impressed me during my fieldwork in San Ramon was the large number of respondents who have little to no contact with their siblings. At first, I suspected that these people did not want to divulge any information about their brothers or sisters who were living in the United States. However, I eventually noticed that this phenomenon also extends to respondents whose siblings are in Mexico. To the best of my knowledge, no researcher has fully examined the cohesiveness of the extended family in Mexico as it relates to international migration.

Second, individuals who live in communities where a high proportion of families have U.S. migration experience may benefit from migration networks, even if their own families and close friends lack such experience. To account for this phenomenon, Massey, Goldring, and Durand (1992) create a "prevalence ratio" using the Mexican Migration Project's data to measure the proportion of families in each survey community with U.S. experience at a given point in time.

I once considered using this variable in my own research. However, I abandoned the idea after realizing that some household heads studied by the project have spent considerable time outside the community in which they were interviewed. Some respondents were not born in their survey community, and others moved away before returning later in life. Thus, it seems improper to attach a prevalence ratio or any other characteristic of the survey community to persons whose link to the community may be weak or non-existent. A rough examination of the life histories of the household heads interviewed by the project yields a startling result. As a group, they have spent roughly one quarter of their combined lifespans in Mexican locations outside their respective survey communities. Although this tally includes episodes of internal migration, it seems substantial nonetheless. Moreover, because several of the communities are clustered together, a few respondents have lived in more than one survey community.

2.4.2. "Bad" Migration Networks

Most of the research on migration networks emphasizes the good experiences of migrants. Recently, however, observers have pointed out that some migrants have profoundly negative experiences with their networks. These range from dealing with relatives who are merely unpleasant to instances of outright abuse and exploitation.

A male respondent from my fieldwork in the Los Angeles area related an experience that illustrates this point. The man entered the United States without papers, and family members referred him to an acquaintance who owned a restaurant. She agreed to hire him to work in the kitchen, despite his undocumented status. Her connections to the respondent's family, however, did not prevent her from verbally berating him on a regular basis. In fact, one day she became so incensed that she thrust a casserole dish upon his head.

Sometimes family members in the United States do not wish to receive their recently arrived kin from Mexico. A female respondent in Las Vegas indicated that her father essentially turned her away when she arrived at his home in southern California. She followed some acquaintances to Las Vegas, but there, too, she felt unwelcome. Without legal immigration status and the support of family and friends, she found it virtually impossible to find work, and she spent a great deal of time desperately wandering the streets. "There was a time," she noted, "when I would have gotten into anybody's car in exchange for a glass of water." Finally, she met a man who worked at a laundry and found work there. They soon became lovers and eventually married. Since the interview, however, she and her husband have separated and are now filing for divorce.

Some migrants intentionally limit contact with their *paisanos* in the United States. For instance, one respondent in the Los Angeles area maintains extremely close ties with relatives in both the United States and Mexico. Outside of his family, however, he largely avoids the company of persons from San Ramon who live in the United States. His primary reason for doing so is that he does not wish to be around persons who drink too much.

These anecdotes suggest that migration networks do not exist simply because someone in Mexico has a friend or relative in the United States or because someone knows someone else who once was a migrant. Instead, migration networks reflect the state of interpersonal relationships between migrants and potential migrants.

2.4.3. Complex Theory, Simple Data

A third research issue, and one that should be of great importance to econometricians studying migration, is the problem of conducting empirical work that matches the complexity of its underlying theoretical foundation. A number of the studies that I reviewed contain elegant economic models that are not tested econometrically. Taylor (1984) considers various elements involving risk, including the variability of remittances, fluctuations in commodity prices, and crop insurance. Sprouse (1991) looks at a household's allocation of time among various productive and leisure activities. Olea (1987) postulates a shadow price for additional income that follows a Martingale process. Fulfilling the promise of these elaborate models necessarily requires additional survey research to collect data for the models. Such endeavors are likely to be more costly than previous surveys, especially if the researcher wishes to conduct a longitudinal analysis or if so much information is solicited that it becomes necessary to compensate the respondent.

2.5. UNEXPLORED ISSUES

Many aspects of migration networks are relatively unexplored. One general topic of interest is the relationship between networks and migrant earnings in the United States. Specifically, how much are family connections and other networks worth to a migrant in the U.S. labor market? A related question is the impact of networks on migrant earnings over time. Do networks facilitate the convergence of migrant incomes on the earnings of native-born workers with similar attributes?

Or do they have the opposite effect by discouraging integration into U.S. society, as well as the acquisition of the English language? A second issue involves the possible influence of migration networks on family cohesion. Networks may alleviate pressures that might otherwise divide migrants from their families in Mexico. For instance, a married migrant whose spouse and dependent children live in Mexico may be less likely to abandon the family if he or she is in immediate contact with relatives while in the United States. In subsequent research, I hope to examine the impact of migration networks on remittances and the dissolution of marriages during the migration process.

The experiences of female migrants constitute a third subject that merits further exploration. Indeed, the existing literature on Mexican migration to the United States is frequently criticized for its general neglect of this subject. Although several case studies in fields other than economics are devoted to female migrants, little to no econometric work has been done in this area. Such work will require the collection of new data sets that are specially designed for studying female migrants. Unfortunately, the data collected by the Mexican Migration Project are not well suited for this task. The project collects only limited information about persons other than the head of household, and in the vast majority of cases, the head of household is male. To address this shortcoming, the project has added questions to its survey instrument that specifically target women, including a retrospective life history of the head of household's spouse. However, the spouse typically has no migration experience. The head of household's daughters are more likely to have such experience. Finally, because female migrants often assume substantial household responsibilities while in the United States, future empirical studies should pay more attention to housework.

NOTES

1. I am indebted to several review articles about the theory of international migration: Massey (1990), Massey, et al. (1993) and Massey, et al. (1994).

2. García España and Massey (1987) offer a more extensive discussion of this subject.

3. Taylor (1984), in particular, emphasizes the influence of networks on various types of risks.

4. The Mexican Migration Project's survey instrument seeks the manner in which the migrant obtained work during the individual's most recent trip to the United States. Since migrants probably rely less on migration networks to find work as they accumulate more migration experience, the project's figures may understate the importance of networks.

5. The Mexican Secretariat of Foreign Relations (*Secretaría de Relaciones Exteriores*—SRE) compiles a lengthy directory of immigrant associations and clubs throughout the United States. See SRE (1995).

6. See, for instance, Massey and Parrado (1994), Massey, Goldring, and Durand (1992), Massey, et al. (1987), and García España and Massey (1987).

7. Completed examples include García España (1992), Goldring (1992), and Zahniser (1996).

8. *Ejidos* are a type of collective farm particular to Mexico that was instituted following the Mexican Revolution. Although the state retains ownership of *ejidal* lands, it grants individuals title to their use.

9. Taylor offered this assessment during a conversation in March 1996.

10. Two related works on relative deprivation and international migration are Stark, Taylor, and Yitzhaki (1988, 1986).

CHAPTER 3
Survey Methodology

3.1. INTRODUCTION

This chapter details the methodology of my fieldwork in Mexico and the United States. Because Massey, et al. (1987) describe the general methodology of the Mexican Migration Project in some detail,[1] this chapter focuses on the work that my assistants and I conducted in San Ramon, Colima, and the metropolitan areas of Los Angeles, California and Las Vegas, Nevada. The chapter is organized as follows. Section 3.2 focuses on the survey research carried out in San Ramon. In addition to describing the methodology of our work, the section offers a few glimpses into what life was like in San Ramon during our brief stay there. Section 3.3 examines the fieldwork conducted in the Los Angeles and Las Vegas areas. Finally, Section 3.4 contemplates the strengths and weaknesses of the methodology.

3.2. MEXICAN INTERVIEWS

I arrived in San Ramon on the morning of December 7, 1994, accompanied by Mr. Víctor Espinoza of the Mexican Migration Project and Mr. Percy Ríos of the University of Guadalajara. Mr. Espinosa stayed for several days, providing instruction about the proper use of the project's survey instrument and the manner in which to conduct a housing census of the community. Mr. Espinosa also returned about a week into the actual interviews in order to check our progress and to proofread our work.

The fieldwork in San Ramon contained three stages. The first stage was to conduct a housing census of the entire community. This consisted of walking through the community and drawing a map depicting every possibly inhabited dwelling in San Ramon. Mr. Ríos and I carried out this activity on December 8 and 9, 1994. The municipal government provided us with street maps of the city, which greatly facilitated our work.[2]

Often, it was difficult to determine whether a particular building or lot was actually inhabited. A well-maintained dwelling with its front door and metal windows shut offered few clues as to whether the building was actually occupied. Imposing walls of brick or adobe surrounded many larger properties. In many of these cases, a tall metal gate ensured that the view of the interior was fully obstructed. Also, some persons operated businesses out of their homes. Thus, it was impossible to eliminate certain places of business as dwellings without speaking to the owner or someone else from the neighborhood. In addition, many neighboring homes share a common wall facing the street. Some of these homes were created when parents gave parcels of their property to their sons and daughters as they married. Often, the most effective means of determining where one of these homes ended and the next began was simply to see where the wall was painted a different color. For these reasons, I included in the housing census all places that were possibly inhabited, even if there was some doubt that they were actually inhabited, rather than to eliminate them from the pool from which the survey sample would be drawn.

The second stage was the random selection of the households to be interviewed. Each dwelling identified in the housing census was given a number. A total of 1,961 possibly inhabited dwellings were enumerated, although we discovered afterwards that we had neglected to number 31 additional dwellings that we had identified in the housing census. These 31 were not included in the pool of addresses from which the survey sample was drawn. We then used a list of randomly generated numbers to select 200 addresses along with 30 reserve addresses to form the original survey sample. As the interview process progressed, we added 61 more addresses to the reserves as the original addresses were depleted, largely due to rejections and the discovery of duplicate addresses and uninhabited dwellings.

The third stage was to conduct the actual interviews. These were performed from December 11 to December 22, 1994 and from January 5 to January 23, 1995. In addition to myself, the interviewers were Ms. Aurora Monterrubio and Ms. Theresa Monterrubio, both of the

University of Chapingo, and Mr. Ríos. Although no firm script was used when the interviewers contacted the potential respondents, the interviewers were instructed to identify themselves by name, to indicate for whom the work was being done, to explain the purpose of the survey, and to inform potential respondents of the interview's voluntary nature. Potential respondents were also told that the interview could be done at a time was convenient to them.

During the course of the interviews, we determined that a large number of the addresses in the survey sample were either uninhabited or otherwise not suitable for conducting interviews. Table 3.1 identifies the outcomes for the first 200 addresses selected as well as the 91 reserve addresses. Of these 291 addresses, 72 were deemed as not suitable. Thirty-five addresses were uninhabited and 12 addresses were duplicates or parts of other dwellings. Four addresses were solely places of business and one was the public library. Five houses were not currently occupied and were owned by persons who had their permanent residence elsewhere.

Table 3.1: Outcomes of Contacting Addresses in Sample

Outcome	First 200	Reserves	Total
Completed interview	144	56	200
Declined to be interviewed	9	10	19
Unsuitable addresses	47	25	72
• Uninhabited dwellings	22	13	35
• Duplicate addresses/Part of another dwelling	9	3	12
• Business or library	4	1	5
• Permanent residence in Colima	2	1	3
• Address did not exist	4	0	4
• U.S. citizens	3	0	3
• Permanent residence in the U.S.	1	0	1
• Decided not to interview	1	1	2
• Visiting somewhere in Mexico	1	1	2
• Permanent residence elsewhere in Cuauhtémoc	0	1	1
• Visiting the U.S.	0	2	2
• Not contacted	0	2	2
TOTAL	200	91	291

We eliminated three addresses from the sample because their inhabitants were U.S. citizens who have settled in San Ramon and thus were not part of the population to be studied. We also decided not to interview two households because we felt that it would have imposed an undue burden on the prospective respondents. The occupants of four addresses were out of town during the period of our fieldwork. Finally, once we completed 200 interviews, we did not try to contact two of the last households that we had selected.

At the 219 suitable addresses where we asked to conduct an interview, nineteen persons declined to be interviewed. This translates into a refusal rate of 8.68 percent,[3] which falls into the upper range of the refusal rates of the communities previously surveyed by Professor Massey's research project. Table 3.2 lists the observable features of the persons who refused to be interviewed. Almost all of the persons who refused appeared to be married, but the vast majority of the persons who agreed to be interviewed also were married. The persons who declined to be interviewed ranged from being younger adults (age 25 to 35) to being elderly (age 75 and up). Four appeared to be between 25 and 35 years of age and seven appeared to be older than 60. Thus it seemed that older persons were more likely to decline to be interviewed. Persons who appeared to be extremely impoverished generally did not refuse to be interviewed, unless they were in poor health or burdened by too much housework.

Table 3.3 contains a distribution of the number of interviews completed by each interviewer and the number of refusals experienced by each interviewer, as well as the refusal rate for each interviewer. The fact that my individual refusal rate was higher than the overall refusal rate suggests that prospective respondents were less confident in dealing with me than with my assistants from Mexico.[4] The appearance of an interviewer from the United States may have discouraged some prospective respondents from participating. In addition, a few respondents indicated that they had mistaken me for a Mormon missionary, perhaps due to my clean-cut appearance.

Table 3.2: Persons in Mexico Who Declined to be Interviewed

1	Male Retiree; age 60 to 70
2	Married couple; age 25 to 35
3	Married couple; age 25 to 35; "too busy"
4	Upper-class couple; possibly ranchers
5	Retired upper-class couple; age 55 to 65; had the flu
6	Alcoholic male; age 40 to 50; said, "No recibo citas" (I don't receive appointments)
7	Male; age 55 to 65
8	Incapacited and impoverished married male; age 70 to 80; said, "No tengo nada que hablar" (I don't have anything to say)
9	Timid female; age 60 to 70; son refused on her behalf
10	Female storeowner; age 55 to 65; described as "unsociable" by neighbor
11	Male retiree; age 65 to 80; said, "Otra ocasión" (Another occasion)
12	Male storeowner; age 60 to 70; adult sons with U.S. migration experience; one said, "Él le dijo que se vaya..." (He's telling you to get out of here)
13	Married couple; age 30 to 40; wife frequently hid herself when I knocked on the door; possible spousal abuse
14	Male; age 25 to 35; said he does not like participating in surveys
15	Married couple; age 25 to 35; paid many visits to house; several broken appointments; wife appeared frightened; male wore sweatshirt of public university in U.S. Northwest
16	Female with children; possibly widowed or divorced; possibly impoverished; age 40 to 50; too occupied with work to participate
17	Characteristics not recorded
18	Male storeowner with children; age 60 to 70; repeatedly said, "No sé como le diría..." (I don't know how to tell you...)
19	Married male; age 35 to 45; said, "Otro día" (Another day)

26 Mexican Migration to the United States

The survey instrument itself contained two parts: the most recent version of the Mexican Migration Project's standard questionnaire and an addendum with questions that I selected (see Appendices A and B). For households with few children and limited international migration experience, the interview typically lasted between 40 and 50 minutes. Interviews with larger households and households with substantial migration experience normally ranged in length between an hour and an hour and a half. A few interviews lasted no more than 15 minutes. These were with single males in their early to mid twenties who had little to no migration experience.

Table 3.3: Interviews and Refusals among Interviewers

Interviewer	Number of Interviews	Number of Refusals	Refusal Rate
Aurora Monterrubio	39	3	7.14%
Teresa Monterrubio	17	1	5.56%
Percy Ríos	66	1	1.49%
Steven Zahniser	78	14	15.22%
Total	200	19	8.68%

The purpose of the addendum was twofold. First, I sought to obtain more precise information about some of the subjects explored by the standard questionnaire. For instance, the standard questionnaire collects extensive data about the head of household's relatives and their first and most recent trips to the United States. However, it is difficult to discern from this information if these people were actually present in the United States during the head of household's first journey there. For this reason, I added a question which asked whom the head of household knew in a given community when he first moved there.

Another example pertains to remittances. The standard questionnaire records the types of goods and services purchased using income remitted by the head of household during his or her most recent trip to the United States. Follow-up questions in the addendum inquired whether these goods and services still would have been purchased in the absence of the remittances and whether any part of the remittance was saved rather than spent. These questions allowed a more precise definition of the impact of remittances on household consumption and investment behavior.

Second, I wanted to gather information about several topics that are not covered in the standard questionnaire. To capture seasonal variations in employment, I solicited information about the number of hours that the head of household worked per week and any periods of unemployment or disability that he or she experienced during the 12 months prior to the interview. In addition, I asked respondents to detail their household's use of credit during this period. This section of the addendum was closely patterned on part of the survey instrument used by Sprouse (1991).

On a typical day, it was possible for a single interviewer to complete questionnaires for four households. During the beginning of the interview process, it was relatively easy to find households to interview since one had the entire list of prospective households to work with. Indeed, Mr. Ríos finished eight interviews during a single day in December. As the interviews progressed, fewer addresses remained on the selection list, and much of the last week of interviews was spent walking between a handful of addresses hoping to find the occupants at home.

The vast majority of the interviews went extremely smoothly. Mr. Ríos and I each initially concentrated our efforts in a handful of neighborhoods. In Mr. Ríos's case, this resulted in his becoming familiar to the people of one particular neighborhood and may have facilitated his work there. With respect to the households that I visited, many respondents seemed to enjoy the novelty of a visit of someone from the United States. Also, several respondents said they had participated in a previous survey conducted by a nearby university, and practically all respondents had participated in the most recent national census. Thus the notion that a student from the United States would come to conduct a survey was not so far-fetched. All in all, the respondents were generally friendly and quite hospitable, and sometimes they would offer the interviewer a glass of water or a soft drink, and in a few cases, something to eat.

Several of the older respondents (age 70 and up) had trouble remembering the answers to certain questions, including questions about their work and migration histories and the names and ages of their adult children. This was especially true for two individuals who had each raised more than 12 children and for several respondents with elaborate migration and work histories. Interviews with older respondents usually took longer than average and sometimes required several visits. In one instance, it was necessary to end an interview at the request of an infirm respondent who could not remember his work history for the 1970s.

My assistants and I unwittingly conducted duplicate interviews for three households. This mistake occurred because some houses located on street corners would have an entrance with a unique house number on each cross street. Surprisingly, only one of the three respondents indicated that he or she had already been interviewed prior to the completion of the duplicate interview. Despite the inconvenience to the respondents, this accidental experiment yielded some interesting insights. At the first household, the first interview was conducted primarily with the head of the household and the duplicate interview was conducted solely with his wife. The wife indicated that she had recently borrowed money from a *prestamista*,[5] but the husband, who may not have known about the loan, made no mention of it. At the second household, the respondent, an older woman, gave different ages for some of her children. At the third household, the information recorded on the two survey instruments was virtually identical.

The tone of the respondents interviewed in December 1994 was generally upbeat, perhaps because people were looking forward to the Christmas season. Quite a few of the December respondents also took the opportunity to express their profound disgust with the State of California's Proposition 187. In January 1995, however, respondents tended to be far more somber. The Mexican peso was sharply devalued in late December, and many persons in San Ramon recognized that a severe recession of unknown length was about to get underway. One January respondent indicated that her son, whose trucking business had boomed during the first year of the North American Free Trade Agreement (NAFTA) due to increased freight volume between the Port of Manzanillo and the city of Guadalajara, was now planning to sell all but one of his three rigs. At the taco stand run by one respondent, the price of tacos climbed from one new peso (NP) to 1.30 NP. The number of patrons in the city's bars dropped substantially. Photocopies of a political cartoon asking outgoing President Carlos Salinas de

Gortari to return the money he had allegedly stolen also appeared in several businesses.
Perhaps due to this deteriorating economic climate, one respondent appeared frightened by a question in the addendum. Question 3 in the addendum's supplement to Chart H in the standard questionnaire asks the respondent to imagine a hypothetical situation such as a medical emergency or an upcoming long voyage in which he or she needs to borrow $500. This respondent, a married woman with several children, repeatedly asked why I was asking such a question and seemed concerned that I might know that something bad was about to happen.
Of the 200 households surveyed in San Ramon, only at two did we encounter anyone belligerent. At one household, the son of the elderly female respondent arrived about halfway through the interview. He was extremely untrusting of me, even after I introduced myself and clearly explained the purpose of the interview. I rapidly drew the interview to a close and did not seek clarification of any unusual answers. I later learned that the son was a former police officer and that he had secretly recorded my questions but not his mother's answers using a small, handheld tape recorder. At the other household, the respondent was extremely intoxicated and gruffly insisted that the interviewer really didn't want to know who he was. Strangely, the respondent eventually agreed to answer to all of the questions.

3.3. U.S. INTERVIEWS

In July 1995, I traveled to the metropolitan areas of Los Angeles, California, and Las Vegas, Nevada, to conduct interviews with relatives of persons whom we interviewed in San Ramon. The names of these persons and information about how to contact them were provided voluntarily by a number of the survey respondents in San Ramon. In most cases, these respondents provided the address and telephone number of the prospective respondents in the United States. In a few cases, they provided only the name and the address or the name and telephone number of the prospective respondent. In one instance, the person in San Ramon only provided the name of his sons' workplace.
The purpose of the U.S. interviews is to compensate for a selection problem in the sample of households interviewed in San Ramon and the other Mexican communities studied by the Mexican Migration Project.

Although the households contacted in Mexico are randomly selected, they do not include families who have moved from Mexico to the United States. For this reason, the Mexican Migration Project conducts 20 interviews in the United States for each community surveyed in Mexico. I completed nine of the 20 U.S. interviews for San Ramon, five in the Los Angeles metropolitan area and four in Las Vegas. The Los Angeles interviews took place July 5-12, and the Las Vegas interviews occurred July 13-16. In addition, a researcher from the Mexican Migration Project conducted another 11 interviews in the Los Angeles area sometime in August 1995.

I used the same survey instrument as in San Ramon except with one modification: I added to the addendum a series of questions about the head of household's first job in the United States. The purpose of these questions was to explore the role of migration networks in the migrant's first U.S. job search. The researcher from the Mexican Migration Project who conducted the other 11 U.S. interviews did not collect information for any of the questions in my addendum.

The U.S. interviews were fraught with problems not experienced in San Ramon. First, the prospective respondents were spread out over a much larger area, especially with respect to the Los Angeles interviews. A great deal of time was spent driving around in the rental car from one address to another. Second, a number of leads did not pan out. One prospective respondent had moved since December 1994, and the address for another did not exist. Third, several prospective respondents were highly suspicious of my intentions and declined to be interviewed. This was presumably due to fears that I was somehow connected with the Immigration and Naturalization Service.

Fourth, the interviews that I did complete did not generate many subsequent interviews. For the U.S. interviews, the Mexican Migration Project tries to locate additional persons from each Mexican community using the technique known as "snowball" sampling, in which respondents are asked to provide the names of other prospective respondents. In my case, the snowball melted very quickly under the California summer sun. The few new contacts provided by the respondents in the Los Angeles area yielded no additional interviews. Surprisingly, in Las Vegas I was able to obtain several new contacts at a household where the original prospective respondent did not wish to be interviewed. These new contacts eventually resulted in the completion of three interviews. Table 3.4 lists the observable features of the individuals in the U.S. who declined to be interviewed. Because the number of these persons is relatively small, it is not possible to observe any pattern regarding their demographic characteristics. However, it is possible to comment on the relationship between the method used to contact prospective respondents in the U.S. and whether they agreed to be interviewed. In several instances, I had met the prospective respondents during my fieldwork in Mexico while they were visiting their families in San Ramon for the Christmas holidays. These persons without exception were willing to be interviewed in the United States. For prospective respondents whom I had not yet met, I was most successful in obtaining an interview when my first contact with them occurred when I presented myself at their front door. Making first contact via telephone resulted in an interview in only one of four attempts.

Table 3.4: Persons in U.S. Who Declined to be Interviewed

1	Male restaurant worker, age 25 to 35, did not return phone calls
2	Male horse groom, age 30 to 40, did not return phone calls nor respond to pages
3	Male landscaper, age 40 to 50, preferred to be interviewed once his wife and children had returned from visiting Mexico
4	Male construction worker, age 30 to 40, appeared very untrusting and did not wish to provide information about himself

All of the U.S. interviews went very smoothly. As in San Ramon, the respondents were in almost all instances quite hospitable and generously sacrificed part of their leisure time to meet with me. One interview was conducted over beer, another during lunch, and at one household, I was even invited to stay for a child's birthday party. It is my belief that many of these respondents would be willing to speak with me again about their migration experiences, either on a formal or an informal basis.

3.4. STRENGTHS AND WEAKNESSES OF THE METHODOLOGY

Despite the difficulties that we experienced in trying to identify and distinguish prospective households for interview in San Ramon, the method used to select the Mexican sample was fundamentally sound. Persons with certain socioeconomic characteristics may have been more likely than others to decline to be interviewed, but the process used to select prospective respondents in the first place was essentially random. The same analysis applies only in part to the generation of the initial list of contacts for the U.S. interviews. Particular types of respondents may have been less likely to provide contact information about family members or friends in the United States. However, the interviewers were allowed some leeway in deciding whether to solicit contact information for the U.S. interviews, especially if the respondent seemed uncomfortable or to have lingering doubts about the interviewer's trustworthiness.

There are also several other ways in which the U.S. sample may have been unrepresentative of the population of persons from San Ramon who were in the United States at the time of my interviews in Mexico. First, research costs forced the U.S. interviews to be conducted in only two metropolitan areas. While Los Angeles and Las Vegas were the two places with the largest number of contacts, there were also contacts in other parts of the country, including northern California, North Carolina, South Carolina, and Texas.

Second, because the initial contacts for the U.S. interviews were obtained from respondents in San Ramon, these contacts naturally did not include anyone who no longer had ties to San Ramon. However, my efforts to expand the original contact list though "snowball" sampling did result in several interviews with persons whose connections to San Ramon were rather limited.

Third, the "snowball" sampling technique itself introduced a certain non-random element into the U.S. interviews. The new contacts provided by the U.S. respondents frequently resembled the respondents themselves. Indeed, the new contacts often were co-workers or siblings, and their socioeconomic characteristics and employment and migration experiences were quite similar to the original respondents.

For my fieldwork in Mexico and the United States, I had the advantage of using a well proven survey instrument. The standard questionnaire had already been used to study some 30 previous communities in Mexico, and I tested the questionnaire along with my addendum on two Mexican immigrant families in the Boulder area before departing for Mexico.

The standard questionnaire contained a wide variety of questions, some of which were of direct interest to me and others which were more of interest to other scholars. The vast majority of the questions did not allow the respondent to elaborate, so I was glad that I included several additional questions crafted by another researcher which sought the respondents' opinions regarding migration to the United States. As Section 3.2 indicated, I was concerned that the length of some interviews was burdensome to some respondents, especially older individuals, large families, and respondents with extensive migration and employment histories. This problem offered no easy solution, since these respondents usually had extremely compelling information to relate.

Despite the large number of questions in the standard questionnaire, the instrument itself was rather compact, which occasionally caused me to forget to ask a question or two and to have to return to the household a second time to obtain the missing answers. My addendum contained fewer questions per page than the standard questionnaire, which made it easier to read but also required the interviewers to lug around more paper.

A number of questions in the standard questionnaire allowed for several possible interpretations. For instance, some persons from San Ramon work in the nearby city of Colima. Since Colima is only 20 minutes away from San Ramon using the regional bus line, it would seem reasonable to view these persons as commuters and not to list them as internal migrants in Chart C. However, since Colima is not part of the Municipality of San Ramon, the Mexican Migration Project treats these individuals as internal migrants. Although Professor Massey and Mr. Espinoza were able to provide a clear interpretation of each question that I found confusing, it would have been helpful to have had a field manual that anticipated many of my questions.

One intriguing subject that was not substantially addressed by either the standard questionnaire or my addendum was the experiences of female migrants. The Mexican Migration Project focuses on the head of household, who is defined as the primary breadwinner in the household. In most instances, this person is male. The project has made some efforts to expand its study of female migrants. For example, the standard questionnaire has included for several years work history charts for both the head of household and his or her spouse. However, a woman who migrates to the United States and becomes married usually escapes the project's search process altogether, unless she is the head of household or is married to another person from her community in Mexico.

All in all, my fieldwork in Mexico and the United States went fairly well. The time that was spent in San Ramon was particularly productive, and in hindsight it seems somewhat remarkable that our small group conducted so many interviews in such a small amount of time. While I had hoped to conduct more interviews myself in the United States, the nine interviews that I did carry out were generally of high quality and provided some unique insights into the family relationships of Mexican migrants to the United States. These will be discussed in the next chapter.

NOTES

1. See Chapter 2, "Study Design," pp. 10-21.

2. The city of San Ramon is also the seat of government for the Municipality of San Ramon. In Mexico, the activities of local government take place in municipalities or *municipios*. *Municipios* correspond in size to counties in the United States. However, in Mexico municipal authorities carry out some responsibilities that typically belong to city or village governments in the United States, such as police protection and the construction and maintenance of streets, water mains, and sewers.

3. I calculated the refusal rate by dividing the number of rejections (19) by the total number of interviews plus the number of rejections (200 + 19 = 219).

4. Mr. Ríos actually is a Peruvian living in Mexico. The other two interviewers are Mexican.

5. A *prestamista* is an informal lender.

CHAPTER 4

Data Profile

4.1. INTRODUCTION

One may easily describe the data collected by the Mexican Migration Project as an embarrassment of riches. The project's data sets present the researcher with so many opportunities for statistical and econometric study that it is virtually impossible to scrutinize every variable and to contemplate every issue prompted by the data. Therefore, this data profile concentrates on those variables that are central to the econometric models of Chapters 5, 6 and 7.

Following this introduction, the chapter is divided into four sections. Section 4.2 provides an overview of the Mexican Migration Project's data sets. It also briefly describes the communities of origin surveyed by the project. Section 4.3 focuses on several characteristics of the head of household that are likely to influence the migration decision. These characteristics include U.S. immigration status, migration networks, gender, the presence of minor-age children in the household, and single parenthood. Section 4.4 shows the relation between these characteristics and the head of household's migration decision, both at the time of the interview and over the years of adult life leading up to the interview. Section 4.5 offers a brief conclusion.

4.2. OVERVIEW OF THE DATA SETS

The data collected by the Mexican Migration Project are stored in several SPSS data sets. This book relies upon the following data sets:

LIFEFILE—a retrospective life history of each head of household;

HOUSFILE—a description of household characteristics at the time of the interview;

MIGFILE—a collection of data detailing the head of household's migration experiences;

PERSFILE—a description of each member of the household;

COMCROSS—a data set that contains various time-invariant characteristics of the Mexican communities surveyed by the project; and

COMYEAR—a data set that measures time-varying characteristics of the communities.

Published information from the International Monetary Fund's *International Financial Statistics*, the *Statistical Yearbook of the Immigration and Naturalization Service*, and other sources is used to create additional variables.

Table 4.1 lists the 31 Mexican communities of origin that had been surveyed by the project at the time that I started the data analysis for this book in early 1996. Since that time, the Mexican Migration Project has studied at least ten other communities. This book does not utilize information about these additional communities. The 31 survey communities range greatly in size, from small rural villages of less than 1,000 persons to urban centers of 400,000 inhabitants and more. Some communities are the sites of state or municipal governments. Nineteen communities are the *cabeceras* of their respective *municipios*, [1] and two are state capitals. Community 23, a small town in the State of Jalisco, may be thought of as the "median community." Its population in the survey year of approximately 10,000 is the median for the 31 communities, and the town is a *cabecera* as well. San Ramon is somewhat smaller in size with roughly 7,000 inhabitants, but it is also a *cabecera*. A total of 6,359 interviews were conducted for the 31 communities, 5,853 in Mexico and 506 in the United States.

The Mexican Migration Project is the continuation of a research project conducted in the early 1980s by Professor Massey, Professor Durand, Humberto González, and Rafael Alarcón. The four investigators interviewed persons in five communities in the States of

Table 4.1: Overview of Mexican Survey Communities

Community Number	State	Survey Year	Population Survey Year	Population 1993	Political Category	Number of Interviews Mexico	Number of Interviews U.S.	Observations in LIFE26 Mexico	Observations in LIFE26 U.S.
1	Guanajuato	1987	49,000	56,000	*Cabecera*	200	21	200	21
2	Guanajuato	1987	709,000	808,000	*Cabecera*	200	0	199	0
3	Jalisco	1988	3,000	4,000	*Cabecera*	200	22	200	22
4	Guanajuato	1988	16,000	17,000	*Cabecera*	200	22	200	22
5	Guanajuato	1988	2,000	2,000	*Tenencia*	150	10	150	10
6	Jalisco	1988	5,000	5,000	*Cabecera*	200	20	200	20
7	Jalisco	1988	3,000	3,000	*Tenencia*	200	15	200	15
8	Michoacán	1989	6,000	7,000	*Tenencia*	200	20	200	20
9	Michoacán	1989	32,000	35,000	*Cabecera*	200	20	200	20
10	Michoacán	1990	2,000	2,000	*Tenencia*	150	20	150	20
11	Nayarit	1990	20,000	21,000	*Cabecera*	200	20	200	20
12	Nayarit	1990	12,000	12,000	*Tenencia*	200	20	200	20
13	Guanajuato	1990	21,000	23,000	*Cabecera*	200	20	200	20
14	Michoacán	1990	7,000	7,000	*Cabecera*	200	20	200	20
15	Guanajuato	1991	275,000	294,000	*Cabecera*	200	20	200	20
16	Michoacán	1991	1,000	1,000	*Tenencia*	100	10	100	10
17	Jalisco	1991	31,000	32,000	*Cabecera*	200	20	200	20
18	Zacatecas	1991	8,000	8,000	*Cabecera*	365	20	365	20
19	Michoacán	1991	442,000	468,000	State Capital	200	20	200	20

Table 4.1 (continued)

Community Number	State	Survey Year	Population		Political Category	Number of Interviews		Observations in LIFE26	
			Survey Year	1993		Mexico	U.S.	Mexico	U.S.
20	Jalisco	1982	3,000	3,000	*Tenencia*	106	14	0	0
21	Jalisco	1982	1,000	2,000	*Tenencia*	94	6	0	0
22	Michoacán	1982	8,000	7,000	*Cabecera*	200	20	0	0
23	Jalisco	1982	10,000	12,000	*Cabecera*	200	20	0	0
24	Jalisco	1982	1,467,000	1,719,000	State Capital	200	16	0	0
25	Jalisco	1992	1,000	1,000	*Tenencia*	100	7	100	7
26	Guanajuato	1992	34,000	35,000	*Cabecera*	200	15	200	15
27	Guanajuato	1992	25,000	26,000	*Cabecera*	200	15	200	15
28	Jalisco	1992	75,000	76,000	*Cabecera*	201	20	200	20
29	Michoacán	1992	201,000	207,000	*Cabecera*	200	13	200	13
30	Zacatecas	1991	1,000	1,000	*Tenencia*	187	0	187	0
33	Colima	1994	7,000	7,000	*Cabecera*	200	20	200	20
					TOTAL	5,853	506	5,051	430

Sources: For list of communities, survey year, and number of interviews per community, Mexican Migration Project, "Table 1: Sample Information," http://www.pop.upenn.edu/mexmig/sampletable.html, downloaded 26 May 1998; for population estimates, COMYEAR (except for the figure for San Ramon, which comes from the road sign on the south end of town); and for political categories, COMCROSS.

Population figures are rounded to the nearest non-zero thousand.

A *cabecera* is a community that is the seat of its municipal government.

A *tenencia* is not the seat of government of the municipality to which it belongs.

Jalisco and Michoacán. This information eventually formed the base of the Mexican Migration Project's data, to which interviews from other communities have been added since 1987.[2]

The data from the first five communities (20, 21, 22, 23, and 24) are noteworthy for several reasons. First, the Mexican Migration Project did not conduct any U.S. interviews for these communities until quite recently. These U.S. interviews were not available when I began the data analysis for this book. Second, the retrospective life histories of the household heads from these five communities lack information about the number of months per year that the individuals spent in the United States. Thus, it is impossible to measure the length of their migration spells. Third, the life histories from these communities contain a few coding errors. For instance, the number of minor-age children in the household is occasionally reported to exceed the head of household's total offspring.

For these reasons, I have eliminated the observations for these communities from the econometric models in Chapters 5 and 6, which are based largely on the data set LIFEFILE.[3] The remaining 26 communities, which include San Ramon, generated a total of 6,359 interviews—5,853 in Mexico and 506 in the United States. Two Mexican observations contain missing values for some variables in the econometric models. Once these are deleted, the resulting data set, which I have named LIFE26, describes 5,481 heads of households— 5,051 in Mexico and 430 in the United States. Most of the descriptive tables in Sections 4.3 and 4.4 are based on LIFE26.

Because parents probably make the migration decisions for most young children, I also delete all observations in which the respondent was 13 years old or younger. The selection of this cutoff point reflects an educated guess as to the earliest age when respondents might have begun to make economic decisions for themselves. Several persons whom I interviewed in San Ramon mentioned that they were orphaned at an early age. These persons and a number of the older respondents indicated that they started to have significant work responsibilities at about age 14. One respondent remembered that he started to carry lunches to his father and other workers in the field at age seven. Several respondents married at age 14 and even younger, and the respondent from one of two trial interviews in Colorado migrated to the United States, mostly under his own volition, when he was only 15.

Even today, Mexican adolescence can be marked by considerable economic responsibility. Public education in Mexico is free only through the end of the *primaria*, which corresponds roughly to a sixth-grade education in the United States. In San Ramon, I met a number of teenagers who had completed the *primaria*, were no longer in school, lived at home, and worked in the family business. In addition, several parents whose children were nearing completion of the *primaria* expressed their concern that they would be unable to afford sending their children to the next level of schooling, the *secundaria*.

Finally, the Mexican Migration Project has produced a set of observation weights by which one may manipulate the data to construct a representative profile of western and central Mexico.[4] I have decided not to use these weights in order to avoid making a lengthy detour into the methodology used to create them and the possible ramifications of their use.

4.3. PROFILE OF SELECTED VARIABLES

4.3.1. Explanatory Notes

Most of the tables discussed in Sections 4.3 and 4.4 are based on the retrospective life histories found in LIFE26. The tables describe the heads of household in the 26-community sample during the survey year and during particular decades. The communities of origin were not all surveyed in the same year.[5] Thus, figures for the survey year indicate the number of household heads with a given characteristic at the time of their respective interviews. Specifically, the figures for the survey year utilize the observations from community 1 for its survey year (1987), the observations from community 2 for its survey year (1987), the observations from community 3 for its survey year (1988), and so on. In contrast, figures for the various decades count the number of observations with the given characteristic during the specified time period. Since each head of household yields one observation for each year recorded in the life history, the number of observations is counted in person-years, not persons.

One should treat the figures for the various decades with care. This information captures changes that occur in the sample over time, but these changes may be the result of numerous factors that are difficult to identify, including cohort effects, the aging of individuals as time advances, and differences in the survey year. Since the household heads were of different ages when they were interviewed, the number of observations in the sample gets smaller and smaller as one moves backwards in time. The data set thus is unbalanced in terms of the number of observations per respondent, an attribute for which I may compensate in econometric work subsequent to this book.[6]

4.3.2. U.S. Immigration Status

Appendix Table C.1 examines the number of household heads in the sample who are legal residents of the United States. For the purposes of this book, legal residents are defined as those persons who legally immigrated to the United States, including both non-citizens and naturalized citizens. Persons who entered the United States legally under the Bracero Program or using a tourist visa are not treated as legal residents. At the time of the interview, 817 of the 5,481 persons in the sample (14.41 percent) were legal residents.

Appendix Table C.2 tabulates the country in which the interview took place by the individual's U.S. immigration status. 316 of the legal residents were interviewed in the United States. Most persons in the sample who have secured legal U.S. immigration status did so within the last 30 years. The percentage of observations (measured in person-years) in which the individual possessed legal residency was 9.47 for the 1980s and only 5.87 for the 1970s. Only 20 heads of household were U.S. citizens at the time of the interview. These persons comprise a mere 0.36 percent of the individuals in the sample. One of the 20 was interviewed in Mexico.

4.3.3. Gender and Family Structure

Appendix Table C.3 indicates the proportion of observations in LIFE26 in which the head of household was female, as well as the proportion of households with and without minor-age children. Because the sampling frame of the Mexican Migration Project focuses on the head of household, males constitute the vast majority of respondents (87.48 percent). Some female heads of household are financially independent women who have never married, and a few are the primary breadwinners in households with two or more incomes. In most instances, however, women become heads of household due to separation from a spouse or the death or incapacitation of the husband.

During the 1970s, 1980s, and 1990s, the proportion of observations in which the head of household was female roughly equals the overall percentage of respondents who are female. As one moves back further in time, this proportion rises, reaching 31.21 percent in the 1920s. This trend is due to the fact that the female heads of household as a group were older than the males in the survey year.

72.94 percent of the households included minor-age children at the time of the interview. The percentage of such households headed by males in the survey year is 77.14, while the corresponding percentage for females is only 43.59. Again, this difference is largely due to the fact that the female heads of household are relatively older.

Appendix Table C.4 resembles Appendix Table C.3, except that the former table details the number of single-parent households with minor-age children. The number of such households is quite small: only 330 of the 3,998 households with minor-age children in the survey year fall into this category. A comparison of the two tables reveals that more than three-fourths of the single-parent households are headed by women. Of the 330 single-parent households, only 78 (23.64 percent) are headed by males. Also, 252 of the 299 female heads of household with minor-age children are single mothers.

4.3.4. Migration Networks

The data sets of the Mexican Migration Project offer two distinct ways of measuring whether a household has access to migration networks. Using the data set LIFEFILE (and hence LIFE26), one may discern whether the individual's father, mother, siblings, and grandparents had any U.S. migration experience as of each calendar year in the head of household's life history. The data set HOUSFILE provides the same information, as well as whether specific relatives and friends were living in the United States at the time of the interview. This information is available not only for the individual's parents, siblings, and grandparents, but also for uncles and aunts, cousins, the mother- and father-in-law, other in-laws, and friends.

The two measures capture different aspects of migration networks with greater precision. Previous migration experience in the family and even experience concurrent to the head of household's own migration experience may result in the transfer of useful information about crossing the border, searching for work in the United States, evading the INS, and so on. Family and friends in the United States may provide the migrant with a place where he or she can initially stay for little to no cost. To some extent, each measure captures the phenomenon directly measured by the other, and to some degree, both measures are likely to reflect the predisposition of certain families to migrate.

The network measures in LIFE26 do not account for the migration experiences of the head of household's sons and daughters. In some families, members of the younger generation may facilitate the subsequent migration of older relatives. In the future, I may use the data set HOUSFILE to craft measures of the U.S. migration experience of the head of household's offspring. These variables could then be used in conjunction with LIFE26.

Table 4.2 displays the number of household heads whose parents, siblings, or grandparents have U.S. migration experience. Such experience is quite common. A little more than half of the respondents (53.38 percent) are closely related to a current or former migrant. Nearly half (46.98 percent) possess at least one sibling with U.S. experience. The head of household's parents and grandparents are far less likely to have participated in migration. 22.37 percent of the respondents' fathers have done so, and an even smaller percentage of respondents (5.27) have at least one grandparent who is a current or former migrant. Relatively few of the respondents' mothers (5.33 percent) have ever migrated to the United States.

Perhaps the most dramatic phenomenon captured by Table 4.2 is the unrelenting growth in the proportion of respondents whose immediate relatives have U.S. migration experience. 16.66 percent of the observations for the 1930s correspond to individuals whose immediate relatives possessed U.S. experience. This percentage nearly doubles by the 1960s, reaching 32.55. For the 1990s, the percentage of such observations is 54.44, more than three times its level in the 1930s. Since these figures are derived from retrospective life histories and not from a panel that is representative of the survey communities across

Table 4.2: Migration Experience of Head of Household's Immediate Relatives

Year/ Decade	Total Heads of Household	Any Immediate Relative		Father		Mother		Sibling(s)		Grandparent(s)	
		Has U.S. Migration Experience	Lacks Migration Experience	Has U.S. Migration Experience	Lacks Migration Experience	Has U.S. Migration Experience	Lacks Migration Experience	Has U.S. Migration Experience	Lacks Migration Experience	Has U.S. Migration Experience	Lacks Migration Experience
Survey Year	5,481	2,926 53.38%	2,555 46.62%	1,226 22.37%	4,255 77.63%	292 5.33%	5,189 94.67%	2,575 46.98%	2,906 53.02%	289 5.27%	5,192 94.73%
1991-94	4,162	2,266 54.44%	1,896 45.56%	821 19.73%	3,341 80.27%	251 6.03%	3,911 93.97%	1,993 47.89%	2,169 52.11%	199 4.78%	3,963 95.22%
1981-90	50,569	25,150 49.73%	25,419 50.27%	11,320 22.39%	39,249 77.61%	2,314 4.58%	48,255 95.42%	20,986 41.50%	29,583 58.50%	2,662 5.26%	47,907 94.74%
1971-80	47,935	19,353 40.37%	28,582 59.63%	9,587 20.00%	38,348 80.00%	1,484 3.10%	46,451 96.90%	14,416 30.07%	33,519 69.93%	2,113 4.41%	45,822 95.59%
1961-70	35,803	11,654 32.55%	24,149 67.45%	6,286 17.56%	29,517 82.44%	696 1.94%	35,107 98.06%	7,650 21.37%	28,153 78.63%	1,164 3.25%	34,639 96.75%
1951-60	23,810	6,514 27.36%	17,296 72.64%	3,505 14.72%	20,305 85.28%	367 1.54%	23,443 98.46%	4,088 17.17%	19,722 82.83%	606 2.55%	23,204 97.45%
1941-50	14,098	2,988 21.19%	11,110 78.81%	1,662 11.79%	12,436 88.21%	163 1.16%	13,935 98.84%	1,662 11.79%	12,436 88.21%	271 1.92%	13,827 98.08%

Table 4.2 (continued)

Year/ Decade	Total Heads of Household	Any Immediate Relative		Father		Mother		Sibling(s)		Grandparent(s)	
		Has U.S. Migration Experience	Lacks Migration Experience	Has U.S. Migration Experience	Lacks Migration Experience	Has U.S. Migration Experience	Lacks Migration Experience	Has U.S. Migration Experience	Lacks Migration Experience	Has U.S. Migration Experience	Lacks Migration Experience
1931-40	6,586	1,097 16.66%	5,489 83.34%	698 10.60%	5,888 89.40%	55 0.84%	6531 99.16%	497 7.55%	6,089 92.45%	92 1.40%	6,494 98.60%
1921-30	2,179	307 14.09%	1,872 85.91%	161 7.39%	2,018 92.61%	14 0.64%	2,165 99.36%	180 8.26%	1,999 91.74%	32 1.47%	2,147 98.53%
1911-20	401	35 8.73%	366 91.27%	20 4.99%	381 95.01%	0 0.00%	401 100.00%	16 3.99%	385 96.01%	0 0.00%	401 100.00%
1905-10	31	0 0.00%	31 100.00%	0 0.00%	31 100.00%	0 0.00%	31 100.00%	0 0.00%	31 100.00%	0 0.00%	31 100.00%

Source: LIFE26

time, one should not interpret them as exact measures of the prevalence of migration. Nevertheless, the numbers indicate an unmistakable upward trend.

In order to provide a more precise measure of the extent of U.S. experience in the various survey communities, Massey, Goldring, and Durand (1994) craft a series of migration prevalence ratios for each of 19 survey communities from 1940 to the community's survey year. This prevalence ratio is defined as the number of persons in the community during a given year with U.S. migration experience divided by the community's total population. The average ratio for the communities in the survey year is 28 percent. The median community (number 12) presents a typical case. There, the earliest instance of U.S. migration recorded in the sample took place in 1943. By 1990, the community's prevalence ratio had reached 29 percent.[7]

When one considers the much broader set of friends and relatives detailed in HOUSFILE, one sees that migration networks may be quite pervasive of Mexican society. 75.12 percent of the respondents had at least one friend or relative in the United States at the time of the interview (see Table 4.3).[8] This percentage is somewhat higher for male heads of household than for females (76.29 versus 66.96). Nearly two-fifths of the household heads (39.95 percent) had a close friend in the United States at the time of the interview.[9]

Almost one-third of the household heads (32.21 percent) had one or more siblings in the United States when the interview took place. In contrast, only 2.27 percent of the household heads' fathers and 1.88 percent of their mothers were in the United States at this time. It was far more common for the head of household to have an uncle or aunt who was living in the United States at the time of the interview. Slightly more than one-fifth of the respondents (20.49 percent) had at least one such uncle or aunt.

4.3.5. Summary

Appendix Table C.5 displays sample statistics for LIFE26. When only observations for the survey year are considered, the typical head of

Table 4.3: Friends and Family in U.S. at Time of Interview by Head of Household's Gender

U.S. Contact	All Heads of Household		Male Household Heads		Female Household Heads	
	Has Specified U.S. Contact	Lacks Specified U.S. Contact	Has Specified U.S. Contact	Lacks Specified U.S. Contact	Has Specified U.S. Contact	Lacks Specified U.S. Contact
Any Close Friend or Relative	4,118 75.12%	1,364 24.88%	3,656 76.29%	1,136 23.71%	462 66.96%	228 33.04%
Any Family Member	3,919 71.49%	1,563 28.51%	3,469 72.39%	1,323 27.61%	450 65.22%	240 34.78%
Close Friend	2,190 39.95%	3,292 60.05%	2,062 43.03%	2,730 56.97%	128 18.55%	562 81.45%
Any Immediate Relative	1,792 32.69%	3,690 67.31%	1,631 34.04%	3,161 65.96%	161 23.33%	529 76.67%
Father	124 2.27%	5,348 97.73%	116 2.43%	4,666 97.57%	8 1.16%	682 98.84%
Mother	103 1.88%	5,379 98.12%	99 2.07%	4,693 97.93%	4 0.58%	686 99.42%
Sibling	1,766 32.21%	3,716 67.79%	1,606 33.51%	3,186 66.49%	160 23.19%	530 76.81%
Grandparent	22 0.40%	5,460 99.60%	21 0.44%	4,771 99.56%	1 0.14%	689 99.86%

Table 4.3 (continued)

U.S. Contact	All Heads of Household		Male Household Heads		Female Household Heads	
	Has Specified U.S. Contact	Lacks Specified U.S. Contact	Has Specified U.S. Contact	Lacks Specified U.S. Contact	Has Specified U.S. Contact	Lacks Specified U.S. Contact
Uncle or Aunt	1,123	4,359	1,056	3,736	67	623
	20.49%	79.51%	22.04%	77.96%	9.71%	90.29%
Cousin	2,193	3,289	1,996	2,796	197	493
	40.00%	60.00%	41.65%	58.35%	28.55%	71.45%
Nephew or Niece	2,214	3,268	1,912	2,880	302	388
	40.39%	59.61%	39.90%	60.10%	43.77%	56.23%
Brother- or Sister-In-Law	1,909	3,573	1,766	3,026	143	547
	34.82%	65.18%	36.85%	63.15%	20.72%	79.28%
Father- or Mother-In-Law	836	4,646	696	4,096	140	550
	15.25%	84.75%	14.52%	85.48%	20.29%	79.71%

Source: HOUSFILE

household is a married male with two minor-age children who lacks legal residency in the United States. At least one of his immediate relatives has U.S. migration experience.

When all observations are considered, the average individual is somewhat different. The typical head of household is still a married male who lacks legal residency and has two minor-age children. But in contrast to the average respondent at the time of the interview, this person is some 13 years younger, has attended three fewer years of school, and lacks an immediate relative with migration experience. In the next section, we shall see how some of these characteristics correspond to the head of household's migration decision.

4.4. RELATION OF CHARACTERISTICS TO THE MIGRATION DECISION

4.4.1. Gender and the Migration Decision

Using the data from HOUSFILE, Appendix Table C.6 distinguishes the household heads by the timing of their most recent U.S. migration experience. 14.90 percent of the respondents migrated to the United States within the three-year period prior to being interviewed. Another 30.79 percent migrated sometime before this period, bringing the total percentage of household heads with U.S. experience to 45.69.

Male heads of household are more likely to have migration experience than females. 16.28 percent of the males migrated to the United States during the three-year period prior to the interview, as compared to 5.36 percent of the females. The proportions of individuals with any U.S. experience are 49.96 percent for the males and 16.08 percent for the females.

Using the data from LIFE26, Appendix Table C.7 indicates the head of household's migration decision by the individual's gender. 18.89 percent of the male household heads and 5.54 percent of the females spent at least part of the survey year in the United States. With respect to the male heads of household, the percentage of observations in which the individual spent some part of the year in the United States drops from 16.73 percent in the 1980s to 14.09 percent in the 1970s. For the 1940s, 1950s, and 1960s, this percentage fluctuates between 8.40 and 9.87. The percentage of observations for females displays a similar pattern as one moves backwards in time, falling at first from the

1980s to the 1970s and then decreasing gradually, for the most part, for the sample's remainder. Interestingly, a fairly large number of older male respondents migrated to the United States between 1911 and 1930, a period that includes both the Mexican Revolution and the *Cristero* Rebellion. These individuals account for more than five percent of the total observations for males during this period.

4.4.2. U.S. Immigration Status

Appendix Table C.8 examines the relationship between legal residency in the United States and the migration decision. 74.91 percent of the household heads with legal residency spent all or part of the survey year in the United States, while only 7.12 percent of the individuals without legal residency did so. For legal residents, the percentage of observations in which the individual spent some part of the year in the United States fluctuates over the decades from the 1950s to the 1990s but remains in a band whose range is less than 15 percentage points. For non-residents, this percentage also fluctuates but appears to experience a gradual upward trend over time. Based on this data alone, it is not possible to assess the efficacy of INS efforts to deter illegal entry into the United States.

From the 1960s to the 1980s, the percentage of observations for legal residents in which the head of household remains in Mexico for the entire year climbs from 13.70 to 22.58. The reason for this upward trend is unclear, although it may be tied to the aging of the respondents in the sample. In any case, it is extremely important to note that many legal residents spend extended periods of time in Mexico. Indeed, the possession of legal U.S. immigration status may facilitate the earlier return of migrants to Mexico, since these persons can return to the United States with relative ease when and if the need or desire arises. Appendix Table C.9 reveals that the U.S. citizens in the sample are not likely to live in Mexico. Presumably, these persons have established permanent roots north of the border.

4.4.3. Family Structure

Appendix Table C.10 details the relationship between minor-age children and the migration decision. Nearly one-fifth of the respondents with minor-age children spent some part of the survey year in the

United States, as opposed to 10.78 percent of the individuals without minor-age children. These percentages are roughly the same when only male heads of household are considered (see Appendix Table C.11). Thus, one possible motive for migration is to earn the income necessary for supporting dependent children. Appendix Table C.12 indicates that these percentages are much smaller for female heads of household (7.02 and 4.39 respectively). One possible explanation of this difference is that females must weigh the benefits of migration against the prospect of placing their children in someone else's care.

At first glance, single parents appear to be far less likely than other household heads to participate in international migration. Only 9.39 percent of the sample's single parents spent some part of the survey year in the United States, in contrast to 17.22 percent of all other respondents (see Appendix Table C.13). However, this result is driven by the fact that the overwhelming majority of single parents in the sample are single mothers. If one examines female respondents separately, there is no discernible difference between the migration rate for single mothers and that for all other household heads. 5.56 percent of the single mothers spent some part of the survey year in the United States, as opposed to 5.53 percent of the other female household heads (see Appendix Table C.14).

Single fathers are somewhat more likely to migrate than other male household heads. 21.79 percent of the single fathers spent some part of the survey year in the United States, in contrast to 18.85 percent of all other male household heads (see Appendix Table C.15). The different migration rates for single fathers and single mothers may be the result of varying attitudes across genders about leaving one's children in someone else's care for extended periods of time. Another possible explanation is that single mothers are less likely to receive long-term childcare assistance from relatives and friends than single fathers.

4.4.4. Migration Networks

First, let us use LIFE26 to examine the relationship between the U.S. migration experience of the head of household's immediate family and the individual's own migration decision. Respondents whose father,

Table 4.4: Head of Household's Migration Decision by U.S. Experience of Immediate Family

Year/Decade	All Heads of Household		Heads of Household Whose Immediate Family Has U.S. Migration Experience		Heads of Household Whose Immediate Family Has No U.S. Migration Experience	
	Spent Part or All of Year in U.S.	Did Not Spend Year in U.S.	Spent Part or All of Year in U.S.	Did Not Spend Year in U.S.	Spent Part or All of Year in U.S.	Did Not Spend Year in U.S.
Survey Year	953	4,528	778	2,148	175	2,380
	17.39%	82.61%	26.59%	73.41%	6.85%	93.15%
1991-94	862	3,600	751	1,791	111	1,809
	19.32%	80.68%	29.54%	70.46%	5.78%	94.22%
1981-90	7,911	42,818	6,406	18,897	1,505	23,921
	15.59%	84.41%	25.32%	74.68%	5.92%	94.08%
1971-80	6,091	41,844	4,577	14,776	1,514	27,068
	12.71%	87.29%	23.65%	76.35%	5.30%	94.70%
1961-70	2,639	33,164	1,817	9,837	822	23,327
	7.37%	92.63%	15.59%	84.41%	3.40%	96.60%
1951-60	1,947	21,863	1,169	5,345	778	16,518
	8.18%	91.82%	17.95%	82.05%	4.50%	95.50%
1941-50	943	13,155	473	2,515	470	10,640
	6.69%	93.31%	15.83%	84.17%	4.23%	95.77%

Table 4.4 (continued)

Year/Decade	All Heads of Household		Heads of Household Whose Immediate Family Has U.S. Migration Experience		Heads of Household Whose Immediate Family Has No U.S. Migration Experience	
	Spent Part or All of Year in U.S.	Did Not Spend Year in U.S.	Spent Part or All of Year in U.S.	Did Not Spend Year in U.S.	Spent Part or All of Year in U.S.	Did Not Spend Year in U.S.
1931-40	75	6,511	31	1,066	44	5,445
	1.14%	98.86%	2.83%	97.17%	0.80%	99.20%
1921-30	83	2,096	25	282	58	1,814
	3.81%	96.19%	8.14%	91.86%	3.10%	96.90%
1911-20	18	383	0	35	18	348
	4.49%	95.51%	0.00%	100 00%	4.92%	95.08%
1905-10	3	28	0	0	3	28
	9.68%	90.32%	n.a.	n.a.	9.68%	90.32%

Immediate family is defined as the head of household's father, mother, siblings, and grandparents.

Source: LIFE26

mother, grandparents, or siblings possessed U.S. migration experience were far more likely to migrate than individuals whose relatives lacked this experience. Table 4.4 shows that 26.38 percent of the heads of household whose immediate family had U.S. experience spent some part of the survey year in the United States, as opposed to 6.73 percent of the individuals whose immediate relatives did not.

Next, let us consider just those observations in LIFE26 for persons whose immediate family had previous migration experience. From the 1940s to the 1980s, the percentage of such observations in which the head of household spent part of the year in the United States steadily climbed, from 15.83 to 24.76. Coupled with the persistent increase in the percentage of Mexican families with previous migration experience (see Table 4.2) and the growth of Mexico's population, this increase in the migration rate translates into a dramatic increase in the number of Mexicans participating in international migration.

Tables 4.5, 4.6, 4.7, and 4.8 allow us to compare the head of household's migration decision to the migration experience of his or her relatives. Among the four types of relatives considered, having a mother who is a current or former migrant appears to be the best predictor of whether the respondent spends some part of the year in the United States. 51.03 percent of the individuals whose mother possessed U.S. experience spent at least part of the survey year in the United States (see Table 4.6). Having one or more grandparents with migration experience is the next best predictor: 43.94 percent of the respondents with at least one such grandparent spent part if not all of the survey year in the United States (see Table 4.8). The number of respondents whose mother or grandparents were actually living in the United States at the time of interview is quite small (see Table 4.9). Nevertheless, it is possible that the past migration of these relatives reflects the existence of other U.S. contacts within the extended family.

Now, let us turn to the information in HOUSFILE about the relationship between the head of household's migration decision and the presence of friends or relatives in the United States. Of the 4,118 heads of household in the data set who had at least one friend or family member in the United States at the time of the interview, 18.19 percent migrated during the three-year period before the interview (see

Table 4.5: Head of Household's Migration Decision By U.S. Experience of Individual's Father

Year/Decade	All Heads of Household		Heads of Household Whose Father Has U.S. Migration Experience		Heads of Household Whose Father Has No U.S. Migration Experience	
	Spent Part or All of Year in U.S.	Did Not Spend Year in U.S.	Spent Part or All of Year in U.S.	Did Not Spend Year in U.S.	Spent Part or All of Year in U.S.	Did Not Spend Year in U.S.
Survey Year	953	4,528	428	798	525	3,730
	17.39%	82.61%	34.91%	65.09%	12.34%	87.66%
1991-94	862	3,600	399	583	463	3,017
	19.32%	80.68%	40.63%	59.37%	13.30%	86.70%
1981-90	7,911	42,818	3,639	7,759	4,272	35,059
	15.59%	84.41%	31.93%	68.07%	10.86%	89.14%
1971-80	6,091	41,844	2,671	6,916	3,420	34,928
	12.71%	87.29%	27.86%	72.14%	8.92%	91.08%
1961-70	2,639	33,164	1,104	5,182	1,535	27,982
	7.37%	92.63%	17.56%	82.44%	5.20%	94.80%
1951-60	1,947	21,863	611	2,894	1,336	18,969
	8.18%	91.82%	17.43%	82.57%	6.58%	93.42%
1941-50	943	13,155	234	1,428	709	11,727
	6.69%	93.31%	14.08%	85.92%	5.70%	94.30%

Table 4.5 (continued)

Year/Decade	All Heads of Household		Heads of Household Whose Father Has U.S. Migration Experience		Heads of Household Whose Father Has No U.S. Migration Experience	
	Spent Part or All of Year in U.S.	Did Not Spend Year in U.S.	Spent Part or All of Year in U.S.	Did Not Spend Year in U.S.	Spent Part or All of Year in U.S.	Did Not Spend Year in U.S.
1931-40	75	6,511	13	685	62	5,826
	1.14%	98.86%	1.86%	98.14%	1.05%	98.95%
1921-30	83	2,096	16	145	67	1,951
	3.81%	96.19%	9.94%	90.06%	3.32%	96.68%
1911-20	18	383	0	20	18	363
	4.49%	95.51%	0.00%	100.00%	4.72%	95.28%
1905-10	3	28	0	0	3	28
	9.68%	90.32%	n.a.	n.a.	9.68%	90.32%

Source: LIFE26

Table 4.6: Head of Household's Migration Decision By U.S. Experience of Individual's Mother

Year/Decade	All Heads of Household		Heads of Household Whose Mother Has U.S. Migration Experience		Heads of Household Whose Mother Has No U.S. Migration Experience	
	Spent Part or All of Year in U.S.	Did Not Spend Year in U.S.	Spent Part or All of Year in U.S.	Did Not Spend Year in U.S.	Spent Part or All of Year in U.S.	Did Not Spend Year in U.S.
Survey Year	953 / 17.39%	4,528 / 82.61%	149 / 51.03%	143 / 48.97%	804 / 15.49%	4,385 / 84.51%
1991-94	862 / 19.32%	3,600 / 80.68%	230 / 65.16%	123 / 34.84%	632 / 15.38%	3,477 / 84.62%
1981-90	7,911 / 15.59%	42,818 / 84.41%	1,204 / 51.50%	1,134 / 48.50%	6,707 / 13.86%	41,684 / 86.14%
1971-80	6,091 / 12.71%	41,844 / 87.29%	734 / 49.46%	750 / 50.54%	5,357 / 11.53%	41,094 / 88.47%
1961-70	2,639 / 7.37%	33,164 / 92.63%	260 / 37.36%	436 / 62.64%	2,379 / 6.78%	32,728 / 93.22%
1951-60	1,947 / 8.18%	21,863 / 91.82%	132 / 35.97%	235 / 64.03%	1,815 / 7.74%	21,628 / 92.26%
1941-50	943 / 6.69%	13,155 / 93.31%	46 / 28.22%	117 / 71.78%	897 / 6.44%	13,038 / 93.56%

Table 4.6 (continued)

Year/Decade	All Heads of Household		Heads of Household Whose Mother Has U.S. Migration Experience		Heads of Household Whose Mother Has No U.S. Migration Experience	
	Spent Part or All of Year in U.S.	Did Not Spend Year in U.S.	Spent Part or All of Year in U.S.	Did Not Spend Year in U.S.	Spent Part or All of Year in U.S.	Did Not Spend Year in U.S.
1931-40	75 / 1.14%	6,511 / 98.86%	6 / 10.91%	49 / 89.09%	69 / 1.06%	6,462 / 98.94%
1921-30	83 / 3.81%	2,096 / 96.19%	4 / 28.57%	10 / 71.43%	79 / 3.65%	2,086 / 96.35%
1911-20	18 / 4.49%	383 / 95.51%	0 / n.a.	0 / n.a.	18 / 4.49%	383 / 95.51%
1905-10	3 / 9.68%	28 / 90.32%	0 / n.a.	0 / n.a.	3 / 9.68%	28 / 90.32%

Source: LIFE26

Table 4.7: Head of Household's Migration Decision by U.S. Experience of Individual's Siblings

Year/Decade	All Heads of Household		Heads of Household With One or More Siblings With U.S. Migration Experience		Heads of Household With No Siblings With U.S. Migration Experience	
	Spent Part or All of Year in U.S.	Did Not Spend Year in U.S.	Spent Part or All of Year in U.S.	Did Not Spend Year in U.S.	Spent Part or All of Year in U.S.	Did Not Spend Year in U.S.
Survey Year	953	4,528	732	1,843	221	2,685
	17.39%	82.61%	28.43%	71.57%	7.60%	92.40%
1991-94	862	3,600	704	1,551	158	2,049
	19.32%	80.68%	31.22%	68.78%	7.16%	92.84%
1981-90	7,911	42,818	5,856	15,278	2,055	27,540
	15.59%	84.41%	27.71%	72.29%	6.94%	93.06%
1971-80	6,091	41,844	3,903	10,513	2,188	31,331
	12.71%	87.29%	27.07%	72.93%	6.53%	93.47%
1961-70	2,639	33,164	1,441	6,209	1,198	26,955
	7.37%	92.63%	18.84%	81.16%	4.26%	95.74%
1951-60	1,947	21,863	867	3,221	1,080	18,642
	8.18%	91.82%	21.21%	78.79%	5.48%	94.52%
1941-50	943	13,155	357	1,305	586	11,850
	6.69%	93.31%	21.48%	78.52%	4.71%	95.29%

Table 4.7 (continued)

Year/Decade	All Heads of Household		Heads of Household With One or More Siblings With U.S. Migration Experience		Heads of Household With No Siblings With U.S. Migration Experience	
	Spent Part or All of Year in U.S.	Did Not Spend Year in U.S.	Spent Part or All of Year in U.S.	Did Not Spend Year in U.S.	Spent Part or All of Year in U.S.	Did Not Spend Year in U.S.
1931-40	75	6,511	27	470	48	6,041
	1.14%	98.86%	5.43%	94.57%	0.79%	99.21%
1921-30	83	2,096	13	167	70	1,929
	3.81%	96.19%	7.22%	92.78%	3.50%	96.50%
1911-20	18	383	0	16	18	367
	4.49%	95.51%	0.00%	100.00%	4.68%	95.32%
1905-10	3	28	0	0	3	28
	9.68%	90.32%	n.a.	n.a.	9.68%	90.32%

Source: LIFE26

Table 4.8: Head of Household's Migration Decision by U.S. Experience of Individual's Grandparents

Year/Decade	All Heads of Household		Heads of Household With One or More Grandparents With U.S. Migration Experience		Heads of Household With No Grandparent With U.S. Migration Experience	
	Spent Part or All of Year in U.S.	Did Not Spend Year in U.S.	Spent Part or All of Year in U.S.	Did Not Spend Year in U.S.	Spent Part or All of Year in U.S.	Did Not Spend Year in U.S.
Survey Year	953 / 17.39%	4,528 / 82.61%	127 / 43.94%	162 / 56.06%	826 / 15.91%	4,366 / 84.09%
1991-94	862 / 19.32%	3,600 / 80.68%	123 / 49.00%	128 / 51.00%	739 / 17.55%	3,472 / 82.45%
1981-90	7,911 / 15.59%	42,818 / 84.41%	1,120 / 41.51%	1,578 / 58.49%	6,791 / 14.14%	41,240 / 85.86%
1971-80	6,091 / 12.71%	41,844 / 87.29%	685 / 32.42%	1,428 / 67.58%	5,406 / 11.80%	40,416 / 88.20%
1961-70	2,639 / 7.37%	33,164 / 92.63%	257 / 22.08%	907 / 77.92%	2,382 / 6.88%	32,257 / 93.12%
1951-60	1,947 / 8.18%	21,863 / 91.82%	127 / 20.96%	479 / 79.04%	1,820 / 7.84%	21,384 / 92.16%
1941-50	943 / 6.69%	13,155 / 93.31%	40 / 14.76%	231 / 85.24%	903 / 6.53%	12,924 / 93.47%

Table 4.8 (continued)

Year/Decade	All Heads of Household		Heads of Household With One or More Grandparents With U.S. Migration Experience		Heads of Household With No Grandparent With U.S. Migration Experience	
	Spent Part or All of Year in U.S.	Did Not Spend Year in U.S.	Spent Part or All of Year in U.S.	Did Not Spend Year in U.S.	Spent Part or All of Year in U.S.	Did Not Spend Year in U.S.
1931-40	75 1.14%	6,511 98.86%	0 0.00%	92 100.00%	75 1.15%	6,419 98.85%
1921-30	83 3.81%	2,096 96.19%	0 0.00%	32 100.00%	83 3.87%	2,064 96.13%
1911-20	18 4.49%	383 95.51%	0 n.a.	0 n.a.	18 4.49%	383 95.51%
1905-10	3 9.68%	28 90.32%	0 n.a.	0 n.a.	3 9.68%	28 90.32%

Source: LIFE26

Table 4.9: Friends and Family in U.S. at Time of Interview by Head of Household's U.S. Experience

Tye of Relative or Friend	Relative or Friend Present In U.S.?	Total	Most Recent U.S. Migration Experience		
			Within Three-Year Period Prior To Interview	More Than Three Years Prior to Interview	No U.S. Migration Experience
Total		5,482	817 14.90%	1,688 30.79%	2,977 54.30%
Any Close Friend or Relative	Yes	4,118	749 18.19%	1,453 35.28%	1,916 46.53%
	No	1,364	68 4.99%	235 17.23%	1,061 77.79%
Any Relative	Yes	3,919	731 18.65%	1,409 35.95%	1,779 45.39%
	No	1,563	86 5.50%	279 17.85%	1,198 76.65%
Close Friend	Yes	2,190	477 21.78%	892 40.73%	821 37.49%
	No	3,292	340 10.33%	796 24.18%	2,156 65.49%

Table 4.9 (continued)

Type of Relative or Friend	Relative or Friend Present In U.S.?	Total	Most Recent U.S. Migration Experience		
			Within Three-Year Period To Interview	More Than Three Years Prior to Interview	No U.S. Migration Experience
Any Immediate Relative (1)					
	Yes	1,792	480 26.79% 337 9.13%	754 42.08% 934 25.31%	558 31.14% 2,419 65.56%
	No	3,690			
Father					
	Yes	124	47 37.90% 770 14.40%	52 41.94% 1,626 30.40%	25 20.16% 2,952 55.20%
	No	5,348			
Mother					
	Yes	103	33 32.04% 784 14.58%	57 55.34% 1,631 30.32%	13 12.62% 2,964 55.10%
	No	5,379			

Table 4.9 (continued)

Type of Relative or Friend	Relative or Friend Present In U.S.?	Total	Most Recent U.S. Migration Experience		
			Within Three-Year Period Prior To Interview	More Than Three Years Prior to Interview	No U.S. Migration Experience
Sibling					
	Yes	1,766	474	745	547
			26.84%	42.19%	30.97%
	No	3,716	343	943	2,430
			9.23%	25.38%	65.39%
Grandparent					
	Yes	22	4	9	9
			18.18%	40.91%	40.91%
	No	5,460	813	1,679	2,968
			14.89%	30.75%	54.36%
Uncle/Aunt					
	Yes	1,123	286	433	404
			25.47%	38.56%	35.98%
	No	4,359	531	1,255	2,573
			12.18%	28.79%	59.03%

Table 4.9 (continued)

Type of Relative or Friend	Relative or Friend Present In U.S.?	Total	Most Recent U.S. Migration Experience		
			Within Three-Year Period To Interview	More Than Three Years Prior to Interview	No U.S. Migration Experience
Cousin	Yes	2,193	501 22.85%	854 38.94%	838 38.21%
	No	3,289	316 9.61%	834 25.36%	2,139 65.03%
Nephew/Niece	Yes	2,214	415 18.74%	899 40.61%	900 40.65%
	No	3,268	402 12.30%	789 24.14%	2,077 63.56%
Brother-/Sister-In-Law	Yes	1,909	459 24.04%	769 40.28%	681 35.67%
	No	3,573	358 10.02%	919 25.72%	2,296 64.26%

Table 4.9 (continued)

Type of Relative or Friend	Relative or Friend Present In U.S.	Total	Most Recent U.S. Migration Experience		
			Within Three-Year Period Prior To Interview	More Than Three Years Prior to Interview	No U.S. Migration Experience
Mother- or /Father-In-Law					
	Yes	836	170 20.33%	401 47.97%	265 31.70%
	No	4,646	647 13.93%	1,287 27.70%	2,712 58.37%

(1) Immediate relatives include the head of household's father, mother, siblings, and grandparents.

Source: HOUSFILE

Table 4.9). In contrast, only 8.32 percent of the respondents who lacked friends and family in the United States migrated during the same period.

Among the various relatives listed in Table 4.9, the best predictor of whether the head of household participated in migration during the three years prior to the interview is the presence of the individual's father in the United States. Of the respondents whose father lived in the United States at the time of the interview, 37.90 percent migrated during this three-year period. In contrast, 20.16 percent of these respondents had never migrated to the United States. For individuals whose mother was in the United States at the time of the interview, the corresponding percentages are 32.04 and 12.62 respectively. Thus, the father's migration experience appears to be more important to the head of household's migration decision than LIFE26 indicates.

4.5. CONCLUSION

Several of the individual characteristics examined in this chapter correspond with being more likely to migrate to the United States. These attributes include legal U.S. immigration status, being male, having minor-age children, and having access to migration networks, as measured by the previous migration experience of one's relatives. The typical individual described by LIFE26 possessed several of these characteristics in the survey year—most notably, being male, having minor-age children, and having someone among his father, mother, siblings, or grandparents with U.S. experience. In Chapters 5 and 6, the head of household's migration decision is modeled using the complete set of explanatory variables available in LIFE26.

NOTES

1. A *cabecera* is similar to a county seat in the United States. Mexican states are generally divided into municipalities or *municipios*, which have the responsibilities of local government.

2. Professor Massey indicates that the initial inspiration for the project resulted from meeting Joshua Reichert in 1978, who was then a graduate student of anthropology at Princeton University. Professor Massey helped code interviews from field research that Reichert conducted in a small town in the State of Michoacán, and the two ultimately collaborated on several papers.

3. The earnings regressions in Chapter 7 rely primarily on the data sets HOUSFILE and PERSFILE. These models do not utilize the data from the first five communities surveyed or communities 2 and 30. This is due to the fact that no U.S. interviews had been conducted for these communities when I began the data analysis for this book.

4. For details on the creation of these weights and their application to estimating migrant remittances to Mexico, see Massey and Parrado (1994).

5. See Table 4.1 for a list of the survey years.

6. For two discussions of the issue of unbalanced panel data, see Chapter 9 of Baltagi (1995) and Verbeek and Nijman (1992).

7. Massey, Goldring, and Durand (1994: 1509).

8. Table 4.3 works with a base of 5,482 heads of household. This total is one less than the number of household heads in LIFE26.

9. One should approach this last statistic with some caution. The survey instrument solicits from the head of household the number of his or her friends who currently live in the United States. In my fieldwork in San Ramon, my assistants and I clarified this question by asking for the number of *amigos muy amigos* (very good friends). Some respondents nevertheless indicated that they had in excess of 100 such friends in the United States.

CHAPTER 5

A Basic Participation Model

5.1. INTRODUCTION

This chapter presents a basic model of the head of household's migration decision. Such models are often called participation models, in reference to the potential migrant's decision regarding whether to participate in migration so as to participate in the labor market of the destination country.

Participation models account for much of the econometric research about migration networks.[1] Nevertheless, this subject warrants another visit for several reasons. Since new communities are added to the data sets of the Mexican Migration Project nearly every year, it is worthwhile from time to time to re-test the hypotheses examined using earlier versions of the data. The models in this chapter utilize the retrospective life histories from 26 of the project's survey communities. To my knowledge, only Massey and Espinosa (1997) draw upon a comparable portion of the histories. García España and Massey (1987) examine the migration decision of the head of household for the 1980-82 period only using data from four survey communities, and García España (1992) looks at the migration decision of each household member in only two survey communities during the same period.

However, there is a far more important reason to revisit this subject. At best, the existing econometric literature identifies a *general* connection between migration networks and Mexican participation in international migration. Typically, these works focus on either the broad presence of friends and relatives in the United States or the existence of U.S. experience within the prospective migrant's family. But the works do not evaluate the relative importance to the migration decision of different family members. For instance, siblings may be in a better position than older relatives to facilitate the head of household's migration since their U.S. contacts and knowledge of migration are relatively fresh.

Moreover, with the exception of Massey and Espinosa (1997), the existing literature does not distinguish the influence of networks on first migration from their influence on repeat migration. If individuals become less likely to rely on networks as they accumulate migration experience, then the U.S. experience of relatives should exercise a stronger influence on first migration than on the repeat phenomenon.

To address these issues, this chapter employs two sets of network variables. Together, they describe the migration experience of the head of household family in far greater detail than has been done previously. The first set is a vector of dummy variables that indicate whether particular relatives migrated to the United States during or prior to the given calendar year. The relatives considered are the parents, grandparents, and siblings of the household head. LIFEFILE lacks comparable information about other relatives, such as aunts, uncles, cousins, and the head of household's offspring. Thus, the influence of these persons is not addressed.

A second vector of dummy variables identifies the presence of family migration experience for household heads who have not yet participated in migration. The two sets of network variables make it possible to assess the separate influences of such experience on first and repeat migration. Gender-specific measures in both sets of network variables distinguish the migration experience of brothers from that of sisters, of fathers from that of mothers, and of grandfathers from that of grandmothers.

This chapter is organized as follows. Section 5.2 presents a simple economic model of the head of household's migration decision. This model is then related to an econometric specification, a standard logit model. Next, the section identifies the explanatory variables used in the logit model and outlines my hypotheses regarding their influence on migration. Section 5.3 analyzes the results from a series of participation models that utilize the data set LIFE26. Finally, Section 5.4 summarizes the chapter's main findings.

5.2. THE MODEL

5.2.1. The Economic Model

Many empirical studies about migration rely upon economic models in which the utility function is not explicitly stated. In these models, the potential migrant evaluates the difference between expected income in the prospective destination and the income available in the individual's current location.[2] This type of modeling belongs to the classic tradition established by Todaro (1969) and is somewhat simpler mathematically than models of utility maximization. However, I wish to infer that the migration decision is predicated, at least in part, on the individual's relative preferences for labor and leisure. Therefore, my underlying economic model, which resembles one developed by Olea (1988), must explicitly involve utility maximization. In addition, the econometric models in this chapter contain only variables that pertain to the year that the prospective migrant is considering spending in the United States. Thus, the migration decision may be cast within a static framework, as the resulting econometric specification is consistent with either a static or a dynamic model.

In my model, the head of household seeks to maximize expected utility for a given time period by choosing between two competing options: migrating to the United States and remaining in Mexico. The individual also selects the optimal combination of labor and leisure for this period. The optimization problem facing the household head may be expressed as follows:

$$\text{Max } E[(1 - d)\, U(C, L_{MX}) + d\, U(C, L_{US})]$$

subject to

$$C = Y + (1 - d)\, p_{MX}\, w_{MX}\, (1 - L_{MX}) + d\, [p_D\, p_{US}\, w_{US}\, (1 - L_{US}) - M].$$

The utility function is assumed to be quasiconcave and a function of two arguments: consumption (C) and leisure (L). C reflects the consumption of the entire household, as the household head is assumed to derive utility not only from his or her own consumption but also from that of other members of the household. Leisure comes in two mutually exclusive forms: L_{US}, leisure experienced as a migrant in the

United States, and L_{MX}, leisure experienced by the individual who remains in Mexico.[3] To keep the model simple, "leisure" is defined as any activity other than wage labor. This definition encompasses some non-wage work activities such as housework and childcare. The dummy variable, d, equals one if the head of household migrates to the United States and zero otherwise.

The budget constraint contains the wage expected by the household head for work in the United States ($p_{US} w_{US}$) and work in Mexico (p_D $p_{MX} w_{MX}$), additional sources of household income (Y), and, for those individuals who migrate, migration costs (M). The variables p_{US} and p_{MX} indicate the probabilities of finding work in the United States and Mexico respectively, while p_D measures that portion of the time period in which the prospective migrant expects to be able to work in the United States without being deported. Additional income sources include agricultural land, a business owned by the household, and gift income received from the head of household's adult offspring. Migration costs are strictly monetary costs incurred by migrants to the United States, such as transportation and the cost of hiring a *coyote*. The psychic costs of migration are captured not by M but instead by the two leisure terms, as leisure time in Mexico is viewed as superior to that passed in the United States.

The head of household migrates when the highest level of expected utility that may be obtained from migration exceeds the highest level that may be secured by remaining in Mexico. This migration rule may be expressed by the inequality

$$E[U(C_{US}{}^*, L_{US}{}^*) - U(C_{MX}{}^*, L_{MX}{}^*)] > 0,$$

where $C_{US}{}^*$ and $L_{US}{}^*$ are the optimal levels of consumption and leisure for the person who migrates, and $C_{MX}{}^*$ and $L_{MX}{}^*$ are the corresponding levels for the person who stays in Mexico.

5.2.2. Relation to the Econometric Model

The econometric specification used in this chapter is a simple logit model. The probability that the head of household migrates to the United States (and hence the probability that the migration rule is met) equals the logistic distribution:

$$P[d = 1] = \exp(\mathbf{x}'\beta) / [1 + \exp(\mathbf{x}'\beta)].$$

The vector of explanatory variables (**x**) acts upon migration through two major routes. First, some variables alter the head of household's relative preferences for labor and leisure. As consumption and hence labor become more appealing relative to leisure, migration becomes more likely. Second, some variables loosen or tighten the budget constraint. Migration becomes less probable when the household has greater access to income sources other than the household head's labor power, since he or she is able to purchase a higher quantity of consumption without sacrificing leisure. Variables that increase the returns to U.S. labor increase the probability of migration. Similarly, variables that increase the returns to labor in Mexico deter migration.

5.2.3. Explanatory Variables

Table 5.1 lists the explanatory variables used in the participation models and the hypothesized direction of their net effect on the migration decision.[4] These variables may be divided into six vectors: (1) individual characteristics, (2) family responsibilities, (3) additional income sources, (4) U.S. immigration status and policies, (5) family migration experience, and (6) national labor market conditions. While most variables in vectors (1), (2), and (3) customarily appear in models of the migration decision, many variables in the other vectors do not.

The vector of individual characteristics describes the gender, age, educational level, and cumulative U.S. migration experience of the individual. The vector also contains a variable that indicates whether the interview was conducted in the United States or Mexico.

Historically, Mexican women have been less likely to participate in international migration than Mexican men. Although this difference has narrowed in recent years, being female should still reduce the probability of migration. Relative to the Mexican population, the household heads of LIFE26 are an old group. Between 1987 and 1994, the median age of the Mexican population ranged between 18 and 22 years (United Nations 1990). In contrast, the median age of the respondents in LIFE26 at the time of the interview is 44 years. In fact, the earliest observation in the sample covers the year 1905.

Table 5.1: Hypothesized Net Effects of Explanatory Variables on Head of Household's Migration Decision

Vector/Variable	Hypothesized Net Effect
Individual characteristics	
Female	Negative
Age (in years)	Positive
Age squared	Negative
Education (in years)	Negative
U.S. migration experience (in months)	Positive
U.S. experience squared	Negative
U.S. interview	Positive
Family responsibilities	
Married	Negative
Single parent	Negative
Single mother	Negative
Number of minor-age children	Positive
Additional income sources	
Number of adult offspring	Negative
Business ownership	Negative
Agricultural land (in hectares)	Negative
U.S. immigration status	
Legal resident of U.S.	Positive
U.S. citizen	Positive
U.S. immigration policies	
Bracero Program in effect	Positive
Amnesty Program in effect	Positive
1968-76	Positive
1977-91	Positive
1992-94	Positive
Deportation ratio	Negative
Relative with U.S. migration experience	
Grandparent	Positive
Grandfather	Positive
Grandmother	Positive
Father	Positive
Mother	Positive
Sibling	Positive
Brother	Positive
Sister	Positive

Table 5.1 (continued)

Vector/Variable	Hypothesized Net Effect
Relatives with U.S. migration experience	
when household head has not yet migrated	
Grandparent	Positive
Grandfather	Positive
Grandmother	Positive
Father	Positive
Mother	Positive
Sibling	Positive
Brother	Positive
Sister	Positive
National economic conditions	
Real GDP growth per capita in Mexico	Negative
Real GDP growth per capita in U.S.	Positive
Real GDP per capita in Mexico	Negative
Real GDP per capita in U.S.	Positive

Within the context of the economic model outlined above, the lower probability of migration for females is associated with their relatively strong preferences for non-wage activities over wage labor. Many of the sample's female heads of household care for an incapacitated spouse. In addition, gender differences may exist in how Mexicans value leaving one's family for extended periods of time. Interestingly, if the wage-earning ability of Mexican women is for some reason less than that of Mexican men (for instance, if women experience a lower degree of human capital accumulation), then females should be more likely to migrate. This may explain the movement of younger Mexican women to areas of high employment within Mexico and their increasing rate of U.S. migration.

With respect to age, the prevalent thinking is that middle-aged persons are more likely to migrate than the very young and the very old (Sprouse 1991; Taylor 1987, 1984; García España 1992; García España and Massey 1987). If this relation holds true, then the probability of migration first climbs as a person initially gets older and then decreases as he or she becomes increasingly aged. The parameter estimates for age and its square should therefore be positive and negative respectively.

Individuals with more schooling should be able to earn higher incomes in Mexico. This should reduce the likelihood that such persons find it worthwhile to migrate to the United States. Thus, the probability of migration should fall as educational level rises. Persons with a college education should be particularly less likely to participate in international migration.

As the household head accumulates work experience in the United States, his or her earnings may converge on but not surpass those of U.S. natives with similar attributes. If this is the case, then U.S. experience should increase the probability of migrating to the United States, and its square should have the opposite effect. Using data from the 1970 U.S. Census, Chiswick (1978) offers evidence that the earnings of the foreign-born of that era eventually exceeded those of similar persons born in the United States. However, he finds that the U.S. earnings of Mexican-born workers are lower than those of other foreign-born workers.

In the last decade, Borjas (1990, 1985) has taken exception not only to Chiswick's conclusions about convergence but also to their entire empirical foundation.[5] Borjas's primary criticism is that Chiswick relies on cross-sectional data of immigrant and non-immigrant earnings to study a phenomenon that calls for a longitudinal analysis. Borjas offers his own evidence that the earnings of more recent immigrant cohorts are not converging on the earnings of their U.S.-born counterparts.

Even if the U.S. earnings of Mexican migrants do not converge, the parameters for migration experience and its square may still be positive and negative respectively. Such experience may coincide with the learning of English, the acquisition of other remunerable skills, and increased familiarity with the labor markets of specific U.S. locales. In turn, these factors may boost the expected earnings from U.S. employment and thus increase the probability of migration.

Family responsibilities (marriage, minor-age children, single parenthood, and single motherhood) should influence the migration decision by altering the household head's preferences for labor relative to leisure. Previous studies have accounted for the number of dependents per adult member of the household (García España and

Massey 1987), the proportion of dependents in the household (García España 1992), or merely household size (Sprouse 1991, Taylor 1984). However, variables measuring marital status and single parenthood have largely been absent from previous participation models. Such data are not hard to collect, so I assume this has been an oversight of earlier researchers.

The migration decisions of married household heads are likely to be influenced by their desire to spend time with their spouses. In addition, through his or her own labor power, a spouse increases the economic resources available to the household, making migration less necessary. For these two reasons, being married should reduce the probability of migration.

As the number of minor-age children increases, the head of household may seek to earn additional income. One possible method of doing so is to work in the United States. However, minor-age children may also deter migration. The head of household may forego migratory opportunities in order to spend time with his or her children. Also, in some households, minors may be put to work. However, if children consume more resources than they bring into the household, then the probability of migration should increase with the number of minors.

In the absence of child support, single parents must find a way to support their families. Unless relatives or friends provide substantial economic assistance, migration to the United States becomes an attractive alternative. Thus, being a single parent should increase the probability of migration. However, if the single parent lacks relatives or friends who can care for the children while he or she is away, migration becomes less viable, as household responsibilities in Mexico become relatively more important than the consumption secured through additional labor in the United States. If single mothers are more likely than single fathers to face such a childcare constraint, then single motherhood should reduce the probability of migration.

Additional income sources alleviate the need to migrate to the United States. Adult offspring are often thought of as potential income sources for the household.[6] Therefore, the probability of migration should decrease as the number of adult offspring rises. Individuals who operate a business or own agricultural land in Mexico should also be less likely to migrate.

The U.S. immigration status of the household head should greatly affect the migration decision. A person with legal residency in the United States is able to cross the border relatively freely, resulting in lower migration costs. In addition, he or she is allowed to participate in the formal U.S. labor market and thus is likely to secure a higher wage. The probability of being deported is much lower for the legal resident than for the undocumented migrant, although it is not zero. The U.S. government is empowered to deport legal resident aliens convicted of serious crimes and in recent years has done so. Also, the probability of finding work may be higher for the legal resident than for the undocumented migrant. For these reasons, legal residency should increase the probability of migration. An individual who obtains U.S. citizenship probably has decided to settle in the United States. These persons should be more likely to reside in the United States.

Several variables assess the impact of U.S. immigration policies. One dummy variable denotes the years 1987 and 1988, which are the first two years following the enactment of the Immigration Reform and Control Act of 1986 (IRCA). White, Bean, and Espenshade (1990) estimate that during the first 23 months after its enactment, the law deterred as many as two million illegal border crossings. The authors explain that potential migrants waited to learn how the U.S. government was going to enforce IRCA's sanctions against the employers of undocumented workers. However, the two years also correspond to the period when the U.S. government initially accepted amnesty applications under the act. During this time, some persons may have come to the United States with the specific intention of making a fraudulent amnesty application. In which direction does the net effect lie? In light of the evidence presented by White, Bean, and Espenshade, I hypothesize that IRCA's overall influence on migration is negative.

Another dummy variable identifies the years in which the Bracero Program was in effect: 1942-64. During its existence, the Bracero Program provided many Mexicans with the opportunity to enter the United States legally and work. Thus, the probability of migration should be higher during the Bracero years, as the program influences the migration decision in a manner similar to legal residency in the United States.

Between 1968 and 1976, U.S. immigration law treated applicants for legal immigration from the Western Hemisphere differently from applicants from the Eastern Hemisphere. Immigration from the Eastern Hemisphere was capped at 170,000 per year, with a limit of 20,000 for each country of origin. In addition, such immigration was subject to a system of preference classes similar to that which is currently in effect for all legal immigration to the United States. In contrast, immigration from the Western Hemisphere was subject only to an annual ceiling of 120,000, with no limits on total immigration from each country and no preference class system. This policy made it much easier for Mexicans to become legal immigrants, including both persons who applied to immigrate while still in Mexico and those who entered the United States illegally with the hope of eventually securing legal residency with the assistance of relatives. Thus, the dummy variable denoting the 1968-76 period should increase the probability of migration.

Beginning in 1977, the policy regime that formerly applied only to the Eastern Hemisphere was extended to the Western Hemisphere as well. This unified framework remains in place today, although the Immigration Act of 1990 raised the ceilings on legal immigration, beginning in Fiscal Year (FY) 1992. Dummy variables for the 1977-91 and 1992-94 periods attempt to capture the effects of these policy changes. I hypothesize that the parameter estimates for these two variables are positive in sign, but less in value than the parameter estimate for the 1968-76 variable.

The deportation ratio equals the number of deportable aliens from Mexico captured by the U.S. Border Patrol divided by Mexico's total population. This ratio is intended to measure the intensity of U.S. efforts to restrict illegal immigration from Mexico. Thus, its parameter estimate should be negative in sign. However, the variable may capture other phenomena as well, such as fluctuations in the annual number of Mexicans who attempt to enter the United States illegally and the number of attempted crossings per illegal entrant per year.

Migration networks may have a number of effects conducive to migration. First, they may reduce the costs of migrating. Previous migration experience within the family may be transferred to the head of household, enabling that person to enter the United States in the most cost-effective manner possible. This knowledge may make the head of household more astute in negotiating with *coyotes* and in avoiding apprehension and deportation by the INS, which force the persistent migrant to incur additional costs in order to re-enter the

United States. Relatives who are living in the United States at the time of migration may provide the migrant with a place to stay initially for little to no cost. Second, as I indicated above, migration networks may reduce the probability of deportation, thus increasing the expected return to migration. Third, migration networks may provide valuable contacts as the migrant searches for work. Indeed, the head of household may even be able to secure U.S. employment prior to arrival. Thus, migration networks may increase the probability of finding work in the United States and perhaps even the actual wage received.

To identify the presence of migration networks, previous researchers have employed a dummy variable measuring the presence of close friends or family in the United States, a dummy variable indicating the previous migration experience of certain relatives (Massey and Espinosa 1997), and the proportion of households in the community with U.S. experience (Massey and Espinosa 1997; Garcia España 1992; and García España and Massey 1987). The results of all previous literature that I have reviewed point to networks having a strongly positive and statistically significant influence on the probability of migration.

To the best of my knowledge, Massey and Espinosa (1997) is the only other work that considers the impact of networks on first versus repeat migration. In general, they find that both types of migration are more likely when the head of household has a parent with U.S. experience and when the number of migrant siblings increases. The only exception to this pattern concerns potential repeat migrants who lack legal immigration status in the United States. For these individuals, the number of migrant siblings has no statistically significant effect on repeat migration.

The participation models of this chapter contain two sets of network variables. The first is a vector of dummy variables that identify the U.S. migration experience of the head of household's father, mother, siblings, and grandparents. If a particular relative (or type of relative) participated in migration during or prior to the given calendar year, then the variable for that relative equals one. Otherwise, the variable equals zero. For example, consider a head of household in 1975 who had at least one sibling with previous U.S. experience. The 1975 observation of the variable for siblings would equal one for this head of household.

The second set of network variables is a vector of dummy variables that equal one when two conditions are met. First, the specific relative (or type of relative) must possess U.S. experience during or prior to the given year. Second, the head of household must not yet have migrated to the United States. The two sets of network variables enable us to distinguish the influence of family migration experience on the probability of first migration from its influence on repeat migration. The net effect on first migration is obtained by adding corresponding pairs of parameter estimates from the two sets of network variables. The effect on repeat migration is simply that measured by the first set of network variables.

Migration networks may be more crucial to first migration than to repeat migration. An experienced migrant should have greater familiarity with the migratory process and thus depend less on networks. For this reason, the second set of network variables may be positively related to migration. However, these variables also identify observations in which the individual has not yet migrated to the United States. Persons with no U.S. experience should be less likely to migrate, all else being equal. Therefore, one cannot easily predict the direction in which the second set of network variables influences migration.

I also estimate models that contain gender-specific variables for the U.S. experience of siblings and grandparents. LIFEFILE provides nearly complete information about the year in which the head of household's father or mother first migrated to the United States (if at all). However, it does not always indicate the gender of the sibling or grandparent with migration experience. For this reason, variables that measure the U.S. experience of siblings or grandparents whose gender is not recorded are also included in these alternative models.

Finally, the participation models include several macroeconomic variables. These are intended to reflect changing labor-market conditions in the United States and Mexico. Each model contains the annual rates of real per capita GDP growth for the two countries. The chance of finding work in either country should increase with its economic growth. Thus, the probability of migration should fall as the Mexican economy accelerates and should rise as the U.S. economy accelerates.

A number of respondents in San Ramon expressed the opinion that Mexican migration to the United States is driven primarily by unemployment and underemployment in Mexico and not by the simple prospect of earning more money in the United States. These conversations led me to believe that some migrants would remain in Mexico if it were possible to earn an adequate income there, even if much higher paying work was available in the United States. For this reason, one set of participation models includes annual measures of real GDP per capita for Mexico and the United States. These variables serve as proxies for w_{MX} and w_{US} and thus should have negative and positive effects respectively on the probability of migration. A second set of models uses the U.S.-to-Mexico ratio of real GDP per capita in place of the two per capita income measures.

5.3. EMPIRICAL RESULTS

5.3.1. Overview

This section analyzes the results from eight different participation models that use the data set LIFE26. As Chapter 4 indicates, LIFE26 is based on the data set LIFEFILE from the Mexican Migration Project. LIFE26 contains 185,574 annual observations from the retrospective life histories of 5,481 heads of household from 26 of the project's survey communities. 20,026 observations correspond with years in which the person spent part (if not all) of the year in the United States as a migrant. The observations for each head of household begin with the year in which the individual was 14 years old and end with the survey year. The earliest observation in the sample is for the year 1905, and the latest is for 1994.

The eight models may be divided into two groups of four. These groups differ in their measures of national economic conditions in Mexico and the United States. The first group utilizes real economic growth and real per capita income for the two countries (see Table 5.2). In the second group, the binational income ratio is used in place of the two measures of per capita income (see Table 5.3). Otherwise, the two groups of models are identical.

Table 5.2: Results from Particpation Models With Four Macroeconomic Variables

Vector/Variable	Gender-Neutral Network Variables		Gender-Specific Network Variables	
	Model 5.1	Model 5.2	Model 5.3	Model 5.4
Intercept	-5.5504***	-5.8718***	-5.6025***	-5.8866***
Individual characteristics				
Age (in years)	0.0830***	0.0964***	0.0854***	0.0977***
Age squared	-0.0022***	-0.0023***	-0.0022***	-0.0023***
Female	-1.1469***	-1.2006***	-1.1451***	-1.2009***
Education (in years)	-0.0173***	-0.0185***	-0.0168***	-0.0174***
College educated	-0.5085***	-0.5187***	-0.5246***	-0.5340***
U.S. interview	1.7743***	1.7321***	1.7818***	1.7373***
U.S. migration experience (in months)	0.0452***	0.0477***	0.0455***	0.0476***
U.S. migration experience squared	-0.0001***	-0.0001***	-0.0001***	-0.0001***
Family responsibilities				
Married	0.0242	0.0540	0.0166	0.0484
Number of minor-age children	0.0080	0.0082	0.0079	0.0082
Single parent	-0.0137	-0.0054	-0.0256	-0.0102
Single mother	0.4963***	0.5090***	0.4749***	0.5083***
Relatives with migration experience				
Grandparent	0.3468***	0.1531***	n.a.	n.a.
Grandfather	n.a.	n.a.	0.3321***	0.1351***
Grandmother	n.a.	n.a.	0.1897	-0.0551
Grandparent (gender not recorded)	n.a.	n.a.	0.3535	0.5825

Table 5.2 (continued)

Vector/Variable	Gender-Neutral Network Variables		Gender-Specific Network Variables	
	Model 5.1	Model 5.2	Model 5.3	Model 5.4
Relatives with migration experience (cont.)				
Father	0.2989***	0.0877***	0.3100***	0.0842***
Mother	-0.4800***	-0.2459***	-0.4407***	-0.2273***
Sibling	0.5901***	0.5041***	n.a.	n.a.
Brother	n.a.	n.a.	0.5653***	0.4937***
Sister	n.a.	n.a.	-0.0565	0.0400
Sibling (gender not recorded)	n.a.	n.a.	0.5229***	0.3969***
Relatives with migration experience when household head has not yet migrated				
Grandparent	-0.5940***	n.a.	n.a.	n.a.
Grandfather	n.a.	n.a.	-0.5987***	n.a.
Grandmother	n.a.	n.a.	-0.5477**	n.a.
Grandparent (gender not recorded)	n.a.	n.a.	0.4283	n.a.
Father	-0.6349***	n.a.	-0.6675***	n.a.
Mother	0.7723***	n.a.	0.7056***	n.a.
Sibling	-0.3044***	n.a.	n.a.	n.a.
Brother	n.a.	n.a.	-0.2717***	n.a.
Sister	n.a.	n.a.	0.2851***	n.a.
Sibling (gender not recorded)	n.a.	n.a.	-0.3494	n.a.

Table 5.2 (continued)

Vector/Variable	Gender-Neutral Network Variables		Gender-Specific Network Variables	
	Model 5.1	Model 5.2	Model 5.3	Model 5.4
Immigration status and policies				
Legal U.S. resident	1.5815***	1.6302***	1.5945***	1.6300***
U.S. citizen	-0.7391***	-0.7264***	-0.6684***	-0.6813***
Bracero Program (1944-64)	0.9035***	0.9181***	0.9057***	0.9161***
Amnesty Program (1987-88)	-0.1254**	-0.1175**	-0.1239**	-0.1177**
Western Hemisphere favored (1968-76)	0.6794***	0.6777***	0.6839***	0.6822***
Similar treatment of hemispheres (1977-91)	0.5984***	0.6106***	0.6057***	0.6137***
Immigration Act of 1990 (1992-94)	0.5925***	0.5939***	0.6078***	0.5948***
Deportation ratio	0.1237***	0.1284***	0.1245***	0.1282***
Additional income sources				
Number of adult offspring	0.0685***	0.0730***	0.0680***	0.0724***
Agricultural land (in hectares)	-0.0092***	-0.0090***	-0.00901***	-0.0090***
Business ownership	-0.7824***	-0.7951***	-0.7828***	-0.7959***
National economic conditions				
Real per capita GDP in Mexico x 10^{-1}	0.0007***	0.0007***	0.0007***	0.0007***
Real per capita GDP in U.S. x 10^{-1}	0.0004***	0.0004***	0.0004***	0.0004***
Real per capita growth in Mexico x 10^{-1}	0.0895***	0.0862***	0.0891***	0.0861***
Real per capita growth in U.S. x 10^{-1}	-0.0713**	-0.0776**	-0.0712**	-0.0766**
Log-likelihood (intercept and covariates)	-30,692.05	-30,873.49	-30,699.69	-30,879.07

Results for community dummy variables are not reported.

Results of Wald Chi-squared test on significance of parameter estimate:

***Passes at 99-percent level; **passes at 95-percent level; and *passes at 90-percent level.

Table 5.3: Results from Particpation Models With Three Macroeconomic Variables

Vector/Variable	Gender-Neutral Network Variables		Gender-Specific Network Variables	
	Model 5.5	Model 5.6	Model 5.7	Model 5.8
Intercept	-4.8955***	-5.2264***	-4.9318***	-5.2281***
Individual characteristics				
Female	-1.1592***	-1.2132***	-1.1578***	-1.2138***
Age (in years)	0.0840***	0.0974***	0.0864***	0.0986***
Age squared	-0.0022***	-0.0023***	-0.0022***	-0.0023***
Education (in years)	-0.0138***	-0.0149***	-0.0132***	-0.0138***
College educated	-0.5290***	-0.5395***	-0.5461***	-0.5556***
U.S. interview	1.7799***	1.7379***	1.7870***	1.7428***
U.S. migration experience (in months)	0.0452***	0.0476***	0.0455***	0.0476***
U.S. migration experience squared	-0.0001***	-0.0001***	-0.0001***	-0.0001***
Family responsibilities				
Married	0.0338	0.0634*	0.0265	0.0579*
Number of minor-age children	0.0085	0.0088	0.0085	0.0088
Single parent	-0.0049	0.0033	-0.0163	-0.0014
Single mother	0.5146***	0.5270***	0.4931***	0.5262***
Relatives with migration experience				
Grandparent	0.3511***	0.1566***	n.a.	n.a.
Grandfather	n.a.	n.a.	0.3352***	0.1377***
Grandmother	n.a.	n.a.	0.1946	-0.0517
Grandparent (gender not recorded)	n.a.	n.a.	0.3793	0.6025

Table 5.3 (continued)

Vector/Variable	Gender-Neutral Network Variables		Gender-Specific Network Variables	
	Model 5.5	Model 5.6	Model 5.7	Model 5.8
Relatives with migration experience (cont.)				
Father	0.3028	0.0919	0.3135	0.0882
Mother	-0.4868	-0.2518	-0.4496	-0.2351
Sibling	0.5982	0.5117	n.a.	n.a.
Brother	n.a.	n.a.	0.5721	0.5002
Sister	n.a.	n.a.	-0.0479	0.0480
Sibling (gender not recorded)	n.a.	n.a.	0.5264	0.4005
Relatives with migration experience when household head has not yet migrated				
Grandparent	-0.5962***	n.a.	n.a.	n.a.
Grandfather	n.a.	n.a.	-0.5995***	n.a.
Grandmother	n.a.	n.a.	-0.5332**	n.a.
Grandparent (gender not recorded)	n.a.	n.a.	0.4134	n.a.
Father	-0.6337***	n.a.	-0.6660***	n.a.
Mother	0.7785***	n.a.	0.7131***	n.a.
Sibling	-0.3059***	n.a.	n.a.	n.a.
Brother	n.a.	n.a.	-0.2726***	n.a.
Sister	n.a.	n.a.	0.2831***	n.a.
Sibling (gender not recorded)	n.a.	n.a.	-0.3484	n.a.

Table 5.3 (continued)

Vector/Variable	Gender-Neutral Network Variables		Gender-Specific Network Variables	
	Model 5.5	Model 5.6	Model 5.7	Model 5.8
Immigration status and policies				
Legal U.S. resident	1.5842***	1.6328***	1.5969***	1.6322***
U.S. citizen	-0.7544***	-0.7429***	-0.6856***	-0.6996***
Bracero Program (1944-64)	0.8994***	0.9115***	0.9013***	0.9096***
Amnesty Program (1988-89)	-0.0720	-0.0671	-0.0694	-0.0662
Western Hemisphere favored (1968-76)	0.9077***	0.9074***	0.9154***	0.9124***
Similar treatment of hemispheres (1977-91)	0.9762***	0.9898***	0.9891***	0.9946***
Immigration Act of 1990 (1992-94)	1.0909***	1.0947***	1.1136***	1.0978***
Deportation ratio	0.1046***	0.1088***	0.1051***	0.1086***
Additional income sources				
Number of adult offspring	0.0692***	0.0736***	0.0687***	0.0730***
Agricultural land (in hectares)	-0.0092***	-0.0091***	-0.0092***	-0.0090***
Business ownership	-0.7823***	-0.7952***	-0.7828***	-0.7960***
National economic conditions				
Binational income ratio	-0.0181**	-0.0168**	-0.0188**	-0.0177**
Real per capita growth in Mexico	0.0095***	0.0093***	0.0094***	0.0092***
Real per capita growth in U.S.	-0.0061*	-0.0068**	-0.0060*	-0.0067*
Log-likelihood (intercept and covariates)	-30,709.71	-30,891.42	-30,717.94	-30,897.25

Results for community dummy variables are not reported.

Results of Wald Chi-squared test on significance of parameter estimate:

***Passes at 99-percent level; **passes at 95-percent level; and *passes at 90-percent level.

Another distinction exists within each group of four models. The variables that measure family migration experience and hence migration networks differ from one model to the next. The first model contains both sets of network variables described previously. The second model omits the second set of network variables. The third and fourth models resemble the first and second respectively, except that gender-specific measures for siblings and grandparents are used.

5.3.2. Basic Results

Table 5.2 lists the parameter estimates from the logit models with four macroeconomic variables. One thing that immediately stands out is that the results are extremely consistent across specifications. The signs of the estimates do not change as one moves from one model to the next, and there are no dramatic changes in the size of the estimates or their significance levels. Let us treat Model 5.1 as the basic model. Then, we can discuss any important differences among the models when necessary.

With respect to the individual characteristics, the parameter estimates for all seven have the hypothesized sign. Moreover, all seven estimates are significant at the 99-percent level or better using a Wald Chi-squared test with one degree of freedom in which the specified parameter is restricted to equal zero.

The parameter estimates for age and its square indicate that the probability of migration increases until age 38 and decreases thereafter. This threshold corresponds closely to that identified in previous cross-sectional studies: age 34 in Taylor (1987) and age 37 in Taylor (1984) and Sprouse (1991).[7] Female heads of household are far less likely than males to participate in international migration. This result is consistent with studies about potential migrants of both genders (Sprouse 1991; and Taylor 1984, 1987). With respect to migration experience, the parameter estimates for U.S. experience and its square are positive and negative respectively, as was the case in Taylor (1987). However, the estimate for the squared term is so tiny that the probability of migration increases until the individual possesses 49 years of such experience.

There is less unanimity in the literature regarding the relationship between education and migration. Taylor (1984) finds no significant relationship between educational level and migration, while Sprouse

(1991) discovers the contrary. Sprouse employs measures of both years of education and its square. His results show that the probability of migration first rises and then falls as education increases. García España and Massey (1987) use a trio of dummy variables that indicate different levels of education. Their results mirror those of Sprouse: persons with one to three years of education are more likely to migrate than persons with no education, and persons with four or more years are less likely to migrate than those with no education. My results indicate that education substantially reduces the probability of migration, a finding that supports the conclusions of Sprouse and García España and Massey.

None of the parameter estimates for family responsibilities have the hypothesized sign, and only that for single motherhood is significant. These results are surprising, as Taylor (1984, 1987) finds that the probability of migration increases with the number of minor-age children.[8] Given the statistical evidence in Chapter 4, the possibility that single mothers might be more likely to migrate is quite startling.

Parameter estimates for the three variables indicating additional income sources are significant at the 99-percent level, and two of the three (business ownership and the amount of agricultural land) have the hypothesized sign. Other researchers have obtained similar results. García España (1992) and García España and Massey (1987) find a negative relationship between the ownership of agricultural land or a business and migration. Taylor (1987) also finds a negative relationship between farmland and migration. Sprouse (1991) and Taylor (1984), who employ a variable measuring the value of total assets, discover no significant relationship.

Taylor (1987, 1984), who focuses on all members of the household, also determines that the probability of migration increases with the number of adults in the household. One possible explanation of this relationship is that adult offspring assume responsibilities in Mexico of the household head, thus enabling that person to migrate.

Persons with legal residency in the United States are more likely to participate in international migration. However, the additional attribute of U.S. citizenship reduces this likelihood somewhat. With respect to U.S. immigration policy, the dummy variables for the Bracero Program and the periods 1968-76, 1977-91, and 1992-94 all obtain highly significant parameter estimates with the anticipated sign. As was hypothesized, the parameter estimate for the 1968-76 period is indeed larger than the estimates for the 1977-91 and the 1992-94 periods. The parameter estimate for the first two years of IRCA is significant at the 95-percent level and has the hypothesized sign. This suggests that IRCA initially discouraged migration to the United States—a finding that is consistent with the work of White, Bean, and Epenshade (1990). Although the parameter estimate for the deportation ratio is statistically significant, its sign is opposite from what was hypothesized. Apparently, this variable does a poor job of measuring the intensity of U.S. efforts to prevent undocumented migration.

Finally, the parameter estimates for 16 of the community dummy variables are significant at the 90-percent level or better. The excluded community in this vector of dummy variables is community 1, a municipal seat of some 55,000 people in the State of Guanajuato. Regarding the statistically significant estimates, five are positive in sign, and 11 are negative. The parameter estimate for San Ramon is positive and significant at the 99-percent level.

5.3.3. Migration Networks

Table 5.4 indicates the net effects of family migration experience on first and repeat migration. As was indicated above, the parameter estimates for the first set of network variables indicate the effect of family migration experience on the probability of repeat migration. The net effect on first migration is calculated by adding the parameter estimates for corresponding pairs of variables from the two sets of network variables. For instance, according to Model 5.1, the net effect of a father with U.S. experience on first migration is 0.2989 + (-0.6349) = -0.3360. Because each net effect is the sum of two randomly distributed parameter estimates, any test of its statistical significance must account for the variances of the two estimates and their covariance. Table 5.4 displays the results of an appropriate set of significance tests.

Let us continue to focus on Model 5.1. The parameter estimates for the first set of network variables are generally consistent with the conclusions of previous research. Having a father, grandparent, or sibling with U.S. experience increases the probability of repeat migration. In the first set of network variables, the parameter estimates for these relatives are all positive and highly significant. In contrast, having a mother with U.S. experience discourages repeat migration. This finding contrasts with the cross-tabulations of Chapter 4, which indicate that participation in international migration is positively associated with the U.S. experience of one's mother. Why the head of household's migration decision should be negatively related to the mother's migration experience is not immediately clear. Perhaps mothers are less likely to work in the United States and thus have fewer job contacts to offer.

The significance of the first set of network variables may not entirely be due to a causal relationship between migration networks and the head of household's migration decision. Instead, the decision may be correlated to family migration experience for some other reason. For example, in a particular Mexican family, one generation after another may take part in migration because the family's job opportunities in Mexico are consistently inferior to those in the United States. It does not need to be the case that older generations assist the migratory efforts of younger ones.

The second set of network variables produce some fascinating results. The parameter estimates for these variables are opposite in sign from corresponding estimates for the first set of network variables. Moreover, the effects measured by the second set of variables completely overwhelm the effects measured by the first set, except for the variables for siblings. For persons who have not yet migrated, having a father or grandparent with U.S. experience reduces the probability of migration. In contrast, having a mother or sibling with U.S. experience increases the probability of first migration. Interestingly, only the migration experience of siblings increases the likelihood of both first and repeat migration.

The negative relationship between first migration and the U.S. experience of fathers and grandparents is especially intriguing. When it comes to migration, some persons may try not to follow in their fathers' footsteps. In San Ramon, several older respondents with U.S. experience expressed a strong desire that their children never migrate to the United States. These individuals believe that migrants are exposed

Table 5.4: Net Effects of Family Migration Experience on Repeat and First Migration

Vector/Variable	Model 5.1	Model 5.3	Model 5.5	Model 5.7
Net effect on repeat migration of relative with migration experience				
Grandparent	0.3468***	n.a.	0.3511***	n.a.
Grandfather	n.a.	0.3321***	n.a.	0.3352***
Grandmother	n.a.	0.1897	n.a.	0.1946
Grandparent (gender not recorded)	n.a.	0.3535	n.a.	0.3793
Father	0.2989***	0.3100***	0.3028***	0.3135***
Mother	-0.4800***	-0.4407***	-0.4868***	-0.4496***
Sibling	0.5901***	n.a.	0.5982***	n.a.
Brother	n.a.	0.5653***	n.a.	0.5721***
Sister	n.a.	-0.0565	n.a.	-0.0479
Sibling (gender not recorded)	n.a.	0.5229***	n.a.	0.5264***
Net effect on first migration of relative with migration experience				
Grandparent	-0.2472**	n.a.	-0.2451**	n.a.
Grandfather	n.a.	-0.2666***	n.a.	-0.2643**
Grandmother	n.a.	-0.3580	n.a.	-0.3386
Grandparent (gender not recorded)	n.a.	0.7818	n.a.	0.7927
Father	-0.3360***	-0.3575***	-0.3309***	-0.3525***
Mother	0.2923***	0.2649**	0.2917**	0.2635**
Sibling	0.2857***	n.a.	0.2923***	n.a.
Brother	n.a.	0.2936***	n.a.	0.2995***
Sister	n.a.	0.2286***	n.a.	0.2352***
Sibling (gender not recorded)	n.a.	0.1735	n.a.	0.1780

Results of t-test on significance of net effect:

***Passes at 99-percent level; **passes at 95-percent level; and *passes at 90-percent level.

in the United States to increased dangers, such as violent crime and AIDS. Such negative assessments may be passed down to the next generation, which becomes less likely to participate in migration.

In addition, the economic lifestyles of previous generations of migrants may not have been conducive to the development of migration networks. Employment in seasonal agricultural activities in the United States, coupled with continued subsistence farming in Mexico, may have provided few opportunities for migrants to establish roots in the United States. Moreover, during the first two decades following World War II, the Bracero Program encouraged a pattern of migration that was both routinized and temporary.

Finally, some years have passed since the most recent U.S. voyage of many former migrants. These individuals are less likely to have information about the migratory process that is useful to potential migrants, and they may have few remaining U.S. contacts.

The inclusion of the gender-specific network variables in Model 5.3 yields results similar to Model 5.1. Previous U.S. experience among the individual's grandfather, father, or brother increases the probability of repeat migration. Despite any warnings about the dangers associated with migration, repeat migration becomes more likely when these male relatives have migration experience. Again, repeat migration is less likely when the head of household's mother has U.S. experience.

Depending on the relative with U.S. experience, the net effect of family migration experience on first migration can be either negative or positive. Someone who lacks U.S. experience is less likely to migrate if the grandfather, grandmother, or father was ever a migrant. Such an individual is more likely to become a first-time migrant if the mother, brother, or sister has U.S. experience. Also, the gender-specific models reveal that only the U.S. experience of the individual's brother increases the probability of both first and repeat migration.

The empirical results for the U.S. experience of siblings and particularly brothers make sense. Siblings are more likely than the head of household's older relatives to have recent migration experience. Thus, they are in the position to have more timely information to share about the migration process. Moreover, migrant siblings are more likely than parents and grandparents with migration experience to be living in the United States at the time that the head of household is making the migration decision.

However, the results for the migration experience of sisters are a bit puzzling. The parameter estimates for the migration experience of sisters are not statistically significant, but they have the same sign as the estimates for the mother's experience. Given the historical predominance of males in Mexican migration to the United States, the head of household is likely to have fewer sisters with migration experience than brothers with such experience. Even so, should not a sister with U.S. experience facilitate migration to a similar extent as a brother with U.S. experience? The participation models offer no evidence that sisters play such a role.

5.3.4. National Economic Conditions

Regarding the four macroeconomic variables in Model 5.1, only the parameter estimate for U.S. per capita GDP has the hypothesized sign, although all four estimates are significant at the 95-percent level or better. In Model 5.5, the three macroeconomic variables fare even worse. Although the parameter estimates for all three are significant at the 90-percent level or better, none garners the hypothesized sign.

All in all, these variables do not appear to be good proxies for labor market conditions in the United States and Mexico. In either country, the earnings of the average household head in the sample are likely to be substantially less than the GDP per capita, so measures of per capita income may not reflect the economic prospects facing the typical prospective migrant. For future work, it should be possible to create new indices based on the wages in the United States and Mexico for occupations in which the respondents in the sample predominate.

5.3.5. Relative Importance of the Explanatory Variables

A comparison of standardized parameter estimates reveals the relative importance of the explanatory variables.[9] Judging from the size of the absolute values of the standardized estimates, the most important factors are age and cumulative migration experience. In Model 5.1, the absolute values for these variables and their squares all exceed 0.5698. A second set of explanatory variables rank next in terms of their impact on the migration decision. The absolute values of the standardized estimates for gender, legal immigration status, whether the Bracero Program was in effect, and the country in which the interview took place are roughly of the same magnitude, ranging between 0.2200 to 0.2400 in Model 5.1. Interestingly, the magnitude of the standardized estimates for national economic conditions is relatively small, suggesting that marginal changes in macroeconomic conditions have a limited effect on the migration decision.

The standardized parameter estimates for the two sets of network variables are generally small in comparison to the estimates for age, U.S. experience, gender, and legal residency. With two exceptions, the standardized estimates for the network variables in Model 5.1 range in absolute value between 0.0367 and 0.0558. The standardized estimate for the father's migration experience when the household head has no such experience is 0.1038, and that for the U.S. experience of siblings, regardless of the household head's migration experience, is –0.1457. This latter result is largely driven by the migration experience of brothers. In Model 5.3, the standardized estimate for brothers when the household head has no U.S. experience is –0.1348. These results provide additional evidence of the importance of siblings to the migration decision. Among the head of household's immediate family, the relationship with one's brothers may be the most important migration network of all.

5.4. CONCLUSIONS

This chapter provides new insights into the precise nature of migration networks. For the head of household who has never participated in international migration, having a mother or at least one sibling with U.S. experience increases the probability of migration. Brothers with migration experience appear to play an important role in the first migration of siblings. In contrast, having a father or at least one grandparent with U.S. experience reduces the probability of first migration. These older relatives may have been poorly situated to establish lasting migration networks, especially if their most recent migration experience took place during the first two decades following World War II. In some instances, former migrants actively discourage younger relatives from migrating.

With respect to repeat migration, having a father, grandparent, or sibling with U.S. experience encourages this phenomenon. Again, having a brother with migration experience appears to be especially important. Curiously, the head of household whose mother is a current or former migrant is less likely to participate in repeat migration. This relationship is hard to explain and warrants further investigation.

The chapter also generates intriguing results about the relative influence of various factors on the head of household's migration decision. Although family migration experience and legal U.S. immigration status increase the probability of migration, the head of household's age and total amount of U.S. experience exercise a stronger influence on the migration decision. Family responsibilities such as marriage and having larger numbers of dependent children do not appear to motivate migration.

The variables measuring national economic conditions in the United States and Mexico also fare poorly in the participation models. This result is quite striking given the wild fluctuations experienced by the Mexican economy over the past half century. These macroeconomic variables simply may not capture the changing economic prospects of potential migrants. Another possibility, one that should disturb the makers of U.S. immigration policy, is that Mexican migration to the United States is largely insensitive to marginal changes in the macroeconomic performance of the two countries. If this is the case, then external efforts to improve the Mexican economy may not appreciably reduce migration unless the results are quite dramatic. Such a rosy scenario seems highly unlikely in the foreseeable future.

NOTES

1. See, for example, Taylor (1984), Sprouse (1991), and using the data of the Mexican Migration Project, and García España and Massey (1987) and García España (1992).

2. See García España and Massey (1987) and Taylor (1987), for example.

3. The idea of having location-specific types of leisure comes directly from Olea (1988). Olea's modeling efforts in his dissertation are particularly noteworthy. In one section, he views the migration decision as a dynamic optimization problem in which the prospective migrant knows the beginning and end points of each migration spell throughout his or her lifetime and then selects the appropriate combination of labor and leisure. After reading his dissertation, I suspected that Olea aspired to create a model in which the

prospective migrant also selects in advance the beginning and end points of each contemplated migration spell. Crafting such a model is difficult.

4. A detailed description of the variables and their sources is located in Appendix 5.1.

5. With respect to Borjas (1990), see Chapter 6, "Assimilation and Earnings of Immigrants," pp. 97-114.

6. Taylor (1987, 1984) routinely includes the number of adults in the household in his econometric models.

7. In the comparable models in García España and Massey (1987) and García España (1992), the parameter estimates for age and its square are not statistically significant.

8. García España (1992), Sprouse (1991) and García España and Massey (1987) obtain insignificant parameter estimates for their measures of the number of dependents in the household.

9. Standardized estimates are measured in terms of the number of standard deviations of the dependent variable per standard deviation of the explanatory variable. The values of these estimates for Models 5.1 through 5.8 are reported in Appendix Tables D.1 and D.2.

CHAPTER 6

The Duration of Migration Spells

6.1. INTRODUCTION

Limited dependent variable models of the migration decision, such as the participation models of Chapter 5 and most previous econometric studies of migration networks, are unable to address one key aspect of the migration process: the decision of how long to stay in the United States and how long to stay in Mexico. This chapter studies the influence of networks and other factors on the length of migration spells in the United States and Mexico. A series of duration models is estimated in order to determine the direction and magnitude of these effects.

This chapter is organized as follows. Section 6.2 discusses the different types of duration models that are employed in this chapter. Special attention is devoted to the apparent distribution of the hazard rate for the migration spells. Section 6.3 presents the empirical results from the models. Section 6.4 contains a brief conclusion.

6.2. THE MODELS

6.2.1. Measuring Migration Spells

The data for the duration models are drawn from the data set LIFEFILE of the Mexican Migration Project. As we shall see below, this data set is less than ideal for an analysis of this sort. A complex and lengthy process must be used to extract information about the migration spells of each head of household. For this reason, I utilize only the observations for San Ramon. A total of 2,535 migration spells are examined—2,285 spells in Mexico and 250 spells in the United States.

In the future, I may replicate this work using a more extensive portion of the data set.

The problem with LIFEFILE is that it lacks clear-cut measures of the length of each migration spell, when a particular spell ends, and when another begins. Instead, LIFEFILE indicates the number of months that the head of household spent in his or her primary place of employment during a given calendar year. Priority is given first to places in the United States, second to Mexican locations outside the individual's survey community, and third to the survey community itself.

Thus, it is necessary to improvise a reasonable measure of the length of each spell, when the spell began, and when it ended. To this end, I utilize a variable in LIFEFILE that identifies the immigration documents, if any, that the individual used to enter the United States during a given calendar year. Because this variable also indicates whether the individual made no border crossing whatsoever during the specified year, it serves as an adequate indicator of the beginning and end of each migration spell.

To facilitate the calculation of spell length, I make two assumptions about the head of household's border crossings. First, I assume that a migrant crossed the border into the United States no more than once per year. Second, I assume that any visit to the United States began at the start of the calendar year. These assumptions are forced by the limitations of the data and do not result in the significant loss of any information provided by LIFEFILE. The data set indicates neither the particular months of the year that the head of household spent in Mexico nor the specific time when each border crossing occurred.

With respect to the head of household's spells in Mexico, I assume that they began at one of two points in time: (1) the beginning of the calendar year when the respondent turned 14 years of age, or (2) the month following the individual's return to Mexico. Thus, if LIFEFILE indicates that a particular head of household spent five months of the year 1975 in the United States, I assume that the individual spent seven months of the year in Mexico, beginning with the month of June 1975. Once I define the points in time when each spell began and ended, all that remains is to tally the total number of months comprising each spell of migration.

While my approach to calculating the length of the spells is relatively straightforward, it may result in the mismeasurement of some spells. For instance, an individual who made two separate trips to the United States in 1979 is treated as having made a single visit. Thus, I may inadvertently lump several relatively short spells together to form longer spells. However, these combined spells should last no longer than 12 months in total.

Finally, I should note that the survey methodology does not consider casual visits to the United States or Mexico to be migration spells. Examples of casual visits are vacations, brief business trips, visiting relatives, and attending special events such as weddings, primary school graduations, and community festivals. Also, an individual who enters the United States, is soon after deported, and immediately returns to the United States is treated as having made one single visit to the United States rather than two separate visits.

6.2.2. The Duration Models

Two sets of duration models are estimated in this chapter. Each set employs a different groups of migration-network variables. The first set utilizes a general measure of the family's migration experience. This variable indicates whether at least one person among the individual's father, mother, siblings, or grandparents possessed U.S. experience before the individual's migration spell began. The second set contains separate variables for the U.S. experience of these four types of relatives. The duration models examine the transition between two states: residence in the United States and residence in Mexico. The use of a two-state model captures the possible interaction between an individual's U.S. and Mexican spells.

A common research strategy in duration analysis is to estimate the model several times using different distributions for the hazard rate—the conditional probability that a migration spell of length z instantaneously ends, given the spell's existence at that time.[1] Three distributions that are frequently employed are the log-logistic, log-normal, and exponential distributions. The exponential distribution features a memory-less hazard: the hazard rate is constant regardless of spell length. For the log-normal and log-logistic distributions, the hazard rate first increases and then decreases as the length of the spell increases.

In general, there is no clear guide to the selection of the distribution. However, the nature of the migration decision suggests that some distributions may be more appropriate than others. Consider an imaginary sample of U.S. migration spells. Let us assume that the shorter spells in the sample belong to more transitory individuals, while the longer ones belong to persons who settle permanently in the United States. A frequency distribution of the spells reveals that the rate of change in the failure rate increases at first as one examines the spells of the more transitory individuals and then decreases as one examines the spells of more settled individuals.[2] Thus, the hazard rate for U.S. spells first increases and then decreases. This pattern conforms closely to that of the log-normal and log-logistic distributions.

Figures 6.1 and 6.2 depict the relation between spell length and the survival rate for the Mexican and U.S. spells respectively. The shape of the two plots is consistent with the hypothetical story told above, suggesting that the log-normal and log-logistic distributions are appropriate for the study at hand. In this chapter, I will estimate models for all three of the distributions mentioned, but with the belief that the log-normal and log-logistic distributions fit the data better than the exponential distribution.

Table 6.1 details the hazard and survival functions for the three distributions. Recalling that the hazard rate, $\lambda(z)$, equals the probability density function divided by the survival function $[f(z)/S(z)]$, Greene (1993: 719) illustrates how the log-likelihood function may be expressed using one of two general forms:

$$\ln L = \Sigma_{\text{uncensored observations}} \ln f(z|\theta) + \Sigma_{\text{censored observations}} \ln S(z|\theta), \text{ or}$$

$$\ln L = \Sigma_{\text{uncensored observations}} \lambda(z|\theta) + \Sigma_{\text{all observations}} \ln S(z|\theta),$$

where θ is a vector containing the parameters λ and p. To capture the influence of exogenous variables, let λ equal $\exp(-\mathbf{x}'\beta)$.[3] Using the former of these two expressions, the log-likelihood function for my two-state duration model may be written as follows:

Figure 6.1: Distribution of Mexican Spells

(a) All Spells

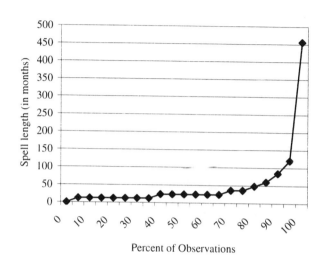

(b) Censored and Uncensored Spells

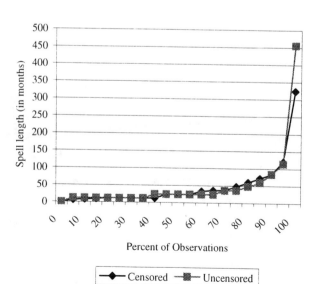

Figure 6.2: Distribution of U.S. Spells

(a) All Spells

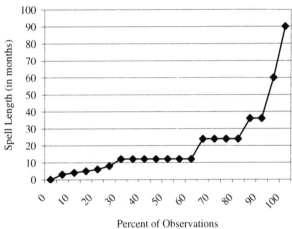

(b) Censored and Uncensored Spells

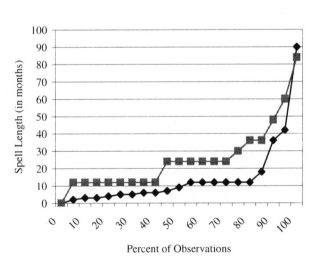

Table 6.1: Three Survival Distributions

Distribution	Hazard Function, $\lambda(z)$	Survival Function, $S(z)$
Exponential	$\lambda(z) = \lambda$	$S(z) = e^{-\lambda z}$
Log-normal	$f(z) = (p/z)\phi(p\ln(\lambda z))$	$S'(z) = \Phi(-p\ln(\lambda z))$
	\multicolumn{2}{l}{$\ln z$ is normally distributed with mean $-\ln \lambda$ and standard deviation $1/p$.}
Log-logistic	$\lambda(z) = \lambda p(\lambda z)^{p-1}/[1+(\lambda z)^p]$	$S(z) = 1/[1+(\lambda z)^p]$
	\multicolumn{2}{l}{$\ln z$ has a logistic distribution with mean $-\ln \lambda$ and variance $\pi^2/(3p^2)$.}

Source: Table 22.6, Greene (1993: 718)
Note: In contrast to Greene, I use z rather than t to indicate the length of the spell.

$\ln L = \ln L_{MX} + \ln L_{US}$, where

$\ln L_{MX} = \Sigma_{\text{uncensored Mexican spells}} \ln f(z_{MX}|\beta_{MX}, p_{MX})$
$\qquad + \Sigma_{\text{censored Mexican spells}} \ln S(z_{MX}|\beta_{MX}, p_{MX})$, and

$\ln L_{US} = \Sigma_{\text{uncensored U.S. spells}} \ln f(z_{US}|\beta_{US}, p_{US})$

$\qquad\quad + \Sigma_{\text{censored U.S. spells}} \ln S(z_{US}|\beta_{US}, p_{US})$.

6.2.3. Explanatory Variables

Table 6.2 lists the explanatory variables for the duration models and the expected signs of their parameter estimates.[4] In a fashion similar to Chapter 5, the explanatory variables may be divided into six vectors: (1) individual characteristics, (2) family responsibilities, (3) additional income sources, (4) U.S. immigration status, (5) U.S. immigration policies, and (6) migration networks. Because the duration models are estimated for a relatively small number of migration spells, some variables from the participation models of Chapter 5 are not included. In subsequent work, I hope to incorporate the omitted variables within duration models based on a larger number of observations.

Also, I had originally hoped to include measures of the number of deportations experienced by the migrant during a given U.S. spell, the costs (if any) of hiring a *coyote* to cross the border, and other migration costs. These variables would have allowed me to compare my duration results to those of Kossoudji (1992). However, to ease the burden on the respondent, the leadership of the Mexican Migration Project decided to ask this information only for the head of household's earliest and latest trip to the United States. This change renders useless many of the subsequently measured spells for a Kossoudji-like specification. In the future, I may re-examine the data to see how many observations contain these desired variables.

The explanatory variables exercise two types of effects on the decision regarding whether to end immediately a spell of residence on either side of the border. The first type of effect is essentially that captured by participation models. Migrating to the United States necessarily means ending one's spell of residence in Mexico. Returning to Mexico (and thus not spending the next time period in the United States) involves terminating one's ongoing spell of U.S. residence.

Table 6.2: Hypothesized Signs of Parameter Estimates in Duration Models

Vector/Variable	Mexican Spells	U.S. Spells
Individual characteristics		
Age	Positive	Positive
Female	Positive	Positive
Education (in years)	Positive	Positive
U.S. interview	Negative	Positive
U.S. migration experience (in months)		
Family responsibilities		
Married	Positive	Negative
Single parent	Positive	Negative
Number of minor-age children	Negative	Negative
Additional income sources		
Number of adult offspring	Positive	Negative
Business ownership	Positive	Negative
Agricultural land (in hectares)	Positive	Negative
U.S. immigration status		
Legal resident of U.S.	Negative	Negative
Bracero	n.a.	Negative
U.S. Immigration Policies		
Bracero Program in effect	Negative	Negative
Amnesty Program in effect	Negative	Positive
Migration networks		
Relative with U.S. experience		
Any immediate relative	Negative	n.a.
Grandparent	Negative	n.a.
Father	Negative	n.a.
Mother	Negative	n.a.
Sibling	Negative	n.a.
Relative with U.S. experience when head of household has not yet migrated		
Any immediate relative	Negative	Negative
Grandparent	Negative	Negative
Father	Negative	Negative
Mother	Negative	Negative
Sibling	Negative	Negative

n.a. = not applicable

Second, the explanatory variables affect the ultimate length of the spells. This may occur through two different mechanisms. First, some variables affect migration costs. Variables that decrease the cost of migration shorten spells of residence on either side of the border, as the head of household realizes that the cost of initiating a new U.S. spell is relatively smaller. Similarly, variables that increase migration costs lengthen spells of residence. Second, certain variables may reflect the migrant's desire to shuttle back and forth across the border. For instance, some individuals may seek to work periodically in Mexico or the United States, while others may wish to spend leisure time in Mexico on a regular basis.

The vector of individual characteristics describes the gender, age, and educational level of the head of household, as well as whether the interview was conducted in the United States or Mexico. For a female head of household, migrating from the United States to Mexico or vice versa may involve additional migration costs. For instance, if her spouse is incapacitated, she must find someone to care for him while she is away. Also, as I mentioned in Chapter 5, Mexican women historically have been less likely to participate in international migration. Therefore, being female should increase the length of both U.S. and Mexican migration spells.

As the head of household gets older, it is reasonable to expect that he or she will become less mobile and thus less likely to end an ongoing spell of residence in either country. Therefore, the probability that the individual instantaneously ends either a U.S. or a Mexican spell should decrease with age.

Persons with more schooling are likely to earn higher incomes on average, regardless of whether they are in the United States or in Mexico. This should provide better educated individuals with a disincentive to ending an ongoing spell on either side of the border.

A dummy variable denoting the country in which the individual was interviewed accounts for the possibility that the persons interviewed in the United States are more prone to migrate there. Thus, the parameter estimates for this variable should be negative for Mexican spells and positive for U.S. spells.

Three variables measure the individual's family responsibilities: marriage, single parenthood, and the number of minor-age children. The migration decisions of married individuals may be influenced by their desire to spend time with their spouses. Also, a spouse's labor power increases the economic resources available to the household, making it less necessary for the head of household to migrate. For these two reasons, being married should have increase the length of Mexican spells and decrease the length of U.S. spells.

Minor-age children are not likely to work much outside the home and usually present a net financial burden for the head of household. Thus, persons with larger numbers of such children should be more likely to end Mexican spells of residence and migrate to the United States. However, if they leave their children behind in Mexico, migrants should be more likely to cut trips to the United States short in order to return home and spend time with their children. Therefore, the number of minor-age children should reduce the length of both Mexican and U.S. spells.

Single parents face the unusual migration cost of either finding someone to take care of their children while they are away or taking their children with them. Thus, single parents should be more likely to extend their Mexican spells of residence and shorten their U.S. spells.

The household's additional economic resources include businesses, the head of household's adult offspring, and agricultural land. Persons who operate a business or possess agricultural land in Mexico should be less likely to migrate to the United States. As Chapter 5 mentions, adult offspring may be thought of as potential sources of net income for the household. Each of these factors should result in longer Mexican spells of residence and shorter U.S. spells.

One dummy variable indicates whether the head of household was a legal resident of the United States at the start of the migration spell. Legal immigration status should translate into lower potential migration costs, as the individual with legal residency is able to cross the border relatively freely. Thus, legal residents should be more likely to end a spell of residence instantaneously on either side of the border.

Another dummy variable denotes whether the individual entered the United States legally under the Bracero Program. This variable directly influences only the length of U.S. spells and thus appears only in the U.S. portion of the model. The Bracero variable distinguishes the spells of non-Braceros who were in the United States during the time of the program from the spells of program participants. Once in the Bracero Program, migrants may have believed that they had a higher probability of being a Bracero again in the future. I hypothesize that program participants acted accordingly by shortening their U.S. spells.

Two dummy variables respectively indicate whether the migration spell began in a year when the Bracero Program or the Amnesty Program under IRCA was in effect. The Bracero Program actively recruited Mexicans to work legally in the United States. This resulted in the early cessation of many Mexican spells of residence. With legal access to the U.S. labor market, numerous Braceros made multiple trips to the United States. Moreover, during the program, it is possible that the U.S. spells of non-Braceros conformed in length to those of Braceros. For these reasons, both Mexican and U.S. spells of residence should be shorter during the Bracero Program.

As Chapter 5 indicates, IRCA may have had competing effects on the migration decision during the two years following the law's enactment. On the one hand, prospective migrants may have delayed ending Mexican spells of residence in order to determine how the law would affect them. Undocumented migrants already in the United States may have stayed there longer, thinking that IRCA would make it harder to get back into the country. On the other hand, some persons in Mexico at the time of the amnesty program may have ended their Mexican migration spells sooner in order to go to the United States and make a fraudulent amnesty application. Individuals already in the United States may have remained longer than they would have otherwise in order to qualify for the program. Thus, IRCA's overall effect on the probability that a U.S. spell ends instantaneously should be negative. However, its effect on Mexican spells is harder to predict. Because White, Bean, and Espenshade (1990) provide evidence of IRCA's initial deterrent effect, I hypothesize that the law decreases the probability that Mexican spells instantaneously ends in 1987 or 1988.

The duration models contain the same type of network variables that are employed in the participation models of Chapter 5. These variables may be divided into two groups. The first measures the presence of U.S. migration experience among the head of household's relatives. The second indicates the presence of this experience for those years in which the individual had not yet migrated to the United States. Since the initiation of a U.S. spell of residence obviously means that the individual possesses U.S. migration experience, the second group of network variables is excluded from the U.S. portion of the duration models.

Two variants of the network variables are employed. In the first set of duration models, the network variables are based on a "catch-all" measure that identifies the previous migration experience of at least one person among the individual's father, mother, siblings, and grandparents. The second set of duration models utilizes specific variables for the previous U.S. experience of these four types of relatives.

Migration networks, as proxied by the U.S. experience of certain relatives, should reduce the costs of migration. Thus, previous migration experience within the family should have an effect similar to that of legal residency in the United States. Crossing the border should become more routine, thus shortening migration spells on either side of the border. Migration networks may have their strongest influence on the length of Mexican spells for those individuals who have not yet participated in migration. However, the results of Chapter 5 caution us in making such a hypothesis. These results also suggest that siblings play an important role influencing the length of Mexican spells.

6.3. EMPIRICAL RESULTS

6.3.1. Primary Results

Table 6.3 displays the parameter estimates from three duration models that contain the general network variables. The results for the exponential distribution largely resemble the results from the two models that utilize a logarithmic distribution. For the 20 parameter estimates in Model 6.3 that are statistically significant at the 90-percent confidence level or better, 19 of the corresponding estimates in Models 6.1 and 6.2 are significant at the same level or better. Since life-table analysis indicates that the logarithmic distributions fit the data better, let us focus our attention on Models 6.1 and 6.2.

Across these two models, there are a number of differences in the significance levels and magnitudes of the parameter estimates. In the Mexican segments of the models, the estimates for single parenthood and agricultural land lose statistical significance as one moves from one specification to the other. In the U.S. segments, the estimates for age,

Table 6.3: Results from Duration Models Using General Network Variables (Observations for San Ramon Only, 1905-94)

Vector/Variable	Log-logistic (Model 6.1)		Log-normal (Model 6.2)		Exponential (Model 6.3)	
	Mexican Spells	U.S. Spells	Mexican Spells	U.S. Spells	Mexican Spells	U.S. Spells
Individual characteristics						
Age	-0.0055	-0.0073	-0.0049	-0.0249***	-0.0062	-0.0139*
Female	1.9163***	0.0837	1.9646***	0.5731	2.278***	0.3948
Education (in years)	0.0057	0.0568***	0.0225	0.0475**	0.0153	0.0627***
U.S. interview	-1.6213***	2.0293***	-1.6039***	1.5665***	-1.8139***	2.3356***
U.S. migration experience (in months)	-0.0041**	0.0113***	-0.0063**	0.0121***	-0.0054**	0.0134***
Family responsibilities						
Married	-0.0253	-0.1378	0.0249	0.0915	0.0528	-0.1020
Single parent	-0.1449	-0.0758	-0.2835***	0.0731	-0.1246	-0.0882
Number of minor-age children	0.0451	0.0602*	0.0232	0.0552*	0.0643	0.0769**
Additional income sources						
Number of adult offspring	0.2474**	-0.0361	0.2082***	0.0283	0.3143***	-0.0059
Business ownership	1.6234***	-0.7680***	1.2561***	-0.7518***	1.7908***	-0.7978***
Agricultural land (in hectares)	0.0190*	-0.0477***	0.0099	-0.0411**	0.0193	-0.0496**
U.S. immigration status						
Legal resident of U.S.	-0.7436***	-1.0019***	-0.4001*	-0.8536***	-0.7945***	-1.0349***
Bracero	n.a.	-0.5649**	n.a.	-0.2251	n.a.	-0.5272*
U.S. immigration policies						
Bracero Program in effect	-0.0832	-0.1838	-0.0909	-0.3699**	-0.0968	-0.1442
Amnesty Program in effect	-0.0118	0.1200**	0.0307	0.2330*	0.0030	0.2048***
Relatives have migration experience	-1.3445***	-0.1530	-1.3756***	-0.1736	-1.5584***	-0.1763
Relatives have migration experience and household head has not yet migrated	0.5578***	n.a.	0.4896***	n.a.	0.6321***	n.a.
Constant	6.3906***	2.7621***	6.2003***	2.7641***	6.7198***	2.7873***
Scale parameter	1.2065***	1.2862***	0.8249***	1.0675***	n.a.	n.a.
Mean log-likelihood		-0.5465		-0.5540		-0.5508

N = 2,535 (2,285 Mexican spells and 250 U.S. spells).

Results of two-tailed *t*-test on significance of parameter estimate:

***Passes at 99-percent level; **passes at 95-percent level; and *passes at 90-percent level.

Braceros, and the Bracero Program lose significance in some specifications.

Female heads of household have longer spells of residence in Mexico, a result that is consistent with the findings of Chapter 5. Age and educational level do not influence the length of Mexican spells, but they do affect the length of U.S. spells. According to Model 6.2, older individuals are more likely to terminate a spell of U.S. residence instantaneously, and both Models 6.1 and 6.2 indicate that more educated persons have longer spells of U.S. residence. This latter result is particularly intriguing, because it suggests that the U.S. labor market offers differential rewards for migrants with higher levels of education, even if those persons are not legal residents of the United States.

As individuals accumulate more U.S. experience, spells of residence in Mexico become shorter and spells of residence in the United States become longer. Persons interviewed in the United States have shorter Mexican spells and longer U.S. spells. This result is further evidence that the U.S. interviews are not representative of the overall sample.

Marital status does not affect the length of migration spells in either country. However, Model 6.2 indicates that single parents have shorter spells of Mexican residence. One possible explanation of this result is that single parents are more likely to participate in migration because their family responsibilities are greater. This result also suggests that single parents are able to address childcare issues to their satisfaction in order to migrate to the United States. The relatively young age of the Mexican population may mean that the typical single parent has able-bodied parents or other relatives who can care for the individual's children while he or she is away in the United States.

The length of U.S. migration spells rises with the number of dependents. However, this result must be approached with caution, since the model does not distinguish between children living in the United States and children living in Mexico.

Additional income sources reduce the incentive for migration and encourage longer spells of residence in Mexico. The parameter estimates in the Mexican part of Models 6.1 and 6.2 are both positive in sign, and all are statistically significant at the 90-percent confidence level or better, with the exception of land in Model 6.2. U.S. spells of residence are shorter for business owners and persons with more farmland.

The variables measuring U.S. immigration status also yield interesting results. As was hypothesized, being a Bracero increases the probability that an ongoing U.S. spell ends instantaneously. Thus, the migration spells of Braceros conformed in length to the program's stipulations. Legal residents of the United States are more likely to shuttle across the border, with shorter spell of residence on both sides of the border. This latter result is particularly striking, since it is thought that most Mexicans who obtain legal residency in the United States want to settle there. Nevertheless, a sizable number of Mexicans with legal residency in the United States choose to spend extended periods of time in Mexico.[5] Indeed, roughly 20 percent of the respondents described by the data set LIFE26 who possess legal U.S. immigration status spent the entire survey year in Mexico.[6]

With respect to U.S. immigration policies, the parameter estimates for the years in which the Bracero Program was in effect are both negative, as was hypothesized. But only the parameter estimate in the U.S. portion of Model 6.2 is statistically significant. This provides some evidence that the migration behavior of non-Braceros conformed to that of program participants during the 1944-64 period. Regarding the primary years in which amnesty applications were accepted, the parameter estimate for U.S. spells is positive in sign and statistically significant in both Models 6.1 and 6.2. This finding supports the hypothesis that migrants delayed ending their U.S. spells of residence until they could evaluate the changes resulting from IRCA. However, the variable for the Amnesty Program may measure the influence of other factors that distinguish migration spells begun in 1987 or 1988, such as difficult economic conditions in Mexico during that time period.

Models 6.1, 6.2, and 6.3 yield similar results for the network variables. The parameter estimates for these variables are significant only with respect to Mexican spells of residence. Table 6.5 indicates the net effects of these variables on first and repeat migration. For persons who have not yet migrated, having an immediate relative with U.S. experience increases the length of Mexican spells. For individuals with U.S. experience, having an immediate relative who is a current or former migrant decreases the length of these spells. Thus, family migration experience discourages first migration and encourages repeat migration. These findings resemble those of Chapter 5 regarding the migration experience of the head of household's father.

The influence of the "catch-all" network variable does not extend to the U.S. spells of residence. The parameter estimates for family migration experience in the U.S. portion of Models 6.1, 6.2, and 6.3 are not statistically significant (see Table 6.3). Thus, the support and assistance provided by migration networks may be limited to crossing the border and establishing one's initial work and living arrangements. After that, the typical migrant may receive little assistance from friends and family.

6.3.2. Relative-Specific Network Variables

Table 6.4 displays results from the three duration models with relative-specific network variables. A comparison of the results from Models 6.4 and 6.5 with those from Models 6.1 and 6.2 reveals two noteworthy differences. First, the parameter estimate for gender in the Mexican portion of Model 6.4 is negative in sign and statistically significant. This result suggests that female heads of household have shorter spells of migration in the Mexico. Second, legal residency in the United States is not found to affect the length of Mexican spells of residence. This evidence is rather startling, in light of the results from the first set of duration models and the participation models of Chapter 5.

A number of the relative-specific network variables garner significant parameter estimates in both the Mexican and U.S. parts of the duration models. Let us first consider the impact of these variables on the Mexican spells of residence, as presented in Table 6.5. For individuals who have not yet migrated, having a mother or sibling with U.S. experience decreases the length of these spells and thus encourages first migration. In contrast, the migration experiences of the head of household's father and grandparents do not have a statistically significant effect on the length of Mexican spells. These results are largely consistent with those in Chapter 5 regarding family migration experience and first migration.

Table 6.4: Results from Duration Models Using Relative-Specific Network Variables (Observations for San Ramon Only, 1905-94)

Vector/Variable	Log-logistic (Model 6.4)		Log-normal (Model 6.5)		Exponential (Model 6.6)	
	Mexican Spells	U.S. Spells	Mexican Spells	U.S. Spells	Mexican Spells	U.S. Spells
Individual characteristics						
Age	-0.0004	-0.0082	-0.0001	-0.0190***	-0.0001	-0.0149**
Female	1.9108***	-0.2707***	1.9371***	-0.0424	2.2825***	0.0106
Education (in years)	-0.0006	0.0490**	0.0150	0.0392**	0.0076	0.0557**
U.S. interview	-1.7959***	2.4591***	-1.9919***	2.1752***	-2.1106***	2.9090***
U.S. migration experience (in months)	-0.0046**	0.0108***	-0.0078**	0.0105***	-0.0063***	0.0128***
Family responsibilities						
Married	-0.0995	-0.2074	-0.0253	-0.1608	-0.0075	-0.1753
Single parent	-0.3278	-0.1707	-0.3857*	-0.1126	-0.3129	-0.2047
Number of minor-age children	0.0363	0.0603**	0.0086	0.0732**	0.0529	0.0806**
Additional income sources						
Number of adult offspring	0.2433***	-0.0392	0.1928***	0.0323	0.3147***	-0.0048
Business ownership	1.6961***	-0.4333***	1.2791***	-0.3756**	1.8675***	-0.3732**
Agricultural land (in hectares)	0.0197*	-0.0435**	0.0095	-0.0467**	0.0198	-0.0473**
U.S. immigration status						
Legal resident of U.S.	-0.2957	-0.7700***	0.0523	-0.4596***	-0.2739	-0.7686***
Bracero	n.a.	-0.5953**	n.a.	-0.2566	n.a.	-0.5700**
U.S. immigration policies						
Bracero Program in effect	-0.0966	-0.2195	-0.0826	-0.2909	-0.0997	-0.1518
Amnesty Program in effect	-0.0513	-0.0888	-0.0078	-0.0592	-0.0514	-0.0403

Table 6.4 (continued)

Vector/Variable	Log-logistic (Model 6.4)		Log-normal (Model 6.5)		Exponential (Model 6.6)	
	Mexican Spells	U.S. Spells	Mexican Spells	U.S. Spells	Mexican Spells	U.S. Spells
Relatives with U.S. migration experience						
Father	1.6684***	0.1221	1.9820***	-0.0985	1.9605***	0.1758
Mother	-0.7364***	-0.9371***	-0.6201*	-0.8573***	-0.7250***	-1.0641***
Grandparents	-0.9210**	-0.9045***	-0.7133	-1.0002***	-1.0559**	-1.0915***
Siblings	-1.6845***	-0.0199	-1.6153***	0.0851	-1.9737***	-0.0222
Relatives have migration experience and household head has not yet migrated						
Father	-1.6067***	n.a.	-1.4919***	n.a.	-1.7384***	n.a.
Mother	0.0367	n.a.	-0.6017	n.a.	-0.0940	n.a.
Grandparents	0.1151	n.a.	-0.0234	n.a.	0.1800	n.a.
Siblings	0.9327***	n.a.	0.6937***	n.a.	1.0577***	n.a.
Constant	6.3518***	2.8329***	6.1223***	2.6246***	6.6795***	2.8377***
Scale parameter	1.2173***	1.3170***	0.8350***	1.1069***	n.a.	n.a.
Mean log-likelihood	-0.5395		-0.5342		-0.5444	

N = 2,535 (2,285 Mexican spells and 250 U.S. spells).

Results of two-tailed *t*-test on significance of parameter estimate:

***Passes at 99-percent level; **passes at 95-percent level; and *passes at 90-percent level.

Table 6.5: Net Effects of Family Migration Experience on Mexican Spells of Residence

Vector/Variable	Model 6.1	Model 6.2	Model 6.3	Model 6.4	Model 6.5	Model 6.6
Net effect of migrant relatives when head of household has U.S. experience						
Any immediate relative	-1.3445***	-1.3756***	-1.5584***	n.a.	n.a.	n.a.
Grandparent	n.a.	n.a.	n.a.	-0.9210**	-0.7133	-1.0559**
Father	n.a.	n.a.	n.a.	1.6684***	1.9820***	1.9605***
Mother	n.a.	n.a.	n.a.	-0.7364***	-0.6201*	-0.7250***
Sibling	n.a.	n.a.	n.a.	-1.6845***	-1.6153***	-1.9737***
Net effect of migrant relatives when head of household has not yet migrated						
Any immediate relative	0.5578***	0.4896***	0.6321***	n.a.	n.a.	n.a.
Grandparent	n.a.	n.a.	n.a.	-0.8059	-0.7367	-0.8759
Father	n.a.	n.a.	n.a.	0.0617	0.4901	0.2221
Mother	n.a.	n.a.	n.a.	-0.6997**	-1.2218*	-0.8190**
Sibling	n.a.	n.a.	n.a.	-0.7518***	-0.9216***	-0.9160***

Results of two-tailed *t*-test on significance of net effect:

***Passes at 99-percent level; **passes at 95-percent level; and *passes at 90-percent level.

For individuals who have already participated in migration, having a mother, grandparent, or sibling with U.S. experience decreases the length of Mexican spells, while having a father who is a current or former migrant increases their length. This latter result contradicts the findings of Chapter 5 regarding the impact of a father's U.S. experience on repeat migration.

The head of household is more likely to have shorter spells of U.S. residence when the individual's mother or siblings have migration experience (see Table 6.4). These relatives should be particularly influential if they reside in the United States and if the migrant expects that they will be there for some time. Thus, the migrant who ends a U.S. spell of residence anticipates having relatively low migration costs should he or she choose to return to the United States. Having a father or grandparent with U.S. experience has no statistically significant effect on the length of U.S. spells. Therefore, the duration models provide no evidence that family migration experience increases the length of U.S. migration spells.

6.4. CONCLUSION

This chapter indicates that migration networks, as proxied by family migration experience, shorten the Mexican spells of residence of household heads who have already participated in migration. The presence of a current or former migrant among one's parents, siblings, and grandparents decreases the length of Mexican spells and thus encourages repeat migration. When specific relatives are considered, having a sibling, mother, or grandparent with U.S. experience spurs the individual to terminate the ongoing Mexican spell of residence and migrate to the United States.

For individuals who have never migrated, having at least one immediate relative with U.S. experience lengthens Mexican spells of residence and thus discourages first migration. However, when specific relatives are considered, having a mother or sibling with U.S. experience decreases the length of these spells. Finally, the chapter offers no evidence that networks increase the length of U.S. migration spells. Instead, having a mother or sibling with U.S. experience is found to decrease their length. This conclusion is consistent with the idea that migration networks facilitate shorter spells of migration by reducing the costs of migration.

Female heads of household have longer spells of Mexican residence, as do heads of households with additional income sources, such as a business, agricultural land, or adult offspring. Older individuals, females, business owners, and persons with more agricultural land all have shorter spells of U.S. residence. Legal residents of the United States and persons with more U.S. experience have shorter spells in Mexico and longer spells in the United States.

What would migration patterns be like if the United States and Mexico forged a pact allowing for the free movement of labor or if the United States instituted a second Bracero program? The results for legal residency suggest that a free labor pact would cause heads of household to have longer spells of residence in the United States and shorter spells in Mexico. If the effects of a new guestworker program resembled that of the Bracero Program, then the U.S. spells of residence for program participants would be relatively short.

The wild card in both scenarios is the proportion of migrants who would decide to settle in the United States. Under a free labor pact, longer spells in the United States could lead to permanent settlement there. Participants in another guestworker program might also choose to remain in the United States indefinitely and even to bring their families across the border, in possible violation of the program's rules. In that event, existing migration networks and new ones forged under the guestworker program would play a key role.

NOTES

1. Because some of the explanatory variables in the duration models are indexed according to calendar year t, I use the letter z to refer to the length of the migration spells.

2. The failure rate is the proportion of spells whose length is less than or equal to the specified level.

3. Note that the parameter λ is altogether different from the hazard rate, $\lambda(t)$.

4. A more detailed description of the variables and their sources is located in Appendix E.

5. During my fieldwork, I met two such individuals. The first obtained legal residency through IRCA but preferred that he and his family live in Mexico. In a guestworker-like fashion, he migrates legally to the United States when job prospects in Mexico become limited. The second, who lives in the United States, returned temporarily to Mexico for about a year in order to spend her pregnancy in the company of relatives.

6. See Appendix Table C.8.

CHAPTER 7

The Rewards to U.S. Experience in the Mexican Labor Market

7.1. INTRODUCTION

This chapter compares the monthly earnings in Mexico of former migrants who have returned from the United States (often referred to as "return migrants") with those of persons who have never migrated. Chiswick (1978), Borjas (1990, 1985), and others have studied whether the U.S. wages of foreign-born workers converge on those of U.S. natives. However, few scholars have examined the earnings of Mexican migrants after they return home.

The earnings of return migrants constitute an intriguing topic. First, if U.S. experience yields high returns in the Mexican labor market, then the prospect of these returns may further motivate Mexico-U.S. migration. Second, if the earnings of return migrants truly diverge from those of non-migrants, then the very return of these migrants may affect Mexican income inequality. If the typical return migrant would earn a less than average income if he or she remained in Mexico, then migration to the United States may ultimately reduce Mexican income inequality. Third, if migrants accumulate new and productive abilities while in the United States, then temporary migration to the United States may result in a net gain of human capital for Mexico.

To examine the returns to U.S. experience in the Mexican labor market, the log of the head of household's monthly earnings is regressed on a vector of explanatory variables, including total U.S. migration experience. An inverse Mills ratio is used to account for any selection bias that results from not having information about the potential Mexican earnings of persons interviewed in the United States. A separate set of earnings regressions is estimated for males only, since the life circumstances of female heads of household are often quite distinct from those of males. Finally, because U.S. experience and income may be endogenous, a two-stage least squares (2SLS) model is considered in which fitted values for migration experience are substituted for the actual values in the earnings regression.

The chapter is organized as follows. Section 7.2 describes the econometric techniques used in the chapter. Special attention is given to the selection problem presented by the data and my response to this problem. Section 7.3 presents the results from the primary set of earnings regressions. Section 7.4 examines the regressions for males only, as well as the models using two-stage least squares. Finally, Section 7.5 offers some closing remarks.

7.2. THE MODEL

7.2.1. Overview of the Model

The Mexican Migration Project collects data about the head of household's monthly earnings at the time of the interview. For most individuals, this amount reflects only income obtained through wage labor. However, some observations may include income from other sources, such as the sale of agricultural output or earnings from a business. By design, the project does not solicit a detailed account of the household's income. The project's leadership believes that some respondents might view extensive questions about economic matters as intrusive, and the questionnaire already is quite lengthy.

Since this chapter focuses on earnings from the Mexican labor market, persons interviewed in the United States are largely excluded from consideration. This introduces a possible selection bias, as the potential Mexican earnings of U.S. respondents may differ from the actual earnings of similar Mexican respondents. Taylor (1987) confirms that selection bias is a genuine concern when working with community-level data describing Mexican migration and earnings. Using 1983 data from four rural villages in the State of Michoacán, Taylor (1987: 626) finds that persons "who are in the best position to contribute to household income as workers in Mexico are positively selected not to migrate to the United States."

To account for the possibility of selection bias, the chapter specifies an earnings regression that is corrected for selection bias, as described by Killingsworth (1983). This technique contains two steps. The first consists of a probit model in which a dummy variable denoting the country of interview is regressed upon a vector of explanatory variables for all observations in the sample—both U.S. and Mexican. This model is essentially a participation model of whether the respondent took part in migration at the time of the Mexican interviews. As we shall see below, most of the probit model's explanatory variables also appear in the participation models of Chapter 5. The one major difference is that the dependent variable in the probit model equals one if the interview took place in Mexico and zero otherwise.

Using the results from the probit model, the inverse of the Mills ratio (M_i) is calculated for each observation:

$$M_i = f(-\mathbf{x}_i{'}\beta) / [1 - F(-\mathbf{x}_i{'}\beta)] = f(\mathbf{x}_i{'}\beta) / F(\mathbf{x}_i{'}\beta).$$

The functions $f(-\mathbf{x}_i{'}\beta)$ and $F(-\mathbf{x}_i{'}\beta)$ are respectively the probability density function and the cumulative density function of the standard normal distribution. The inverse Mills ratio is then included as an explanatory variable in a regression of the log of monthly income, as measured in 1994 new pesos:

$$\log y_i = \mathbf{z}_i{'}\gamma_1 + M_i\gamma_2 + \varepsilon_i$$

This earnings regression forms the second step of the approach.

The explanatory variables are drawn from the data sets HOUSFILE and PERSFILE of the Mexican Migration Project. When I started the data analysis for this book, no U.S. interviews had been conducted for seven of the project's survey communities. Therefore, the observations for these communities are excluded from the sample. Also dropped from the sample is any head of household whose monthly earnings were zero, as well as any individual older than 65 years. The remaining data set contains 3,138 observations—2,767 in Mexico and 371 in the United States.

7.2.2. Hypotheses

Several variables in the probit model do not appear in the participation models of Chapter 5 or the duration models of Chapter 6. In place of the number of minor-age children and the number of adult offspring, the probit model includes the number of workers and the number of non-workers in the household. The model also contains a dummy variable that indicates whether the individual's spouse was working at the time of the interview. A network variable denotes whether the individual had at least one close friend or relative in the United States at the time of the interview. This differs from the network variables of Chapters 5 and 6, which indicate whether certain relatives possessed U.S. experience at a given point in time. Otherwise, the probit model largely resembles the participation models of Chapter 5. Table 7.1 summarizes my hypotheses regarding the probit model's explanatory variables. Since the reasoning behind these hypotheses is essentially the same as for the participation models, I will not elaborate on them further.

Table 7.1: Hypothesized Net Effects of Explanatory Variables on Interview Location

Vector/Variable	Hypothesized Net Effect
Individual Characteristics	
Age	Negative
Age squared	Positive
Female	Positive
Education (in years)	Positive
Family Responsibilities	
Married	Positive
Number of non-workers in household	Negative
Additional Income Sources	
Business ownership	Positive
Agricultural land (in hectares)	Positive
Number of non-workers in household	Positive
Spouse works	Positive
Legal resident of U.S.	Negative
Migration network	Negative

Table 7.2 lists the hypothesized signs of the parameter estimates for the earnings regression. The regression's explanatory variables may be divided into several smaller vectors: (1) individual characteristics, (2) family responsibilities, (3) additional income sources, (4) migration-experience interaction terms, (5) the inverse Mills ratio, (6) occupational variables, and (7) community dummy variables. Precise definitions of these variables and an identification of their sources are located in Appendix F.

The vector of individual characteristics measures the age, gender, education, and U.S. experience of the head of household. If age may be used as a proxy for work experience, then income should increase with age. To account for the possibility that this marginal return diminishes as age increases, the earnings regression includes the square of age. Regarding education, earnings should rise with additional schooling.

Previous chapters note that the female heads of household studied by the Mexican Migration Project typically become the head of household due to separation, divorce, or the incapacitation of the husband. During my fieldwork in San Ramon, I observed that many of these women had limited work experience outside the home prior to becoming the head of household. For this reason, the earnings of females should be lower than those of males, else being equal.

Migrants may acquire new skills and abilities while in the United States. They may also build upon existing ones. If these skills and abilities are transferable to the Mexican labor market, then U.S. experience should have a positive effect on Mexican earnings. The model includes the square of U.S. experience to account for the possibility that this effect tapers off as experience increases. However, if the skills and abilities are not transferable, then migration experience should have, at best, a negligible effect on Mexican earnings. In the worst-case scenario, U.S. experience may reduce these earnings, as time passed in the United States could have been better spent developing and maintaining one's Mexico-specific human capital.

With respect to family responsibilities, married individuals and persons with more dependents may work longer hours or increase their work effort in order to support their families. If this is the case, then the variables denoting marriage and the number of non-workers in the household should positively affect the log of monthly earnings.

Table 7.2: Hypothesized Net Effects of Explanatory Variables on Mexican Earnings

Vector/Variable	Hypothesized Net Effect
Individual characteristics	
Age	Positive
Age squared	Negative
Female	Negative
Education (in years)	Positive
U.S. interview	Positive
Family responsibilities	
Married	Positive
Number of non-workers in household	Positive
Additional income sources	
Business ownership	Positive
Agricultural land (in hectares)	Positive
Number of workers in household	?
Spouse works	?
Migration-experience interaction terms	
Education times experience	Positive
Business ownership times experience	Positive
Agricultural land times experience	Positive
Inverse Mills ratio	Positive
Occupational variables	
Irregularly employed	Negative
Technician	Negative
Office worker or nonmanual worker	Negative
Salesperson	Negative
Industrial owner or supervisor	Negative
Skilled manual laborer	Negative
Unskilled manual worker	Negative
Agricultural worker	Negative
Service worker or unknown occupation	Negative

These two variables may also be positively related to earnings for another reason: people may evaluate prospective mates on their potential to be good breadwinners.

Several variables identify potential sources of household income in addition to the head of household's labor power. These are a business, agricultural land, employment of the individual's spouse, and the number of workers in the household. A head of household who owns a business or more agricultural land than average should enjoy higher earnings. Harder to predict is the influence of spousal employment and the number of workers in the household. On the one hand, the head of a household with more workers may choose to enjoy more leisure time. Such a decision presumably reduces monthly earnings. On the other hand, these workers may assume home responsibilities that would otherwise belong to the head of household, thus enabling that person to work more. There may also be economies of scale with respect to the number of workers, especially if the household is engaged in agriculture or operates a business. Thus, earnings may rise with the number of workers.

Three variables measure the possible interaction between migration experience and education, business ownership, and agricultural land. To create these interaction terms, the variables measuring business ownership, educational level, and agricultural land are each multiplied by a dummy variable that equals one if the head of household has ever migrated to the United States and zero otherwise. The three terms respectively measure the difference in earnings of return migrants and non-migrants who have the same educational level, who both own a business, and who possess the identical amount of agricultural land.

As I indicated above, the purpose of the inverse Mills ratio is to capture any influence of selection bias on the log of monthly earnings. Killingsworth (1983: 144) notes that the parameter estimate for the inverse Mills ratio is an estimate of the standard deviation of the dependent variable—in this case, the log of monthly earnings. A statistically insignificant parameter estimate provides no evidence of selection bias.

A group of nine dummy variables denotes different categories of professions. A relatively high-income employment classification, professionals and administrators, is selected as the excluded occupational category to ensure that the earnings regression is of full rank. Therefore, the parameter estimates for all nine occupational dummy variables should be negative in sign.

7.3. EMPIRICAL RESULTS

7.3.1. Overview

This section reports the empirical results from several variants of the earnings model. Two specifications (Models 7.1b and 7.1c) are based on a probit model that includes dummy variables for the various survey communities (Model 7.1a). Two other versions (Models 7.2b and 7.2c) follow a probit model in which these variables are absent (Model 7.2a). In addition, Models 7.1b and 7.2b contain interaction terms for U.S. experience and education, business ownership, and agricultural land. Otherwise, the four earnings models are identical.

7.3.2. Probit Model

Table 7.3 displays the results from four specifications of the probit model. Models 7.1a and 7.2a utilize observations for both genders, while Models 7.3a and 7.4a deal only with males. Let us focus for the moment on the probit models for both genders. Corresponding parameter estimates across the two models are of identical sign, and there is no substantial difference in their significance levels.

Two important variables in the participation models of Chapter 5— age and its square—are insignificant in both Models 7.1a and 7.2a. Age may be a poor predictor of interview location due to the snowball sampling method used to select the U.S. respondents. As Chapters 3 and 4 indicated, the U.S. respondents are not likely to be representative of the population of interest: Mexican household heads from the various survey communities who were in the United States at the time of the interviews.

The parameter estimates for marital status and the number of non-workers in the household are both highly significant and positive in sign, which is opposite from what I hypothesized. The number of non-workers in the household is statistically insignificant, just as the number of minor-age children was insignificant in Chapter 5.

Table 7.3: Results from Probit Models Used to Generate Inverse Mills Ratio

	Both Genders		Males Only	
Vector/Variable	Model 7.1a	Model 7.2a	Model 7.3a	Model 7.4a
Intercept	0.6335	1.0754***	0.4577	0.8768*
Individual characteristics				
Age	0.0369	0.0288	0.0407	0.0338
Age squared	-0.0003	-0.0002	-0.0004	-0.0003
Female	0.7043***	0.7502***	n.a.	n.a.
Education (in years)	-0.0355***	-0.0416***	-0.0339**	-0.0386***
College educated	0.8409***	0.9306***	0.7939***	0.8811***
Family responsibilities				
Married	0.6845***	0.7407***	0.7387***	0.7939***
Number of non-workers in household	0.0814***	0.0676***	0.0873***	0.0712***
Additional income sources				
Business ownership	0.3254***	0.3276***	0.2956***	0.2964***
Agricultural land (in hectares)	-0.0018	-0.0013	-0.0017	-0.0011
Number of workers in household	0.0387	0.0271	0.0555	0.0444
Spouse works	-0.6136***	-0.5919***	-0.6074***	-0.5890***
Legal resident of U.S.	-1.7683***	-1.5435***	-1.7767***	-1.5446***
Migration network	-1.2414***	-1.0068***	-1.2225***	-0.9900***
Community variables				
3	0.1371	n.a.	0.1763	n.a.
4	-0.0928	n.a.	-0.0929	n.a.
5	0.2456	n.a.	0.2820	n.a.
6	0.6584**	n.a.	0.6547**	n.a.
7	0.6134*	n.a.	0.5187	n.a.
8	0.8828***	n.a.	0.8542***	n.a.

Table 7.3 (continued)

Vector/Variable	Both Genders		Males Only	
	Model 7.1a	Model 7.2a	Model 7.3a	Model 7.4a
Community variables (cont.)				
9	0.7861**	n.a.	0.7637**	n.a.
10	1.3948***	n.a.	1.3659***	n.a.
11	0.5451*	n.a.	0.5258	n.a.
12	0.4498	n.a.	0.4493	n.a.
13	0.8672***	n.a.	0.8601***	n.a.
14	0.1066	n.a.	0.1051	n.a.
15	0.2358	n.a.	0.2078	n.a.
16	0.7853**	n.a.	0.7782**	n.a.
17	0.8826***	n.a.	0.8886***	n.a.
18	1.1958***	n.a.	1.2478***	n.a.
19	0.5853*	n.a.	0.5900*	n.a.
25	0.4587	n.a.	0.6229	n.a.
26	0.9280***	n.a.	1.0151***	n.a.
27	0.5122*	n.a.	0.4678	n.a.
28	0.5024	n.a.	0.5048	n.a.
29	0.5118	n.a.	0.5558*	n.a.
33	0.4480	n.a.	0.4256	n.a.
N	3,138	3,138	2,910	2,910
Mexican interviews	2,767	2,767	2,552	2,552
U.S. interviews	371	371	358	358
Log-likelihood	-677.2849	-715.4962	-643.8901	-681.6134

Results of Wald Chi-squared test of parameter estimate's significance:

***Passes at 99-percent confidence level; **passes at 95-percent level; and *passes at 90-percent level

Household heads who own a business are more likely to be interviewed in Mexico, while individuals whose spouse is employed are less likely to be interviewed there. The latter result may be due to the fact that it is less common in Mexico than in the United States for both husband and wife to work outside of the home. If the direction of causation indeed runs from country of interview to spousal employment, then this variable should be dropped from the probit model.

Persons who lack legal residency in the United States and persons who have no close friends or relatives there are more likely to be interviewed in Mexico. These findings are consistent with the results of Chapter 5. With respect to the community dummy variables in Model 7.1a, the parameter estimates for 13 of the 23 are significant at the 90-percent level or better. All 13 significant estimates are positive in sign. The parameter estimate for San Ramon is not significant.

7.3.3. Earnings Regression

Table 7.4 presents the results from four specifications of the earnings regression. Across these models, corresponding parameter estimates have the identical sign. However, there are a few noteworthy differences in their significance levels. College education and spousal employment are significant only in the models without community variables (Models 7.2b and 7.2c). The squared term for migration experience and business ownership are significant only in the models containing interaction terms for U.S. experience (Models 7.1b and 7.2b). Otherwise, the results from the four models are quite similar.

Migration experience has a positive effect on Mexican earnings. The estimated return from the first year of such experience ranges from 4.0 to 5.9 percent. According to Model 7.1b, the net effect of U.S. experience and its square rises for the first 53 years of such experience. These results provide initial evidence that the returns to international migration are not limited to a migrant's U.S. earnings. Instead, migration experience has a more lasting impact on the Mexican earnings of return migrants.

Unfortunately, the regressions do not reveal the precise route by which migration experience influences the earnings ability of the return migrant. The individual may learn new skills at work in the United

Table 7.4: Results from Earnings Regressions for Both Genders

Vector/Variable	With Community Variables			Without Community Variables		
	Model 7.1b	Model 7.1c		Model 7.2b	Model 7.2c	
Intercept	5.9311***	5.9805***		5.4684***	5.5186***	
Individual characteristics						
Age	0.0414***	0.0417***		0.0450***	0.0453***	
Age squared	-0.0005***	-0.0005***		-0.0005***	-0.0005***	
Female	-0.3882***	-0.3960***		-0.3485***	-0.3558***	
Education (in years)	0.0359***	0.0318***		0.0336***	0.0292***	
College educated	0.0986	0.1003		0.1605*	0.1557*	
U.S. migration experience (in years)	0.0566***	0.0397***		0.0589***	0.0415***	
U.S. experience squared	-0.0011***	-0.0005		-0.0011***	-0.0005	
Family responsibilities						
Married	0.2829***	0.2632***		0.3187***	0.2981***	
Number of non-workers in household	0.0096	0.0086		0.0077	0.0058	
Additional income sources						
Business ownership	0.1171**	0.0469		0.1324***	0.0647	
Agricultural land (in hectares)	0.0041***	0.0024**		0.0044***	0.0023**	
Spouse works	-0.0483	-0.0400		-0.1035**	-0.0910*	
Number of workers in household	0.0214	0.0226		0.0204	0.0215	
Interaction terms						
Education and U.S. experience	-0.0161***	n.a.		-0.0181***	n.a.	
Business ownership and U.S. experience	-0.1662**	n.a.		-0.1571**	n.a.	
Agricultural land and U.S. experience	-0.0035*	n.a.		-0.0042**	n.a.	
Inverse Mills ratio	0.4594***	0.3860***		0.7063***	0.6288***	

Table 7.4 (continued)

Vector/Variable	With Community Variables		Without Community Variables	
	Model 7.1b	Model 7.1c	Model 7.2b	Model 7.2c
Occupational variables				
Irregularly employed	-0.1241	-0.1383	-0.1259	-0.1394
Technician	0.0033	0.0081	0.0171	0.0272
Office worker or nonmanual worker	-0.1245	-0.1288	-0.1247	-0.1291
Salesperson	-0.2001**	-0.2100**	-0.1965**	-0.2051**
Industrial owner or supervisor	0.4201*	0.4084	0.4747*	0.4760*
Skilled manual laborer	-0.1529**	-0.1737**	-0.1335*	-0.1537**
Unskilled manual worker	-0.2753***	-0.2918***	-0.2850***	-0.3038***
Agricultural worker	-0.3443***	-0.3619***	-0.3249***	-0.3394***
Service worker or unknown occupation	-0.1229	-0.1429*	-0.0899	-0.1092
N	2,767	2,767	2,767	2,767
R-squared	0.2294	0.2218	0.2011	0.1921

Results of two-tailed t-test of parameter estimate's significance:

***Passes at 99-percent level; **passes at 95-percent level; and *passes at 90-percent level

Results for community dummy variables are not reported.

States that would not have been acquired in Mexico. This may especially be the case for migrants whose U.S. occupation is substantially different from what it would have been in Mexico. Also, migrants may obtain additional education in the United States. Training at the technical- or community-college level may be particularly important.

Mexican experience offers economic benefits of its own. The parameter estimates for age and its square, which serve as proxies for Mexican experience, are both highly significant. According to Model 7.1b, the marginal effect of the 20th year of life is a 2.2-percent increase in monthly earnings. The marginal effect of the 30th year is 1.2 percent. Because the parameter estimate for age-squared is small, the net effect of age and its square rises for the first 83 years of life.

The Mexican labor market also rewards the better educated. The estimated return to each year of Mexican education ranges from 3.0 to 3.6 percent. The variable denoting college-educated heads of household is marginally significant in only Models 7.2b and 7.2c.

As was hypothesized, female household heads have substantially lower earnings than males. One cannot emphasize enough that the typical female in the sample faces difficult economic circumstances. Many of these women have limited work experience outside the home and must weather a challenging family crisis such as widowhood, divorce, or the incapacitation of one's spouse.

Married heads of household earn higher incomes than their single counterparts. The model does not indicate whether this is due to the head of household working more in order to support the family, a selection issue regarding the ability of high-income individuals to marry, or some other factor. The number of non-workers in the household is not found to influence earnings.

The four models provide clear evidence that earnings rise with the amount of agricultural land. Business ownership is statistically significant in two of the regressions and is also found to boost earnings. Spousal employment predicts lower earnings in Models 7.2b and 7.2c.

The migration-experience interaction terms yield parameter estimates that are significant at the 95-percent level or better (see Models 7.1b and 7.1c). Interestingly, their signs are negative. In the case of education, this means that persons who migrate to the United States and then return to Mexico experience lower returns to education than non-migrants with similar levels of schooling. This factor may have motivated their migration in the first place. A similar relation apparently exists between migration and the productivity of agricultural land. Persons who cultivate less productive plots of land may be more likely to participate in international migration.

With respect to business ownership, the negative parameter estimate for its interaction term suggests that return migrants who own businesses earn less money in Mexico than non-migrant business owners. One possible explanation of this result is that return-migrant business owners are more likely to be first-time entrepreneurs and thus are less likely to succeed. However, the earnings model might generate different results if it contained explanatory variables that distinguish among various types of businesses. In San Ramon, for instance, businesses ranged from selling soft drinks out of the home to partial ownership of the local bank.

The inverse Mills ratio is significant at the 99-percent confidence level. This provides strong evidence that selection bias is a problem due to a lack of data about the potential Mexican earnings of U.S. respondents.

Four of the dummy variables denoting occupational categories are statistically significant in all four earnings regressions. These categories are salesperson, skilled manual worker, unskilled manual worker, and agricultural worker. A fifth category, industrial owner or supervisor, is significant in Models 7.1b, 7.2b, and 7.2c. A sixth category, service worker or unknown occupation, is significant in Model 7.1b only. Particularly noteworthy are the results for unskilled manual workers and agricultural workers. Their parameter estimates are negative, and the absolute values of the estimates are the second and third highest among the nine variables. In San Ramon, the poorer respondents typically alternated between farm labor and less skilled construction work, with little to no differentiation in the wage according to the amount of experience.[1]

Table 7.4 does not report the results for the 23 community variables used in Models 7.1b and 7.1c. In both models, the parameter estimates for 20 of these variables (including that for San Ramon) are significant at the 90-percent level or better. Nineteen of the 20 significant estimates are negative in sign. The 20 estimates are quite large in terms of their absolute values, ranging from −0.2307 (community 8) to –0.6574 (community 5) using the results of Model 7.1b. The parameter estimate for San Ramon is –0.2714 in Model 7.1b and –0.2711 in Model 7.1c. Thus, the average head of household in San Ramon earns 27 percent less than the average respondent overall.

Why is location so important to Mexican earnings? Differences in the cost of living may offer a partial explanation, but they are unlikely to tell the whole story. One possible explanation is that poorer Mexicans find it difficult to secure the resources necessary to migrate to the United States or at least to move to a different part of Mexico where job prospects are superior. If they cannot save or borrow these resources, they may get locked into low-wage locales.

7.4. VARIATIONS OF THE BASIC MODEL

7.4.1. Male Heads of Household Only

Table 7.5 lists the results from four earnings regressions that use only the observations for the male heads of household. The vector of explanatory variables used in these models is virtually identical to that employed in the models for both genders. Thus, Model 7.3b may be compared to Model 7.1b, Model 7.3c to Model 7.1c, and so on.[2]

Only one female household head in the sample was interviewed in the United States. Therefore, it is not possible to run a similar set of regressions for females only, since there are not enough observations to estimate the probit model necessary for obtaining the inverse Mills ratio.

The empirical results for males only are extremely similar to those for both genders. Migration experience is highly significant and exerts a positive influence on the Mexican earnings of return migrants. The first year of U.S. experience yields an estimated increase in Mexican earnings ranging from 3.7 to 6.1 percent. The magnitude of this effect is roughly equal to that obtained from the models for both genders. The squared term for U.S. experience is significant in Models 7.3b, 7.4b, and 7.4c. According to Model 7.3b, the net effect of migration experience and its square rises until 60 years of such experience have been accumulated.

The inverse Mills ratio is also highly significant. Thus, the selection-bias issue concerning the potential Mexican earnings of U.S. respondents is also a valid concern in the earnings regressions for males.

One noteworthy difference between the two sets of regressions concerns the dummy variable for the irregularly employed. The parameter estimate for this variable becomes statistically significant when only males are considered. Apparently, gender captures some of this variable's influence in the earnings regressions for both sexes.

7.4.2. Two-Stage Least Squares

Since migration experience and Mexican earnings may be endogenous, two-stage least squares is used to estimate another set of earnings models. The first stage is a tobit model that regresses U.S. experience on the entire set of explanatory variables from the earnings regression, as well as four other variables:

1. the age at which the individual first migrated to the United States or, in the case of non-migrants, the individual's age at the time of the interview;

2. the square of this variable;

3. a dummy variable that equals one if the individual's father migrated to the United States prior to the individual's first migration experience (if any); and

4. a dummy variable that equals one if one or more of the individual's siblings migrated to the United States prior to the individual's first migration experience.

These four variables are included in order to boost the tobit model's explanatory power.

Parameter estimates from the tobit model are used to calculate the predicted level of U.S. experience for each observation. These fitted values are then substituted for the actual measures of migration experience in the earnings regression, which constitutes the second stage of 2SLS.

Persons whose first migration experience occurs earlier in life should have the opportunity to accumulate more U.S. experience overall. Thus, the age at first migration should be an effective predictor of total U.S. experience. Given the presence of the individual's age and its square in the original vector of explanatory variables, one should carefully evaluate the tobit model's parameter estimates for the four

Table 7.5: Results from Earnings Regressions for Males Only

Vector/Variable	With Community Variables		Without Community Variables	
	Model 7.3b	Model 7.3c	Model 7.4b	Model 7.4c
Intercept	5.9500***	5.9971***	5.5164***	5.5682***
Individual characteristics				
Age	0.0411***	0.0411***	0.0439***	0.0438***
Age squared	-0.0005***	-0.0005***	-0.0005***	-0.0005***
Education (in years)	0.0326***	0.0297***	0.0303***	0.0268***
College educated	0.1274	0.1321	0.1875**	0.1873**
U.S. migration experience (in years)	0.0510***	0.0370***	0.0610***	0.0459***
U.S. experience squared	-0.0009**	-0.0005	-0.0011***	-0.0007*
Family responsibilities				
Married	0.2685***	0.2517**	0.3067***	0.2885***
Number of non-workers in household	0.0057	0.0049	0.0029	0.0019
Additional income sources				
Business ownership	0.1362***	0.0669*	0.1502***	0.0788*
Agricultural land (in hectares)	0.0041***	0.0024**	0.0043***	0.0022**
Spouse works	-0.0576	-0.0520	-0.1015**	-0.0918*
Number of workers in household	0.0112	0.0125	0.0113	0.0125
Interaction terms				
Education and U.S. experience	-0.0113**	n.a.	-0.0138**	n.a.
Business ownership and U.S. experience	-0.1607**	n.a.	-0.1628**	n.a.
Agricultural land and U.S. experience	-0.0035*	n.a.	-0.0041**	n.a.
Inverse Mills ratio	0.4656***	0.4099***	0.7011***	0.6383***

Table 7.5 (continued)

Vector/Variable	With Community Variables		Without Community Variables	
	Model 7.3b	Model 7.3c	Model 7.4b	Model 7.4c
Occupational variables				
Irregularly employed	-0.3250***	-0.3343***	-0.2960**	-0.3047**
Technician	0.0171	0.0160	0.0331	0.0377
Office worker or nonmanual worker	-0.1376	-0.1433	-0.1320	-0.1376
Salesperson	-0.1777**	-0.1861**	-0.1749**	-0.1824**
Industrial owner or supervisor	0.4432*	0.4302	0.4993	0.4964**
Skilled manual laborer	-0.1470*	-0.1630**	-0.1189	-0.1353*
Unskilled manual worker	-0.2577***	-0.2703***	-0.2656***	-0.2815***
Agricultural worker	-0.3581***	-0.3734***	-0.3305***	-0.3431***
Service worker or unknown occupation	-0.1117	-0.1269	-0.0761	-0.0917
N	2,552	2,552	2,552	2,552
R-squared	0.2148	0.2085	0.1771	0.1689

Results of two-tailed *t*-test of parameter estimate's significance:

***Passes at 99-percent level; **passes at 95-percent level; and *passes at 90-percent level

Results for community dummy variables are not reported.

age-based variables. However, since the purpose of this model is to generate fitted values for U.S. experience, the interpretation of these estimates is of secondary concern.

The two indicators of family migration experience are different from the network variables of Chapter 5 and 6. The variables in the tobit model equal one when the specified relative has migration experience that predates the first U.S. experience (if any) of the household head. These variables are therefore time-invariant, in contrast to the network variables of Chapters 5 and 6. Table 7.6 displays the results from the second-stage earnings regressions, and Appendix Table G.1 presents the results from the first-stage tobit models.[3] Each 2SLS earnings model has a corresponding ordinary least-squares (OLS) earnings regression in either Table 7.4 or Table 7.5. The earnings models containing the three interaction terms for U.S. experience are not replicated using 2SLS, since these variables would also have to be fitted using their own reduced-form equations.

The 2SLS earnings regressions produce much weaker evidence regarding the returns to migration experience in the Mexican labor market. The fitted value for U.S. experience is statistically insignificant in each of the 2SLS models. But the squared term yields a positive parameter estimate that is significant at the 95-percent level in Models 7.1e and 7.2e and at the 90-percent level in Model 7.4e.

The return to the first year of U.S. experience is relatively meager. According to Model 7.1e, the first year of such experience increases earnings by only 0.27 percent. However, this return becomes more substantial as the individual head accumulates additional migration experience. Five years of U.S. experience raise monthly earnings in Mexico by 6.8 percent, and ten years of such experience yield a 27.2-percent return.

Because the parameter estimate for the squared fitted value is so small, the income gains from U.S. experience are initially inferior to the gains from Mexican experience (i.e., age). At 15 years, the rewards of U.S. experience finally exceed the rewards of an equivalent amount of Mexican experience. More precisely, the net effect on monthly earnings of 15 years of migration experience is slightly greater than the net effect of being 15 years old. How the head of household evaluates these returns in light of the fact that one typically earns a higher wage while accumulating U.S. experience is not readily apparent.

The 2SLS earnings regressions suggest that the OLS models may overstate the relationship between migration experience and Mexican earnings. Nevertheless, the 2SLS models clearly indicate evidence that experience as a U.S. migrant generates positive returns in the Mexican labor market. The associated income gains in Mexico appear to be substantial for persons with many years of U.S. experience.

Alternate specifications of the 2SLS model may yield results that more closely resemble the findings of the OLS regressions. From an econometric standpoint, the key is to specify a first-stage model that does a good job of predicting U.S. experience. As the Mexican Migration Project adds new communities and hence new observations to its data sets, this task should become easier. In addition, the inclusion of new variables in the first-stage tobit model might boost its predictive power. In some ways, this task is more difficult than conducting more interviews, as the earnings regressions already contain many of the project's relevant variables.

7.5. CLOSING REMARKS

This chapter offers preliminary evidence that U.S. experience has a significant and positive effect on monthly earnings in Mexico. If migration experience and Mexican earnings are truly endogenous, then the economic rewards in the Mexican labor market to small amounts of such experience may be rather limited. However, as the individual accumulates additional migration experience, the rewards become increasingly appealing. Therefore, one must consider the possibility that the accumulation of human capital while in the United States is an additional factor that motivates Mexican participation in international migration.

Return migrants who become entrepreneurs earn less money than their non-migrant counterparts. Businessowners who are also return migrant may be first-time entrepreneurs and thus less likely to succeed. Moreover, return migrants obtain lower returns than non-migrants to schooling and to agricultural land. These differences may exist prior to migration. Thus, some Mexicans may migrate to the United States because their educational training is inadequately rewarded or because their farmland is relatively unproductive. One possible avenue for future research is to identify the factors for which these lower returns

Table 7.6: Results from Earnings Regressions Using Two-Stage Least Squares

Vector/Variable	Both Genders		Males Only	
	Model 7.1e	Model 7.2e	Model 7.3e	Model 7.4e
Intercept	5.8946***	5.2599***	5.9024***	5.5063***
Individual characteristics				
Age	0.0460***	0.0538***	0.0451***	0.0485***
Age squared	-0.0006***	-0.0006***	-0.0005***	-0.0058***
Female	-0.3989***	-0.3131***	n.a.	n.a.
Education (in years)	0.0315***	0.0348***	0.0294***	0.0260***
College educated	0.0959	0.1289	0.1273	0.1864**
Fitted U.S. experience (in years)	-0.0024	0.0243	-0.0003	-0.0057
Fitted U.S. experience squared	0.0027**	0.0035**	0.0021	0.0040*
Family responsibilities				
Married	0.2725***	0.3453***	0.2650***	0.2956***
Number of non-workers in household	0.0085	0.0070	0.0050	0.0017
Additional income sources				
Business ownership	0.0534	0.1168***	0.0742*	0.0861**
Agricultural land (in hectares)	0.0024**	0.0040***	0.0024**	0.0021**
Spouse works	-0.0538	-0.1321***	-0.0668	-0.1072**
Number of workers in household	0.0210	0.0211	0.0110	0.0126
Inverse Mills ratio	0.4273***	0.7998***	0.4679***	0.6418***

Table 7.6 (continued)

| Vector/Variable | Both Genders | | Males Only | |
	Model 7.1e	Model 7.2e	Model 7.3e	Model 7.4e
Occupational variables				
Irregularly employed	-0.1379	-0.1392	-0.3348***	-0.3260***
Technician	0.0048	-0.0074	0.0141	0.0307
Office worker or nonmanual worker	-0.1251	-0.1379	-0.1392	-0.1357
Salesperson	-0.2004**	-0.1983**	-0.1757**	-0.1730**
Industrial owner or supervisor	0.4072	0.4392*	0.4302*	0.4877**
Skilled manual laborer	-0.1663**	-0.1404*	-0.1548**	-0.1317*
Unskilled manual worker	-0.2780***	-0.2859***	-0.2558***	-0.2749***
Agricultural worker	-0.3470***	-0.3352***	-0.3574***	-0.3334***
Service worker or unknown occupation	-0.1348*	-0.1041	-0.1195	-0.0854
N	2,767	2,767	2,552	2,552
R-squared	0.2146	0.1930	0.2002	0.1597

Results of two-tailed *t*-test of parameter estimate's significance:

***Passes at 99-percent level; **passes at 95-percent level; and *passes at 90-percent level

Models 7.1e and 7.3e also include a vector of community dummy variables. Results for these variables are not reported.

exist. Any future work should account for the probable endogeneity of U.S. experience and Mexican earnings.

Another direction for future research is to specify the earnings regression in a way that yields greater insight into the routes by which migration experience influences Mexican earnings. One improvement would be to include a variable that indicates whether the return migrant's Mexican occupation differs from his or her U.S. occupation. A second improvement would be to include dummy variables that distinguish among the various types of businesses for return-migrant and non-migrant entrepreneurs.

NOTES

1. In a simplified version of Model 7.1b that uses only the observations for San Ramon, the parameter estimates for age and its square are statistically indistinguishable from zero.

2. The regressions for males only omit the variable denoting gender. A less obvious difference concerns the inverse Mills ratio: Models 7.3b and 7.3c utilize the ratio produced by Model 7.3a, and Models 7.4b and 7.4c use the ratio from Model 7.4a.

3. The tobit models 7.1d, 7.2d, 7.3d, and 7.4d respectively correspond to the earnings regressions 7.1e, 7.2e, 7.3e, and 7.4e. Models 7.1d and 7.1e employ the inverse Mills ratio generated by Model 7.1a, Models 7.2d and 7.2e use the ratio from Model 7.2a, and so on.

CHAPTER 8
Conclusion

8.1. THE CONTEXT OF MEXICO-U.S. MIGRATION

One of the major developments in U.S.-Mexican economic relations during the twentieth century has been the growth and intensification of labor migration from Mexico to the United States. Since the Second World War, Mexico-U.S. migration has taken place under both legal and extralegal auspices. Under the Bracero Program, the U.S. government intentionally fostered the migration of Mexican laborers to the United States. During the three-and-a-half decades since the end of this program, the United States has adopted various and often conflicting policies regarding Mexico-U.S. migration, particularly with respect to undocumented migration. At different times, the U.S. government has tacitly allowed illegal immigration from Mexico, granted legal residency to roughly two million undocumented entrants under IRCA, and more recently, stepped up its enforcement of immigration restrictions.

Migration networks have played an important role in the expansion of Mexico-U.S. migration. Early migrants accumulated experience and know-how related to the migration process and passed this knowledge on to subsequent migrants. Once in the United States, these migrants provided a base of support for other migrants. Over time, the development of such networks and the expansion of migration have become reinforcing processes, with migration leading to the extension and intensification of networks and networks in turn causing greater migration. One result of this process is that Mexican migration to the United States has become commonplace. According to the retrospective life histories of the Mexican Migration Project, the proportion of

Mexican families in which the head of household's parents, siblings, or grandparents have previous U.S. migration experience has climbed steadily during the course of the twentieth century, from approximately 15 percent in the 1920s to roughly 55 percent in the 1990s.

This book provides fresh empirical evidence about the relationship between networks and migration. Beneath the descriptive statistics that link these two phenomena, the book uncovers a complex set of relationships between the migration experience of certain relatives and the head of household's migration decision. Although the U.S. experience of parents and grandparents increases the likelihood of some aspects of migration, having a sibling with U.S. experience is shown to facilitate all aspects of migration studied in this book. A migrant sibling increases the probability of both first and repeat migration. Similarly, Mexican spells of residence are shorter when the head of household has at least one migrant sibling. Having a migrant sibling also shortens the head of household's U.S. spells of residence. This result suggests that migrant siblings reduce the expected cost of re-entering the United States, especially if the head of household believes that these siblings will still be in the United States when he or she returns.

For individuals who have not yet migrated, having a father or grandparent with U.S. experience decreases the probability of migration. To the best of my knowledge, this book is the only work that provides convincing econometric evidence of such a relationship with respect to Mexican migration to the United States. The empirical results do not offer a precise explanation of this phenomenon. However, it is well known that some former migrants discourage their children from following in their footsteps. Also, the children of some migrants may have drawn negative conclusions about migration on their own. Another possibility is that the migration of previous generations of Mexicans was relatively temporary. This characterization seems particularly applicable to fathers and grandfathers who participated in the Bracero Program. If so, then the relationship described above may fade with time.

To some extent, the impact of family migration experience varies with the gender of the relative with U.S. experience. For instance, a migrant mother and a migrant father have opposite effects on both first and repeat migration. Also, a migrant brother increases the likelihood of repeat migration, while a migrant sister has no significant effect.

Overall, there seems to be a pattern in which the migratory "coattails" of female migrants are shorter than those of males. These differences may be related to how migrants constitute households in the United States. A married woman may be willing to accept additional migrants into her home. An unmarried female migrant may not. An alternative configuration of the network variables might yield different results. With respect to the migration experience of the head of household's parents, one could use a trio of dummy variables. The first would indicate that only the individual's father had U.S. experience; the second would indicate that only the mother had U.S. experience; and the third would indicate that both parents were current or former migrants. In any case, the possible connection between a migrant's gender and the subsequent migration of family and friends warrants further attention.

Finally, migration networks are not the most important factor influencing Mexican migration to the United States. According to the standardized estimates from the participation models, age and total U.S. experience have a greater impact on the head of household's migration decision than networks. The effect of legal residency in the United States is also larger in magnitude than that of migration networks.

8.2. LESSONS FOR U.S. POLICYMAKERS

This book offers several important lessons for the makers of U.S. immigration policy. First, one revelation that perhaps is obvious is that some factors driving migration are not under the control of U.S. policymakers. For instance, in the participation models, one of the most important factors is the age of the prospective migrant. Given the continued although slowing growth of the Mexican population, the increasing number of young Mexicans who are entering the workforce translates into a growing pool of potential migrants. Table 8.1 illustrates that the growth rate of the Mexican population is gradually decreasing, from an estimated 2.22 percent per annum during the 1985-90 period to a projected 1.33 percent during the 2005-10 period. This change should eventually lessen Mexico-U.S. migration. For some time to come, however, most Mexicans will have not yet entered their prime migratory years. Even in 2025, the median age in Mexico is predicted to be 32 years.

Table 8.1: Estimates and Projections of Mexico's Population, Median Age, and Population Growth (1950-2025)

Year	Total Population (Thousands)	Median Age (Years)	Period	Population Growth Rate (Percent)
Estimates				
1950	27,297	18.3		
1955	31,330	17.9	1950-55	2.76
1960	36,530	17.2	1955-60	3.07
1965	42,864	16.8	1960-65	3.20
1970	50,328	16.6	1965-70	3.21
1975	58,876	16.6	1970-75	3.14
1980	67,046	17.5	1975-80	2.60
1985	75,594	18.6	1980-85	2.40
1990	84,486	20.0	1985-90	2.22
Projections				
1995	93,670	21.7	1990-95	2.06
2000	102,555	23.2	1995-2000	1.81
2005	110,810	24.8	2000-05	1.55
2010	118,455	26.5	2005-10	1.33
2015	125,484	28.3	2010-15	1.15
2020	131,885	30.1	2015-20	0.99
2025	137,483	32.0	2020-25	0.83

Projections are the medium-variant projections.
Source: United Nations (1993).

Second, the participation models cast doubt on the notion that marginal changes in national economic conditions substantially alter the probability of migration. This finding may be disconcerting to U.S. policymakers who hope to influence undocumented Mexican migration through free-trade agreements, short-term refinancing of Mexico's public debt, and the like. Many economists, such as Martin (1993), believe that the North American Free Trade Agreement (NAFTA) will ultimately lead to a decrease in Mexico-U.S. migration, after a brief upturn in such migration. Such predictions usually are based on the theory that NAFTA will bring accelerated economic growth to Mexico, which will eventually outweigh any deleterious effects of the agreement on small-scale agricultural producers.

The first four years following NAFTA's enactment have provided an untidy atmosphere in which to assess the agreement's influence on migration. An armed rebellion in the southern state of Chiapas (partially in response to NAFTA), several unsolved political assassinations, an awkward devaluation of the Mexican peso beginning in December 1994, and a sharp recession in Mexico in 1995 have complicated the evaluation of the agreement. Weintraub (1996) argues that the expanded trade relations between the United States and Mexico resulting from NAFTA insulated the Mexican economy from the travails of its recent recession. If this is true, then the trade agreement may also have partially offset any increase in migration caused by the recession.

One should remember that the econometric models in this work allow predictions to be made about the effects of the explanatory variables on the average individual described by the data. Macroeconomic conditions in Mexico and the United States may exert a more profound influence on the prospective migrant who is at the margin of deciding whether to migrate to the United States. For instance, drought conditions may force such individuals into the migrant stream for the first time, including persons whose families have little U.S. experience.

Third, since migration is in part a cumulative process, one way to reduce future migration from Mexico is to discourage current migration. This hinders the accumulation of additional U.S. experience and the further growth of migration networks, two factors that significantly affect the probability of migrating in the participation models of Chapter 5. Contemplated reforms such as further immigration amnesties and new guestworker initiatives are thus likely to result in greater migration, not less. Persons who enter the United States legally will be more likely to stay, and some legal entrants may provide support for family members and friends who wish to enter the United States illegally.

Table 8.2: Legal Immigration to United States of Persons Born in Mexico (Fiscal Years 1981-96)

Fiscal Year	Total	Total Minus IRCA Legalizations	Subject To Numerical Limitations	Immigrants Exempt From Numerical Limitations							
				Total Exempt	All Immediate Relatives	Immediate Relatives			IRCA Legalizations	Other
						Parents of adult U.S. citizens	Spouses of U.S. citizens	Children of U.S. citizens		
1996	163,572	159,967	102,661	116,396	55,485	9,950	34,811	10,724	3,605	1,821
1995	89,932	86,960	63,585	48,363	22,016	4,348	13,824	3,844	2,972	1,359
1994	111,398	106,995	42,392	99,152	30,146	4,941	19,828	5,377	4,403	34,457(1)
1993	126,561	109,027	36,754	121,332	31,525	4,995	20,401	6,129	17,534	40,748(2)
1992	213,802	91,332	36,587	201,655	24,440	3,470	15,350	5,620	122,470	30,305(3)
1991	946,167	52,866	19,683	926,484	30,455	4,570	17,794	8,091	893,301	2,728
1990	679,068	56,549	20,134	658,934	31,876	4,242	19,185	8,449	622,519	4,539
1989	405,172	66,445	20,922	384,250	36,126	3,974	24,380	7,772	338,727	9,397
1988	95,039	95,039	20,341	74,698	42,689	3,857	30,755	8,077	n.a.	32,009(4)
1987	72,351	72,351	21,558	50,793	44,618	4,123	32,328	8,167	n.a.	6,175
1986	66,533	66,533	20,369	46,164	44,201	3,355	32,757	8,089	n.a.	1,963
1985	61,290	61,290	20,748	40,542	38,064	2,476	29,032	6,556	n.a.	2,478
1984	57,557	57,557	19,576	37,981	35,284	2,033	27,077	6,174	n.a.	2,697
1983	59,079	59,079	21,000	38,079	35,394	2,156	26,514	6,724	n.a.	2,685
1982	56,106	56,106	21,504	34,602	32,282	1,789	23,466	7,027	n.a.	2,320
1981	101,268	101,268	72,433	28,835	26,517	1,581	18,390	6,546	n.a.	2,318

(1) Includes 33,136 legalization dependents; (2) includes 39,425 legalization dependents; (3) includes 28,449 legalization dependents;
(4) includes 30,319 immigrants admitted under the 1972 Registry provision

Source: U.S. Immigration and Naturalization Service, *Statistical Yearbook of the Immigration and Naturalization Service*, various issues.

In addition, U.S. immigration law is intentionally structured to facilitate the reunification of legal immigrants with their families, a quality that further amplifies the power of migration networks. IRCA provides a good illustration of this relationship. As Table 8.2 indicates, IRCA legalizations account for the lion's share of persons born in Mexico who immigrated legally to the United States between Fiscal Year (FY) 1981 and FY 1992. From FY 1989 to FY 1996, 2,005,531 persons born in Mexico became permanent residents of the United States under IRCA legalizations. This constitutes 60.68 percent of all legal immigration by persons born in Mexico during the entire FY 1981-96 period.

Had the United States allowed the legal framework governing immigration prior to the Immigration Act of 1990 to remain in place, persons legalized under IRCA would have had to seek the admittance of relatives using the same channels available to other legal immigrants. Permanent residents are entitled to apply for the entrance of various family members under the numerically limited categories of admission. Also, immigrants who obtain U.S. citizenship may apply for the admission of their parents, children, and spouses, a type of admission that currently is exempt from numerical limitations. However, the Immigration Act of 1990 created a third route specifically for immigrants who legalized their residency status through IRCA. The law entitles them to apply for the admission of certain family members under the category of "legalization dependents." From FY 1992 to FY 1994, 101,010 such dependents were admitted from Mexico. Thus, the total number of Mexicans who will indirectly obtain legal residency in the United States as a result of IRCA is potentially quite large, and many of these individuals will enter the United States sooner than they would have otherwise if it were not for the Immigration Act of 1990.

Fourth, the denial of legal entry to the United States definitely has a deterrent effect on undocumented migration. Thus, to some extent, the current U.S. policies of restricting legal entry and trying to apprehend and deport illegal entrants do achieve the intended result. According to the duration models of Chapter 6, persons without legal residency in the United States are more likely to remain in Mexico for longer periods of time. However, undocumented migrants have longer spells of residence in the United States. This unintended consequence of U.S. immigration policies is also identified by Kossoudji (1992).

Fifth, despite the many obstacles that the U.S. government has placed in the way of undocumented migration, many Mexicans still view working in the United States for some length of time as superior to remaining in Mexico. This book has identified another benefit of migrating to the United States: return migrants earn higher incomes in Mexico than non-migrants with similar attributes. Unfortunately, the earnings regressions of Chapter 7 do not identify the exact route by which this occurs. Two possibilities are that migrants accumulate new abilities and skills while on the job in the United States, perhaps in different occupations from what they would have done in Mexico, and that migrants receive formal education and training in the United States.

Sixth, Mexicans who persist in migrating to the United States in the face of tightening U.S. restrictions often incur additional costs, such as the hiring of a *coyote*, in order to enter the United States. While migration networks presumably reduce some of these costs, the end result may be that prospective migrants who have less to gain through migration will not participate. Thus, U.S. immigration restrictions may have the unintended consequence of altering the qualities of the typical undocumented Mexican migrant.

Finally, for the vast majority of the migrants studied in this book, the principal reason for their coming to the United States was to work. Care should be taken in extending this conclusion to the entire population of migrants, especially since this book focuses on the head of the household and not all its members. Some migrants come to the United States for other reasons, such as reuniting with family members, experiencing an adventure, and even finding a mate. Nevertheless, most participants in Mexico-U.S. migration, especially those who enter the United States illegally, come with the expressed intention of working.

The primacy of this economic objective appears to elude some participants in the current debate surrounding U.S. immigration policy. Many of the most strident voices in this debate ascribe other motives to the migrants, such as securing welfare benefits and the utilization of other government services in the United States. These characterizations are far from the mark and most likely will lead to poorly crafted policy.

Survey Instrument of the Mexican Migration Project

This appendix contains a reproduction of the survey instrument currently utilized by the Mexican Migration Project. Except for some minor revisions, it is essentially identical to the one that I used during my fieldwork in San Ramon, Colima, and in the Los Angeles, California, and Las Vegas, Nevada, areas.

PROCESOS MIGRATORIOS ENTRE
MÉXICO Y ESTADOS UNIDOS.

LUGAR:_____

DIRECCIÓN:_____

ETNOENCUESTA No._____

FECHA:_____

ENCUESTADOR:_____

_____
_____
_____
_____
_____
_____

CUADRO A   INFORMACIÓN SOBRE LOS MIEMBROS DE LA FAMILIA Y TODAS LAS PERSONAS QUE HABITAN EN LA CASA. (Comenzar por (1) el jefe de familia, (2) la esposa, (3) todos los hijos vivos del mayor al menor y (4) otras personas que habitan en la misma casa.

Nombre:	Sexo:	Rela-ción al jefe:	Año en que nació:	Lugar donde nació: (Municipio y estado).	Edo. ci-vil:	Es-cuela años:	Ocupación principal:	Especificación laboral:
1								
2								
3								
4								
5								
6								
7								
8								
9								
10								
11								
12								
13								
14								
15								
16								
17								
18								
19								
20								

1. Nombre del informante: _____
2. Hijos que viven en otra casa aparte: _____
Números en cuadro A: _____

Salario o ingreso del jefe:
En pesos: _____
En dólares: _____
Por: _____

ESTADO CIVIL:
1. Soltero(a).   5. Divorciado(a).
2. Casado(a).   6. Separado(a).
3. Unión libre.   9. Desconocido.
4. Viudo(a).

GUÍA PARA ESCOLARIDAD:
(Escribir arriba años terminados):
Primaria terminada = 6 años.
Secundaria terminada = 9 años.
Preparatoria terminada = 12 años.
Universidad terminada = 17 años.

CUADRO B INFORMACIÓN SOBRE CADA PERSONA DEL CUADRO A CON EXPERIENCIA MIGRATORIA A ESTADOS UNIDOS.

Primera visita a Estados Unidos:

Nombre:	No. en A:	Año en que se fue:	Duración: año y meses:	Documentación:	Principal lugar de destino: (Ciudad y estado).	Ocupación principal:	Salario por hora: dóls.

Visita más reciente (o actual) a Estados Unidos:

Año en que se fue:	Duración: año y meses:	Documentación:	Principal lugar de destino: (Ciudad y estado).	Ocupación principal:	Salario por hora: dóls.	No. total de viajes:

DOCUMENTACIÓN:
1 = Documentado.
2 = Indocumentado.
3 = Contratado/Bracero.
4 = Turista.
5 = Ciudadano.
6 = Amnistía.
7 = Programa de Trabajadores Agrícolas (SAW).
8 = Carta Silva.
9 = Desconocido.

EN BASE A:
1 = Esposo/a.
2 = Hijo/a.
3 = Padre/madre.
4 = Hermano/a.
5 = Amnistía.
6 = Programa de Trabajadores Agrícolas (SAW).
7 = Por medio del trabajo (no SAW).
8 = Otro: _____
9 = Desconocido.

PARA LAS PERSONAS DE ARRIBA QUE TIENEN RESIDENCIA LEGAL EN E.U.

No. en A:	Año de aplicación:	Año en que recibió sus documentos:	En base a:

CUADRO C   INFORMACIÓN SOBRE CADA PERSONA DEL CUADRO A CON EXPERIENCIA MIGRATORIA DENTRO DE MÉXICO. (Incluir todos los empleos fuera del municipio donde se localiza el lugar de la muestra a partir del establecimiento de la persona en ese lugar).

			Primer empleo fuera del municipio o primera salida a otro lugar dentro México para trabajar:					Última (o actual) salida fuera del municipio a otro lugar dentro México para trabajar:			
Nombre:	No. en A:	Año en que se fue:	Duración: año y meses:	Principal lugar de destino: (Municipio y estado).	Ocupación principal:	Sala-rio por día: (Pesos).	Año en que se fue:	Duración: año y meses:	Principal lugar de destino: (Municipio y estado).	Ocupación principal:	Sala-rio por día: (Pesos).	No. total de via-jes:

CUADRO D HISTORIA MATRIMONIAL DEL JEFE DE LA FAMILIA E INFORMACIÓN SOBRE LOS HIJOS QUE YA NO VIVEN.

Unión:	Año en que co-menzó:	Año que finalizó (muerte o separación).	Tipo de unión:	1 Año de naci-miento:	1 Año de falleci-miento:	2 Año de naci-miento:	2 Año de falleci-miento:	3 Año de naci-miento:	3 Año de falleci-miento:	4 Año de naci-miento:	4 Año de falleci-miento:
1											
2											
3											

TIPO DE UNIÓN:
1 = Religioso.   3 = Unión libre.
2 = Civil.   4 = Religioso y civil.

CUADRO E HISTORIA DE PROPIEDADES AGRÍCOLAS A LOS LARGO DE LA VIDA DEL JEFE.

Parcela No.	Extensión en hectáreas:	Clase de tierra:	Tenencia:	Año de adquisición:	Año de venta:	¿Financiado con migradólares?
1						
2						
3						
4						
5						

CLASE DE TIERRA: 1 = Riego.   4 = Agostadero.   TENENCIA: 1 = Ejidal.
                     2 = Humedad.   5 = Huerta.   2 = Privada.
                     3 = Temporal.   6 = Otro:_____   3 = Comunal.

CUADRO F   INFORMACIÓN SOBRE LA VIVIENDA QUE HABITAN E HISTORIA DE OTRAS PROPIEDADES DE LA FAMILIA.

Tipo de propiedad:	Materiales de construcción:	Tipo de suelo:	Número de cuartos:	Tenencia:	Año de adquisición:	Año de venta:	¿Financiado con migradólares?	¿Localizado en E.U.?	* ¿Cómo la compró?
1 Casa que habitan:									

TIPO DE PROPIEDAD:
1 = Casa que habita.
2 = Casa propia.
3 = Lote propio.
4 = Local para negocio.
5 = Edificio de departamentos.

MATERIALES DE CONSTRUCCIÓN:
1 = Adobe y teja.
2 = Ladrillo y teja o lamina.
3 = Ladrillo y techo de cemento.
4 = Madera.

TIPO DE SUELO:
1 = Tierra.
2 = Cemento.
3 = Mosaico.
4 = Madera.

TENENCIA:
1 = Prestada.
2 = Rentada.
3 = Propia.
4 = Otro.

¿CÓMO LA COMPRÓ?
1 = Ahorros.
2 = Hipoteca/prestamo del banco.
3 = Prestamo de familiares.
4 = Prestamo de amigo.
5 = Otro: _____

* Todos los que apliquen.

CUADRO G1 SERVICIOS DE LA CASA:	
Agua corriente:	
Electricidad:	
Drenaje:	
Estufa:	
Refrigerador:	
Lavadora:	
Máquina de coser:	
Radio:	
Televisor:	
Estereo:	
Teléfono:	

CUADRO G2 VEHÍCULOS:

Tipo de vehículo:	Año de adquisición:	¿Financiado con migra-dólares?	¿Comprado en E.U.?	* ¿Como lo compró?

TIPO DE VEHÍCULO:
1 = Auto.
2 = Camioneta.
3 = Camión.
4 = Tractor.
5 = Otro: _____

¿CÓMO LO COMPRÓ?
1 = Ahorros.
2 = Prestamo banco/compañia de autos.
3 = Prestamo de familiares.
4 = Prestamo de amigo.
5 = Otro: _____
* Todos los que apliquen.

CUADRO H INFORMACIÓN SOBRE LA FORMACIÓN E HISTORIA DE PROPIEDADES, NEGOCIOS, EMPRESAS O TRABAJOS POR CUENTA PROPIA DEL JEFE O LA ESPOSA.

Número de negocio:	Descripción, tipo de negocio o empresa:	Año de formación:	Año de venta:	¿Usó migra-dólares para iniciarlo?	Número de miembros de la familia que trabajan o trabajaban:	Número de empleados aparte de los miembros de la familia:	¿Está localizado en E.U.?	* ¿Cómo lo inició?
1								
2								
3								
4								
5								
6								

TIPO DE NEGOCIO:
1 = Comercio ambulante de alimentos.
2 = Comercio ambulante de bienes.
3 = Tienda de abarrotes.
4 = Compra y venta de ganado.
5 = Compra y venta de productos agrícolas.
6 = Compra y venta de productos fabricados.
7 = Molino de masa/tortillería.
8 = Carnicería.
9 = Cenaduría/restaurante.
10 = Taller.
11 = Taller mecánico.
12 = Taller de maquila.
13 = Otro.
99 = Desconocido.

¿CÓMO LO INICIÓ?
1 = Ahorros.
2 = Hipoteca/préstamo del banco.
3 = Préstamo de familiares.
4 = Préstamo de amigo.
5 = Otro:_____

* Todos los que apliquen.

CUADRO I HISTORIA LABORAL DEL **JEFE O JEFA DE FAMILIA** DESDE QUE COMENZÓ A TRABAJAR.

Año:	Edad:	Lugar: (Municipio y estado).	Ocupación principal:	Duración: año y meses.	Documentos: (Para empleos en E.U.).

DOCUMENTOS:
- 1. Documentado.
- 2. Indocumentado.
- 3. Contratado/Bracero.
- 4. Turista.
- 5. Ciudadano.
- 6. Amnistía.
- 7. Programa Trabajadores Agrícolas (SAW).
- 9. Desconocido.

CUADRO IB HISTORIA LABORAL DE LA **ESPOSA DEL JEFE DE FAMILIA** DESDE QUE COMENZÓ A TRABAJAR.

Año:	Edad:	Lugar: (Municipio y estado).	Ocupación principal:	Duración: año y meses.	Documentos: (Para empleos en E.U.).

DOCUMENTOS:

1. Documentado.
2. Indocumentado.
3. Contratado/Bracero.
4. Turista.
5. Ciudadano.
6. Amnistía.
7. Programa Trabajadores Agrícolas (SAW).
9. Desconocido.

CUADRO J EXPERIENCIA MIGRATORIA A ESTADOS UNIDOS DE LA FAMILIA DE ORIGEN DEL **JEFE.**

Relación al jefe:	Sexo:	Año del 1er. viaje:	Año del último viaje:	¿Está vivo?	Lugar donde vive actualmente:
Madre:					
Padre:					
Abuelo/a 1					
Abuelo/a 2					
Hermano/a 1					
Hermano/a 2					
Hermano/a 3					
Hermano/a 4					
Hermano/a 5					
Hermano/a 6					
Hermano/a 7					
Hermano/a 8					
Hermano/a 9					
Hermano/a 10					
Hermano/a 11					
Hermano/a 12					

DIRECCIONES EN ESTADOS UNIDOS:

Nombre:	
Relación:	
Domicilio:	
Ciudad:	
Teléfono:	

Nombre:	
Relación:	
Domicilio:	
Ciudad:	
Teléfono:	

Nombre:	
Relación:	
Domicilio:	
Ciudad:	
Teléono:	

Nombre:	
Relación:	
Domicilio:	
Ciudad:	
Teléfono:	

CUADRO K   MIGRACIÓN A ESTADOS UNIDOS DE PARIENTES, AMIGOS Y PAISANOS DEL JEFE.

Parientes:	Cantidad con experiencia en Estados Unidos:			Cantidad que viven actualmente en Estados Unidos:		
	Hombres:	Mujeres:	Total:	Hombres:	Mujeres:	Total:
Tíos:						
Primos:						
Sobrinos:						
Cuñados: (Familia de origen).						
Cuñados: (Familia política).						
Yernos:						
Nueras:						
Suegros:						
Amigos:						

**CUADROS ESPECIALES PARA JEFES
CON EXPERIENCIA MIGRATORIA A ESTADOS UNIDOS.**

CUADRO L INFORMACIÓN SOBRE LOS CRUCES DE LA FRONTERA A LO LARGO DE LA VIDA DEL JEFE.

Viaje No.	Año:	Documen- tación:	Modo de pasar:	Lugar por donde cruzó: (Ciudad y estado).	¿Cuánto pagó al coyote en dólares?	¿Cuánto dinero necesitó en total para el viaje?	No.de depor- taciones:
1							
2							
3							
4							
5							
6							
7							
8							
9							
10							
11							
12							
13							
14							
15							
16							
17							
18							
19							
20							
21							
22							
23							
24							
25							

DOCUMENTACIÓN:
1 = Documentado.
2 = Indocumentado.
3 = Contratado/Bracero.
4 = Turista.

5 = Ciudadano.

6 = Amnistía.
7 = Programa de Trabajadores Agrícolas (SAW).
8 = Otro:_____
9 = Desconocido.

MODO DE PASAR:
1 = Solo.   6 = Con Coyote y amigos.
2 = Con coyote.   7 = Bracero.
3 = Con familiares.   8 = Legal.
          4 = Con amigos.   9 = Con visa de
                                                          turista
5 = Con coyote   99 = Desconocido.
     y familiares.

CUADRO M INFORMACIÓN DEL **JEFE** SOBRE SU VIAJE MÁS RECIENTE A ESTADOS UNIDOS.

¿En su viaje más reciente a Estados Unidos...		Respuesta:
Estaba su ESPOSA en la casa con usted?		
Cuántos HIJOS e HIJAS estaban en la casa con usted?		
Estaban otros PARIENTES en la misma casa con usted?		
Estaban otros PAISANOS en la misma casa con usted?		
Cuándo usted NECESITÓ DINERO a quien acudió?		
Tenía usted CUENTA BANCARIA en E.U.?	Desde qué año:	
Tenía usted TARJETA DE CREDITO?	Desde qué año:	
Hizo usted DECLARACIONES DE IMPUESTOS?	Desde qué año:	
Perteneció usted a alguna asociación RECREATIVA?	De qué tipo:	
Perteneció usted a alguna asociación SOCIAL?	De qué tipo:	
Tuvo usted relación amistosa con CHICANOS?		
Qué tipo de relación tuvo con CHICANOS?		
Tuvo usted relación amistosa con NEGROS?		
Qué tipo de relación tuvo con NEGROS?		
Tuvo usted relación amistosa con GRINGOS?		
Qué tipo de relación tuvo con GRINGOS?		
Tuvo usted relación amistosa con LATINOS?		
Qué tipo de relación tuvo con LATINOS?		
Quién le dio ALOJAMIENTO cuando llegó?		
Habla y entiende usted el INGLÉS?		
Ha tomado usted CLASES DE INGLÉS?	Cuántos años:	
Cuánto usaba el INGLÉS EN SU CASA?		
Cuánto usaba el INGLÉS EN EL TRABAJO?		
Cuánto usaba el INGLÉS CON SUS AMIGOS?		
Cuánto usaba el INGLÉS EN SU BARRIO (para compras, en la calle, etc.)?		

¿HABLA INGLÉS?
0 = No habla ni entiende.
1 = No habla pero entiende un poco.
2 = No habla pero entiende bien.
3 = Habla y entiende un poco.
4 = Habla y entiende bien.
9 = Desconocido.

USO DEL INGLÉS:
1 = Nada.
2 = Un poco.
3 = Mucho.
4 = Siempre.
9 = Desconocido.

TIPO DE RELACIONES:
1 = Sólo en el trabajo.
2 = Se visitan en la casa o salen a la calle.
3 = Otro: _____
4 = En el trabajo y en la casa o calle.

¿A QUIÉN ACUDIÓ PARA DINERO/ HOSPEDAJE?
1 = Paisano.
2 = Amigo.
3 = Patrón.
4 = Pariente.
5 = Banco
6 = No necesitó.
7 = Otro:_____
9 = Desconocido.

CUADRO M1
INFORMACIÓN SOBRE APOYO MATERIAL RECIBIDO
POR LOS JEFES MIGRANTES.

¿Quién le ha....	* Todas las variables que apliquen.
prestado para alimentación o renta?	
prestado para comprar casa?	
prestado para comprar carro?	
conseguido trabajo?	
prestado carro?	
pagado gastos de coyote?	
prestado para cruzar la frontera?	
recogido de la frontera?	
traido familiares de la frontera?	

CUADRO M2
DATOS SOBRE APOYOS EN INFORMACIÓN RECIBIDOS
POR LOS JEFES MIGRANTES.

¿Quién le ha dado información sobre...	* Todas las variables que apliquen.
trabajos disponibles?	
cómo evitar a la migra?	
cómo obtener documentos para trabajar?	
cómo arreglar los papeles para residencia legal?	
cómo obtener beneficios (desempleo, estampillas de comida, etc.)?	
cómo pasar la frontera?	
cómo encontrar donde vivir?	

¿QUIÉN?	
1 = Padre/madre.	10 = Cuñados.
2 = Hermano/a.	11 = Otros:_____
3 = Hijo/a.	12 = Abogados.
4 = Esposo/a.	13 = Contratista.
5 = Padrino/madrina.	14 = Coyote.
6 = Tío/a.	15 = Sobrino/a.
7 = Primo/a.	
8 = Amigo/a.	
9 = Paisano/a.	
8888 = Él mismo, nadie o N/A.	

CUADRO M3 OPINIÓN DEL JEFE Y LA ESPOSA ACERCA DE LA MIGRACIÓN DE MÉXICO A ESTADOS UNIDOS.

	JEFE: (Sí, no o no sabe)	ESPOSA: (Sí, no o no sabe)
¿Le gusta a Ud. vivir en E.U. más que en México?		
¿Le gustaría a Ud. que sus hijos crecieran en E.U. más que en México?		
¿Le gustaría a Ud. obtener residencia legal en E.U.?		
¿Le gustaría a Ud. obtener ciudadania en E.U.?		
¿Cree Ud. que la migración es buena para E.U.?		
¿Cree Ud. que la migración es buena para México?		

CUADRO N INFORMACIÓN SOBRE EL EMPLEO MÁS RECIENTE EN ESTADOS UNIDOS DE LOS JEFES DE FAMILIA.

¿En su empleo más reciente en Estados Unidos...	Respuesta:
Cómo obtuvo su empleo?	
Cuánto le pagaban por hora?	
Cuántas horas trabajó por semana?	
Cuántas meses trabajó durante el año?	
Le pagaban en cheque o en efectivo?	
Le descontaban impuestos en Seguridad Social?	
Le descontaban impuestos Federales?	
Cuánto gastaba al mes en alojamiento?	Dólares:
Cuánto gastaba al mes en alimentación?	Dólares:
Cuánto mandaba al mes a su familia en México?	Dólares:
* En qué gastó su familia ese dinero?	
Cuánto ahorraba en promedio al mes?	Dólares:
Cuánto dinero trajó de regreso?	
* En qué gastó ese ahorro?	

¿CÓMO OBTUVO EL EMPLEO?
1. Buscandolo.
2. Recomendado por un pariente.
3. Recomendado por un amigo.
4. Recomendado por otro paisano.
5. Por el coyote.
6. Iba contratado.
7. Otro.
9. Desconocido.

¿EN QUÉ GASTÓ ESTE DINERO/AHORRO?
1. Construcción.   9. Vehículos.
2. Deuda.   10. Negocio.
3. Artículos.   11. Herramientas.
4. Casa/Lote.   12. Nada.
5. Terreno agrícola.   13. Otro_____
6. Ganado.
7. Diversión.   * Todas las que apliquen.
8. Sustento.

CUADRO O INFORMACIÓN SOBRE USO DE SERVICIOS PÚBLICOS DE LOS JEFES DE FAMILIA EN ESTADOS UNIDOS.

¿A lo largo de su experiencia de vida o trabajo en Estados Unidos...	Respuesta:
Ha tenido hijos en escuelas públicas?	
Ha recibido usted alguna vez compensación al desempleo?	
Ha recibido usted estampillas de comida?	
Ha recibido usted welfare del gobierno?	
Ha visitado usted o algún miembro de su familia un médico?	
Ha visitado usted o algún miembro de su familia un hospital?	
* Si usted visitó un hospital o médico: Quién pagó?	

¿QUIÉN PAGÓ POR MÉDICO/HOSPITAL?
1. Patrón.
2. Seguro.
3. El entrevistado.
4. Un pariente.
5. Nadie.
6. Otro:_____
9. Desconocido.
* Todos los que apliquen.

**CUADROS ESPECIALES PARA
ENTREVISTADOS QUE REALIZAN ACTIVIDADES AGRÍCOLAS.**

CUADRO P   INFORMACIÓN SOBRE USO DE TIERRA AGRÍCOLA PROPIA Y RENTADA PARA CADA UNIDAD DOMÉSTICA.

Clase de tierra:	Hectáreas de tierra propia:	Número de hectáreas rentadas como aparcero:	Hectáreas sembradas con:			Hectáreas dadas a otros para cultivar:
			Maíz:	Sorgo:	Otro:	
Riego:						
Humedad:						
Temporal:						
Agostadero:						
Huerta:						

CUADRO Q   INFORMACIÓN SOBRE TAREAS DE CULTIVO EN CADA UNIDAD DOMÉSTICA.

Tarea:	Número de miembros de la familia que ayudan:	Número de jornaleros que ayudan:	¿Utiliza maquinaria agrícola?
Desmonte:			
Barbecho:			
Siembra:			
Escarda:			
Cosecha:			

¿Utiliza fertilizantes?		¿Utiliza insecticidas?	
¿Utiliza semilla mejorada?		¿Utiliza migradólares para subsidiar la producción?	

CUADRO R   INFORMACIÓN SOBRE POSESIÓN DE ANIMALES POR CADA UNIDAD DOMÉSTICA.

Tipo de animal:	Número total:	Cantidad animales adquiridos con migradólares:
Vacas:		
Cerdos:		
Caballos:		
Burros:		
Bueyes:		
Gallinas:		

Supplement to the Basic Questionnaire

This appendix contains a reproduction of my supplement to the basic questionnaire of the Mexican Migration Project. The questions about credit access in "Supplement to Chart H" ("Suplemento a Cuadro H") are closely patterned after those in the survey instrument of Sprouse (1991). The last two pages of the supplement, "Cuestiones Adicionales Para el Jefe de la Familia," were used only during my fieldwork in the United States.

Suplemento a Cuadro A

1.   ¿Cuándo empezó su familia a vivir en Cuauhtémoc?

Mes	Año

2.   ¿Ha vivido su familia en otros municipios?

1 = Sí
2 = No
7 = No sé
9 = No quiero contestar

Si la familia ha vivido en otros municipios, ¡pregúntale!—

3.   ¿Donde vivieron Uds.?

Municipio	Estado	Año de Empezar de Vivir en Este Municipio	Año de Terminar de Vivir en Este Municipio

Suplementos a Cuadro B y Cuadro C (Migración en México y Migración a los Estados Unidos)

Si el Jefe de la familia ha visitado o ha vivido en los Estados Unidos, ¡pregúntale!—

1A.   ¿Cómo financió Ud. su visita más reciente a los Estados Unidos?   _____

Si el Jefe pidió un préstamo o recibió un regalo, ¡pregúntale!—

1B.   ¿De quién recibió Ud. el préstamo o regalo?   _____

1C.   ¿Cuánto fue el valor aproximado del préstamo o regalo?   _____

Si el Jefe pidió un préstamo, ¡pregúntale!—

1D.   ¿A qué plazo fue el préstamo concedido?   _____

1E.   ¿Qué tasa de interés tuvo el préstamo?   _____

Si el Jefe de la familia tiene experiencia como un migrante interno, ¡pregúntale!—

2A.   ¿Cómo financió Ud. su viaje más reciente a <lugar en México>?   _____

Si el Jefe pidió un préstamo o recibió un regalo, ¡pregúntale!—

2B.   ¿De quién recibió Ud. el préstamo o regalo?   _____

2C.   ¿Cuánto fue el valor aproximado del préstamo o regalo?   _____

Si el Jefe pidió un préstamo, ¡pregúntale!—

2D.   ¿A qué plazo fue el préstamo concedido?   _____

2E.   ¿Qué tasa de interés tuvo el préstamo?   _____

¿Cómo financió?   1 = Ahorros   4 = Otro   _____
                       2 = Préstamo   7 = No sé
                       3 = Regalo   9 = No quiero contestar

¿De quién?

01 = Banco	06 = Patrón en EE.UU.	12 = Tío(a)
02 = Cooperativa	07 = Amigo(a)	13 = Primo(a)
03 = Alguna dependencia	08 = Compadre	14 = Sobrino(a)
del gobierno	09 = Hermano(a)	15 = Otro
04 = Prestador informal	10 = Padre/Madre	77 = No sé
05 = Patrón en México	11 = Abuelo(a)	99 = No quiero
		contestar

Otro Suplemento a Cuadro B (Migración a los Estados Unidos)

Si el Jefe ha visitado o ha vivido en los Estados Unidos, ¡pregúntale!—

1A. ¿Recibió Ud. alguna educación en los Estados Unidos?

1 = Sí, clases de inglés
2 = Sí, clases de educación vocacional
3 = Sí, clases de ciudadanía
4 = Sí, clases de amnistía
5 = Sí, otro _____
6 = No
7 = No sé
9 = No quiero contestar

Si el Jefe contestó Sí, ¡pregúntale!—

1B. ¿Cuándo?   Año _____

1C. ¿Dónde?   Municipio _____   Estado _____

Suplemento a Cuadro D (Historia Matrimonial y de Fecundidad)

Unión	¿Cómo finalizó la unión?
1	_____
2	_____
3	_____

Como terminó: 1 = Muerte
2 = Separación
7 = No sé
9 = No quiero contestar

Suplemento a Cuadro H (Aceso a Crédito)

1. ¿Quién de su familia recibió dinero prestado durante el año 1994?

¿Quién recibió el préstamo? (Número en Cuadro A)	¿De quién recibió él/élla el préstamo?	¿Cuánto fue el valor aproximado del préstamo?	¿A qué plazo fue el préstamo concedido?	¿Qué tasa de interés tuvo el préstamo?

¿De quién?

01 = Banco	09 = Hermano(a)
02 = Cooperativa	10 = Padre/Madre
03 = Alguna dependencia	11 = Abuelo(a)
del gobierno	12 = Tío(a)
04 = Prestador informal	13 = Primo(a)
05 = Patrón en México	14 = Sobrino(a)
06 = Patrón en EE.UU.	15 = Otro (¡Específique!)
07 = Amigo(a)	77 = No sé
08 = Compadre	99 = No quiero contestar

2A.   ¿Necesita su familia más préstamos?

 1 = Sí

 2 = No

 7 = No sé

 9 = No quiero contestar

Si la persona contestó Sí, ¡pregúntale!—

2B.   ¿Qué tipos de préstamos? _____

3.   ¡Imágine que Ud. necesita $500 (1,650 N.P)! Quizás por una emergencia médica o para hacer un viaje de gran distancia. ¿De cuáles de las siguientes fuentes de crédito podría pedir Ud. un préstamo para obtener parte o todo de los $500?

A. Banco

B. Cooperativa

C. Alguna dependencia del gobierno

D. Prestador informal

E. Patrón en México

F. Patrón en EE.UU.

G. Amigos

H. Compadre

I. Parientes

Códigos: 1 = Sí

                2 = No

                7 = No sé

                9 = No quiero contestar

Columna Adicional Para Cuadro I (Historia Laboral)

¡Pregúnta al Jefe de la familia lo siguiente si ha trabajado en un lugar afuera de Cuauhtémoc!

1. ¿Conoció Ud. a alguien (por ejemplo, parientes o amigos) en ese municipio o cerca de ese municipio antes de empezar a trabajar allá?

Año	Municipio	Parientes (Sí o No)	Amigos (Sí o No)	Otros (Sí o No)

Códigos: 1 = Sí
2 = No
7 = No sé
9 = No quiero contestar

Otro Suplemento a Cuadro I (Historia Laboral)

Si el Jefe de la familia trabajó durante el año 1994, ¡pregúntale las proximas dos cuestiones!

1. ¿Cuántas horas trabaja Ud. pro semana (en su empleo actual o más reciente)?   _____

2A. ¿Hubo algun tiempo durante el año 1994 en que Ud. trabajó menos que <x> horas pro semana o más que <x> horas?
    (1) Sí
    (2) No
    (7) No sé
    (9) No quiero contestar

Si el Jefe contestó Sí, ¡pregúntale!—

2B. ¿Cuándo?   Mes(es)   _____

2C. ¿Por qué?   _____

2D. ¿Cuántos horas?   _____

¡Pregúnta la proxima cuestión al Jefe de la familia!

3A. ¿Hubo algun tiempo durante el año 1994 en que no tuvo Ud. empleo?
    (1) Sí
    (2) No
    (7) No sé
    (9) No quiero contestar

Si la persona contestó Sí, ¡pregúntale!—

3B. ¿Cuándo?   Mes   _____

3C. ¿Por qué?   _____

3D. ¿Trató Ud. actívamente encontrar trabajo durante ese tiempo?

    (1) Sí

    (2) No

    (7) No sé

    (9) No quiero contestar

Suplemento a Cuadro N (Empleo Más Reciente en los Estados Unidos)

¡Pregúnta las proximas cuestiones al Jefe con experiencia en los Estados Unidos!

Después de la pregunta ¿En qué gastó su familia este ahorro?, ¡pregúntale!—

1A. ¿Habría gastado su familia el mismo dinero en las cosas que Ud. mencionó (los bienes comprado con el dinero de las remesas y del ahorro) si no hubiera trabajado en los Estados Unidos?

1 = Sí
2 = No
7 = No sé
9 = No quiero contestar

Si el Jefe contestó Sí, ¡pregúntale!—

1B. ¿En cuáles bienes habría gastado su familia el mismo dinero si no hubiera trabajado en los Estados Unidos?

_____

_____

_____

1C. ¿Tuvo Ud. algún dinero remanente para ahorrar después de que hizo Ud. estos gastos?

1 = Sí
2 = No
7 = No sé
9 = No quiero contestar

Si el Jefe contestó Sí, ¡pregúntale!—

1D. ¿Cuánto?   _____

Suplemento Final

Si el Jefe nunca ha utilizado los servicios de un coyote para cruzar la frontera con los Estados Unidos, ¡pregúntale!—

1. ¿Sabe Ud. como obtener los servicios de un coyote para cruzar la frontera con los Estados Unidos?

   1 = Sí
   2 = No, no tengo idea
   3 = No, pero conozco a personas que saben
   4 = No, pero no sería difícil contactar a un coyote
   5 = No, otra explicación _____
   7 = No sé
   9 = No quiero contestar

Si el Jefe tiene experiencia en los Estados Unidos, ¡pregúntale!—

2A. ¿Sabe Ud. como obtener documentos falsos de inmigración para los Estados Unidos?

   1 = Sí
   2 = No
   7 = No sé
   9 = No quiero contestar

2B. ¿Tiene Ud. una carta de Seguridad Social de los Estados Unidos? ¿Es verdadera o falsa?

   1 = Sí, tengo una carta verdadera
   2 = Sí, tengo una carta falsa
   3 = No, no la tengo
   4 = No, pero tengo un número de Seguro Social
   5 = Otro _____
   7 = No sé
   9 = No quiero contestar

Si el Jefe tiene una carta falsa, ¡pregúntale!—

2C. ¿Cómo lo obtuvo? _____

2D.   ¿Dónde?

    1 = En los Estados Unidos

    2 = En México

    7 = No sé

    9 = No quiero contestar

2E. ¿Cuánto costó la carta?

    _____ Nuevos Pesos

    _____ Dólares

Cuestiones Adicionales Para el Jefe de la Familia Sobre Su Primer Empleo en los EE.UU.

1. Información General Sobre el Primer Empleo (¡Véase a Cuadros B e I!)

Ocupación	Lugar (Ciudad/Estado)	Año	Duración (Años y Meses)	Salario Por Hora	Documentación

2A. ¿Cómo obtuvo Ud. su primer empleo en los EE.UU.?
(1) Buscándolo
(2) Recomendado por un pariente
(3) Recomendado por un amigo
(4) Recomendado por otro paisano
(5) Por el coyote
(6) Iba contratado
(7) Otro
(9) Deconocido

2B. ¿Obtuvo Ud. su primer empleo en los EE.UU. antes de llegar aquí?
(1) Sí — ¿Cómo? _____
(2) No

2C. ¿Cuántas horas trabajó Ud. por semana? _____

2D. ¿Se le pagaba en cheque o en efectivo?   Cheque Efectivo

2E. ¿Se le descontaron impuestos de Seguridad Social? Sí   No

2F. ¿Se le descontaron otros impuestos federales?   Sí   No

3A. ¿Conoció Ud. a la persona que tuvo el empleo antes de Ud.?
(1) Sí — ¿Quién? _____
(2) No

3B. ¿Tuvo él/élla algún papel en encontrarle para el empleo?
(1) Sí — ¿Qué tipo? _____
(2) No
(3) No aplica

3C.   ¿Tuvo él/élla algún papel en su entrenamiento para el empleo?
       (1) Sí — ¿Qué tipo? _____
       (2) No
       (3) No aplica

3D.   ¿Le dio algún consejo informal para el empleo?
       (1) Sí — ¿Qué tipo? _____
       (2) No
       (3) No aplica

4A.   ¿Conoció Ud. a la persona que tuvo el empleo después de Ud.?
       (1) Sí — ¿Quién? _____
       (2) No
       (3) No aplica

4B.   ¿Participó Ud. en encontrarle para el empleo?
       (1) Sí — ¿Cómo? _____
       (2) No
       (3) No aplica

4C.   ¿Participó Ud. en el entrenamiento de esta persona?
       (1) Sí — ¿Cómo? _____
       (2) No
       (3) No aplica

4D.   ¿Le dio Ud. algún consejo informal sobre el empleo?
       (1) Sí — ¿Cómo? _____
       (2) No
       (3) No aplica

5.   ¿Cómo le trató el jefe en su primer empleo?
       (1) Muy bien
       (2) Bien
       (3) Mal
       (4) Muy mal
       (5) Otro
       Comentarios: _____

Supplemental Tables to Chapter 4

Appendix Table C.1: U.S. Immigration Status of Head of Household

Year/Decade	Total Heads of Household	Legal Resident of U.S.		U.S. Citizen	
		Yes	No	Yes	No
Survey Year	5,481	817 / 14.91%	4,664 / 85.09%	20 / 0.36%	5,461 / 99.64%
1991-94	4,162	533 / 12.81%	3,629 / 87.19%	22 / 0.53%	4,140 / 99.47%
1981-90	50,569	4,791 / 9.47%	45,778 / 90.53%	151 / 0.30%	50,418 / 99.70%
1971-80	47,935	2,812 / 5.87%	45,123 / 94.13%	99 / 0.21%	47,836 / 99.79%
1961-70	35,803	1,329 / 3.71%	34,474 / 96.29%	61 / 0.17%	35,742 / 99.83%
1951-60	23,810	304 / 1.28%	23,506 / 98.72%	30 / 0.13%	23,780 / 99.87%
1941-50	14,098	112 / 0.79%	13,986 / 99.21%	19 / 0.13%	14,079 / 99.87%
1931-40	6,586	70 / 1.06%	6,516 / 98.94%	2 / 0.03%	6,584 / 99.97%
1921-30	2,179	44 / 2.02%	2,135 / 97.98%	0 / 0.00%	2,179 / 100.00%
1911-20	401	6 / 1.50%	395 / 98.50%	0 / 0.00%	401 / 100.00%
1905-10	31	0 / 0.00%	31 / 100.00%	0 / 0.00%	31 / 100.00%

Source: LIFE26

Appendix Table C.2: Interview Location by Head of Household's U.S. Immigration Status

Interview Location	Legal Resident of U.S.		U.S. Citizen		Total for Location
	Yes	No	Yes	No	
Mexico					
Percent of Mexican Respondents Belonging to Immigration Category	501	4,550	4	5,047	5,051
	9.92%	90.08%	0.08%	99.92%	
Percent of Respondents in Immigration Category (or Total) Interviewed in Mexico	61.32%	97.56%	20.00%	92.42%	92.15%
U.S.					
Percent of U.S. Respondents Belonging to Immigration Category	316	114	16	414	430
	73.49%	26.51%	3.72%	96.28%	
Percent of Respondents in Immigration Category (or Total) Interviewed in U.S.	38.68%	2.44%	80.00%	7.58%	7.85%
Total for Immigration Category	817	4,664	20	5,461	5,481
Percent of Respondents in Immigration Category	14.91%	85.09%	0.36%	99.64%	

Source: LIFE26

Appendix Table C.3: Presence of Minor-Age Children in Household by Head of Household's Gender

Year/Decade	Total Heads of Household			All Heads of Household		Male Heads of Household		Female Heads of Household	
	Both Genders	Males	Females	With Minor-Age Children	Without Minor-Age Children	With Minor-Age Children	Without Minor-Age Children	With Minor-Age Children	Without Minor-Age Children
Survey Year	5,481	4,795 87.48%	686 12.52%	3,998 72.94%	1,483 27.06%	3,699 77.14%	1,096 22.86%	299 43.59%	387 56.41%
1991-94	4,162	3,614 86.83%	548 13.17%	2,932 70.45%	1,230 29.55%	2,677 74.07%	937 25.93%	255 46.53%	293 53.47%
1981-90	50,569	44,077 87.16%	6,492 12.84%	35,326 69.86%	15,243 30.14%	31,794 72.13%	12,283 27.87%	3,532 54.41%	2,960 45.59%
1971-80	47,935	41,254 86.06%	6,681 13.94%	30,004 62.59%	17,931 37.41%	25,693 62.28%	15,561 37.72%	4,311 64.53%	2,370 35.47%
1961-70	35,803	29,850 83.37%	5,953 16.63%	20,321 56.76%	15,482 43.24%	16,473 55.19%	13,377 44.81%	3,848 64.64%	2,105 35.36%
1951-60	23,810	19,048 80.00%	4,762 20.00%	11,539 48.46%	12,271 51.54%	8,622 45.26%	10,426 54.74%	2,917 61.26%	1,845 38.74%
1941-50	14,098	10,836 76.86%	3,262 23.14%	5,231 37.10%	8,867 62.90%	3,581 33.05%	7,255 66.95%	1,650 50.58%	1,612 49.42%
1931-40	6,586	4,814 73.09%	1,772 26.91%	1,624 24.66%	4,962 75.34%	931 19.34%	3,883 80.66%	693 39.11%	1,079 60.89%
1921-30	2,179	1,499 68.79%	680 31.21%	348 15.97%	1,831 84.03%	157 10.47%	1,342 89.53%	191 28.09%	489 71.91%
1911-20	401	286 71.32%	115 28.68%	24 5.99%	377 94.01%	11 3.85%	275 96.15%	13 11.30%	102 88.70%
1905-10	31	25 80.65%	6 19.35%	0 0.00%	31 100.00%	0 0.00%	25 100.00%	0 0.00%	6 100.00%

Source: LIFE26

Appendix Table C.4: Number of Single-Parent Households by Head of Household's Gender

Year/Decade	Total Heads of Household			All Heads of Household		Male Heads of Household		Female Heads of Household	
	Both Genders	Males	Females	Single-Parent Households	All Other Households	Single-Parent Households	All Other Households	Single-Parent Households	All Other Households
Survey Year	5,481	4,795 87.48%	686 12.52%	330 6.02%	5,151 93.98%	78 1.63%	4,717 98.37%	252 36.73%	434 63.27%
1991-94	4,162	3,614 86.83%	548 13.17%	278 6.68%	3,884 93.32%	67 1.85%	3,547 98.15%	211 38.50%	337 61.50%
1981-90	50,569	44,077 87.16%	6,492 12.84%	3,046 6.02%	47,523 93.98%	1,020 2.31%	43,057 97.69%	2,026 31.21%	4,466 68.79%
1971-80	47,935	41,254 86.06%	6,681 13.94%	2,191 4.57%	45,744 95.43%	872 2.11%	40,382 97.89%	1,319 19.74%	5,362 80.26%
1961-70	35,803	29,850 83.37%	5,953 16.63%	1,308 3.65%	34,495 96.35%	618 2.07%	29,232 97.93%	690 11.59%	5,263 88.41%
1951-60	23,810	19,048 80.00%	4,762 20.00%	776 3.26%	23,034 96.74%	357 1.93%	18,681 98.07%	409 8.59%	4,353 91.41%
1941-50	14,098	10,836 76.86%	3,262 23.14%	315 2.23%	13,783 97.77%	184 1.70%	10,652 98.30%	131 4.02%	3,131 95.98%
1931-40	6,586	4,814 73.09%	1,772 26.91%	83 1.26%	6,503 98.74%	58 1.20%	4,756 98.80%	25 1.41%	1,747 98.59%
1921-30	2,179	1,499 68.79%	680 31.21%	17 0.78%	2,162 99.22%	5 0.33%	1,494 99.67%	12 1.76%	668 98.24%
1911-20	401	286 71.32%	115 28.68%	0 0.00%	401 100.00%	0 0.00%	286 100.00%	0 0.00%	115 100.00%
1905-10	31	25 80.65%	6 19.35%	0 0.00%	31 100.00%	0 0.00%	25 100.00%	0 0.00%	6 100.00%

Source: LIFE26

Appendix Table C.5: Sample Statistics for LIFE26

Vector/Variable	Survey Year Only		All Observations	
	Mean	Standard Deviation	Mean	Standard Deviation
Individual characteristics				
Age (in years)	46.8577	16.0960	34.2542	15.1447
Age squared	2,454.68	1,654.48	1,402.71	1,252.84
Female	0.1252	0.3309	0.1631	0.3695
Education (in years)	4.6893	4.4105	2.1502	3.8775
U.S. migration experience (in months)	34.1887	74.1340	15.3596	46.2597
U.S. experience squared	6,663.71	24,934.45	2,375.86	13,408.20
U.S. interview	0.0785	0.2689	0.0549	0.2278
Family responsibilities				
Married	0.8393	0.3673	0.6452	0.4784
Single parent	0.0602	0.2379	0.0432	0.2033
Single mother	0.0460	0.2095	0.0260	0.1591
Has minor-age children	0.7294	0.4443	0.5785	0.4938
Number of minor-age children	2.3468	2.1905	2.1502	2.5435
Additional income sources				
Number of adult offspring	2.4496	3.2073	0.9369	2.1369
Business ownership	0.2779	0.4480	0.1329	0.3395
Agricultural land (in hectares)	3.5321	30.0228	2.8011	31.3961
U.S. immigration status				
Legal resident of U.S.	0.1491	0.3562	0.0539	0.2258
U.S. citizen	0.0037	0.0540	0.0021	0.0454

Appendix Table C.5 (continued)

Vector/Variable	Survey Year Only		All Observations	
	Mean	Standard Deviation	Mean	Standard Deviation
U.S. immigration policies				
Bracero Program in effect	n.a.	n.a.	0.2679	0.4429
Amnesty Program in effect	n.a.	n.a.	0.0567	0.2314
1968-76 period	n.a.	n.a.	0.2133	0.4096
1977-91 period	n.a.	n.a.	0.3963	0.4891
1992-95 period	n.a.	n.a.	0.0088	0.0933
Deportation ratio	n.a.	n.a.	0.8800	0.6771
Relative with U.S. migration experience				
Any immediate relative	0.5338	0.4989	0.3738	0.4838
Father	0.2237	0.4167	0.1835	0.3871
Mother	0.0533	0.2246	0.0287	0.1672
Sibling	0.4698	0.4491	0.2775	0.4477
Grandparent	0.0527	0.2235	0.0385	0.1923
Economic conditions				
Real GDP growth per capita in Mexico	n.a.	n.a.	2.4408	4.2847
Real GDP growth per capita in U.S.	n.a.	n.a.	1.8621	3.6392
Real GDP per capita in Mexico	n.a.	n.a.	2,246.39	1,019.90
Real GDP per capita in U.S.	n.a.	n.a.	15,954.59	4,274.68
N	5,481		185,574	

Appendix Table C.6: Head of Household's Most Recent Migration Experience by Individual's Gender

| Gender | Total | Most Recent U.S. Migration Experience | | |
		Within Three-Year Period Prior To Interview	More Than Three Years Prior to Interview	No U.S. Migration Experience
All Heads of	5,482	817	1,688	2,977
Household		14.90%	30.79%	54.30%
Males	4,792	780	1,614	2,398
		16.28%	33.68%	50.04%
Females	690	37	74	579
		5.36%	10.72%	83.91%

Source: HOUSFILE

Appendix Table C.7: Head of Household's Migration Decision by Individual's Gender

Year/Decade	All Heads of Household		Male Heads of Household		Female Heads of Household	
	Spent Part or All of Year in U.S.	Did Not Spend Year in U.S.	Spent Part or All of Year in U.S.	Did Not Spend Year in U.S.	Spent Part or All of Year in U.S.	Did Not Spend Year in U.S.
Survey Year	944	4,537	906	3,889	38	648
	17.22%	82.78%	18.89%	81.11%	5.54%	94.46%
1991-94	558	3,604	525	3,089	33	515
	13.41%	86.59%	14.53%	85.47%	6.02%	93.98%
1981-90	7,713	42,856	7,376	36,701	337	6,155
	15.25%	84.75%	16.73%	83.27%	5.19%	94.81%
1971-80	6,066	41,869	5,813	35,441	253	6,428
	12.65%	87.35%	14.09%	85.91%	3.79%	96.21%
1961-70	2,621	33,182	2,507	27,343	114	5,839
	7.32%	92.68%	8.40%	91.60%	1.92%	98.08%
1951-60	1,946	21,864	1,880	17,168	66	4,696
	8.17%	91.83%	9.87%	90.13%	1.39%	98.61%
1941-50	943	13,155	925	9,911	18	3,244
	6.69%	93.31%	8.54%	91.46%	0.55%	99.45%
1931-40	75	6,511	69	4,745	6	1,766
	1.14%	98.86%	1.43%	98.57%	0.34%	99.66%
1921-30	83	2,096	79	1,420	4	676
	3.81%	96.19%	5.27%	94.73%	0.59%	99.41%
1911-20	18	383	18	268	0	115
	4.49%	95.51%	6.29%	93.71%	0.00%	99.41%
1905-10	3	28	3	22	0	6
	9.68%	90.32%	12.00%	88.00%	0.00%	100.00%

Source: LIFE26

Appendix Table C.8: Head of Household's Migration Decision by U.S. Immigration Status

Year/Decade	All Heads of Household		Legal Residents of U.S.		Not Legal Residents of U.S.	
	Spent Part or All of Year in U.S.	Did Not Spend A Year in U.S.	Spent Part or All of Year in U.S.	Did Not Spend Year in U.S.	Spent Part or All of Year in U.S.	Did Not Spend Year in U.S.
Survey Year	944 17.22%	4,537 82.78%	612 74.91%	205 25.09%	332 7.12%	4,332 92.88%
1991-94	558 13.41%	3,604 86.59%	376 70.54%	157 29.46%	182 5.02%	3,447 94.98%
1981-90	7,713 15.25%	42,856 84.75%	3,470 72.43%	1,321 27.57%	4,243 9.27%	41,535 90.73%
1971-80	6,066 12.65%	41,869 87.35%	2,180 77.52%	632 22.48%	3,886 8.61%	41,237 91.39%
1961-70	2,621 7.32%	33,182 92.68%	1,132 85.18%	197 14.82%	1,489 4.32%	32,985 95.68%
1951-60	1,946 8.17%	21,864 91.83%	234 76.97%	70 23.03%	1,712 7.28%	21,794 92.72%
1941-50	943 6.69%	13,155 93.31%	59 52.68%	53 47.32%	884 6.32%	13,102 93.68%
1931-40	75 1.14%	6,511 98.86%	17 24.29%	53 75.71%	58 0.89%	6,458 99.11%
1921-30	83 3.81%	2,096 96.19%	24 54.55%	20 45.45%	59 2.76%	2,076 97.24%
1911-20	18 4.49%	383 95.51%	6 100.00%	0	12 3.04%	383 96.96%
1905-10	3 9.68%	28 90.32%	0 n.a.	0 n.a.	3 9.68%	28 90.32%

Source: LIFE26

Appendix Table C.9: Head of Household's Migration Decision by U.S. Citizenship Status

Year/Decade	All Heads of Household		U.S. Citizens		Not U.S. Citizens	
	Spent Part or All of Year in U.S.	Did Not Spend Year in U.S.	Spent Part or All of Year in U.S.	Did Not Spend Year in U.S.	Spent Part or All of Year in U.S.	Did Not Spend Year in U.S.
Survey Year	944	4,537	16	4	928	4,533
	17.22%	82.78%	80.00%	20.00%	16.99%	83.01%
1991-94	558	3,604	20	2	538	3,602
	13.41%	86.59%	90.91%	9.09%	13.00%	87.00%
1981-90	7,713	42,856	131	20	7,582	42,836
	15.25%	84.75%	86.75%	13.25%	15.04%	84.96%
1971-80	6,066	41,869	85	14	5,981	41,855
	12.65%	87.35%	85.86%	14.14%	12.50%	87.50%
1961-70	2,621	33,182	46	15	2,575	33,167
	7.32%	92.68%	75.41%	24.59%	7.20%	92.80%
1951-60	1,946	21,864	24	6	1,922	21,858
	8.17%	91.83%	80.00%	20.00%	8.08%	91.92%
1941-50	943	13,155	9	10	934	13,145
	6.69%	93.31%	47.37%	52.63%	6.63%	93.37%
1931-40	75	6,511	0	2	75	6,509
	1.14%	98.86%	n.a.	n.a.	1.14%	98.86%
1921-30	83	2,096	0	0	83	2,096
	3.81%	96.19%	n.a.	n.a.	3.81%	96.19%
1911-20	18	383	0	0	18	383
	4.49%	95.51%	n.a.	n.a.	4.49%	95.51%
1905-10	3	28	0	0	3	28
	9.68%	90.32%	n.a.	n.a.	9.68%	90.32%

Source: LIFE26

Appendix Table C.10: Head of Household's Migration Decision by Presence of Minor-Age Children

Year/Decade	All Heads of Household		Heads of Household With Minor-Age Children		Heads of Household Without Minor-Age Children	
	Spent Part or All of Year in U.S.	Did Not Spend Year in U.S.	Spent Part or All of Year in U.S.	Did Not Spend Year in U.S.	Spent Part or All of Year in U.S.	Did Not Spend Year in U.S.
Survey Year	944 / 17.22%	4,537 / 82.78%	783 / 19.58%	3,215 / 80.42%	161 / 10.86%	1,322 / 89.14%
1991-94	558 / 13.41%	3,604 / 86.59%	419 / 14.29%	2,513 / 85.71%	139 / 11.30%	1,091 / 88.70%
1981-90	7,173 / 14.34%	42,856 / 85.66%	5,286 / 15.20%	29,500 / 84.80%	1,887 / 12.38%	13,356 / 87.62%
1971-80	6,066 / 12.65%	41,869 / 87.35%	3,946 / 13.15%	26,058 / 86.85%	2,120 / 11.82%	15,811 / 88.18%
1961-70	2,621 / 7.32%	33,182 / 92.68%	1,752 / 8.62%	18,569 / 91.38%	869 / 5.61%	14,613 / 94.39%
1951-60	1,946 / 8.17%	21,864 / 91.83%	1,181 / 10.23%	10,358 / 89.77%	765 / 6.23%	11,506 / 93.77%
1941-50	943 / 6.69%	13,155 / 93.31%	450 / 8.60%	4,781 / 91.40%	493 / 5.56%	8,374 / 94.44%
1931-40	75 / 1.14%	6,511 / 98.86%	19 / 1.17%	1,605 / 98.83%	56 / 1.13%	4,906 / 98.87%
1921-30	83 / 3.81%	2,096 / 96.19%	9 / 2.59%	339 / 97.41%	74 / 4.04%	1,757 / 95.96%
1911-20	18 / 4.49%	383 / 95.51%	0 / 0.00%	24 / 100.00%	18 / 4.77%	359 / 95.23%
1905-10	3 / 9.68%	28 / 90.32%	0 / n.a.	0 / n.a.	3 / 9.68%	28 / 90.32%

Source: LIFE26

Appendix Table C.11: Migration Decision of Male Household Heads by Presence of Minor-Age Children

Year/Decade	All Male Heads of Household		Male Heads of Household With Minor-Age Children		Male Heads of Household Without Minor-Age Children	
	Spent Part or All of Year in U.S.	Did Not Spend Year in U.S.	Spent Part or All of Year in U.S.	Did Not Spend Year in U.S.	Spent Part or All of Year in U.S.	Did Not Spend Year in U.S.
Survey Year	906	3,889	762	2,937	144	952
	18.89%	81.11%	20.60%	79.40%	13.14%	86.86%
1991-94	525	3,089	399	2,278	126	811
	14.53%	85.47%	14.90%	85.10%	13.45%	86.55%
1981-90	7,376	36,701	5,587	26,207	1,789	10,494
	16.73%	83.27%	17.57%	82.43%	14.56%	85.44%
1971-80	5,813	35,441	3,781	21,912	2,032	13,529
	14.09%	85.91%	14.72%	85.28%	13.06%	86.94%
1961-70	2,507	27,343	1,706	14,767	801	12,576
	8.40%	91.60%	10.36%	89.54%	5.99%	94.01%
1951-60	1,880	17,168	1,151	7,471	729	9,697
	9.87%	90.13%	13.35%	86.65%	6.99%	93.01%
1941-50	925	9,911	445	3,136	480	6,775
	8.54%	91.46%	12.43%	87.57%	6.62%	93.38%
1931-40	69	4,745	18	913	51	3,832
	1.43%	98.57%	1.93%	98.07%	1.31%	98.69%
1921-30	79	1,420	8	149	71	1,271
	5.27%	94.73%	5.10%	94.90%	5.29%	94.71%
1911-20	18	268	0	11	18	257
	6.29%	93.71%	0.00%	100.00%	6.55%	93.45%
1905-10	3	22	0	0	3	22
	12.00%	88.00%	n.a.	r.a.	12.00%	88.00%

Source: LIFE26

Appendix Table C.12: Migration Decision of Female Household Heads by Presence of Minor-Age Children

Year/Decade	All Female Heads of Household		Female Heads of Household With Minor-Age Children		Female Heads of Household Without Minor-Age Children	
	Spent Part or All of Year in U.S.	Did Not Spend Year in U.S.	Spent Part or All of Year in U.S.	Did Not Spend Year in U.S.	Spent Part or All of Year in U.S.	Did Not Spend Year in U.S.
Survey Year	38	648	21	278	17	370
	5.54%	94.46%	7.02%	92.98%	4.39%	95.61%
1991-94	33	515	20	235	13	280
	6.02%	93.98%	7.84%	92.16%	4.44%	95.56%
1981-90	337	6,155	239	3,293	98	2,862
	5.19%	94.81%	6.77%	93.23%	3.31%	96.69%
1971-80	253	6,428	165	4,146	88	2,282
	3.79%	96.21%	3.83%	96.17%	3.71%	96.29%
1961-70	114	5,839	46	3,802	68	2,037
	1.92%	98.08%	1.20%	98.80%	3.23%	96.77%
1951-60	66	4,696	30	2,887	36	1,809
	1.39%	98.61%	1.03%	98.97%	1.95%	98.05%
1941-50	18	3,244	5	1,645	13	1,599
	0.55%	99.45%	0.30%	99.70%	0.81%	99.19%
1931-40	6	1,766	1	692	5	1,074
	0.34%	99.66%	0.14%	99.86%	0.46%	99.54%
1921-30	4	676	1	190	3	486
	0.59%	99.41%	0.52%	99.48%	0.61%	99.39%
1911-20	0	115	0	13	0	102
	0.00%	100.00%	0.00%	100.00%	0.00%	100.00%
1905-10	0	6	0	0	0	6
	0.00%	100.00%	n.a.	n.a.	0.00%	100.00%

Source: LIFE26

Appendix Table C.13: Migration Decision of Single Parents and All Other Household Heads

Year/Decade	All Heads of Household		Single Parents		All Other Heads of Household	
	Spent Part or All of Year in U.S.	Did Not Spend Year in U.S.	Spent Part or All of Year in U.S.	Did Not Spend Year in U.S.	Spent Part or All of Year in U.S.	Did Not Spend Year in U.S.
Survey Year	944 17.22%	4,537 82.78%	31 9.39%	299 90.61%	913 17.72%	4,238 82.28%
1991-94	558 13.41%	3,604 86.59%	23 8.27%	255 91.73%	535 13.77%	3,349 86.23%
1981-90	7,713 15.25%	42,856 84.75%	366 12.02%	2,680 87.98%	7,347 15.46%	40,176 84.54%
1971-80	6,066 12.65%	41,869 87.35%	179 8.17%	2,012 91.83%	5,887 12.87%	39,857 87.13%
1961-70	2,621 7.32%	33,182 92.68%	65 4.97%	1,243 95.03%	2,556 7.41%	31,939 92.59%
1951-60	1,946 8.17%	21,864 91.83%	44 5.67%	732 94.33%	1,902 8.26%	21,132 91.74%
1941-50	943 6.69%	13,155 93.31%	20 6.35%	295 93.65%	923 6.70%	12,860 93.30%
1931-40	75 1.14%	6,511 98.86%	0 0.00%	83 100.00%	75 1.15%	6,428 98.85%
1921-30	83 3.81%	2,096 96.19%	0 0.00%	17 100.00%	83 3.84%	2,079 96.16%
1911-20	18 4.49%	383 95.51%	0 n.a.	0 n.a.	18 4.49%	383 95.51%
1905-10	3 9.68%	28 90.32%	0 n.a.	0 n.a.	3 9.68%	28 90.32%

Source: LIFE26

Appendix Table C.14: Migration Decision of Single Mothers and All Other Female Household Heads

Year/Decade	All Female Heads of Household		Single Mothers		All Other Female Heads of Household	
	Spent Part or All of Year in U.S.	Did Not Spend Year in U.S.	Spent Part or All of Year in U.S.	Did Not Spend Year in U.S.	Spent Part or All of Year in U.S.	Did Not Spend Year in U.S.
Survey Year	38 5.54%	648 94.46%	14 5.56%	238 94.44%	24 5.53%	410 94.47%
1991-94	33 6.02%	515 93.98%	15 7.11%	196 92.89%	18 5.34%	319 94.66%
1981-90	337 5.19%	6,155 94.81%	136 6.71%	1,890 93.29%	201 4.50%	4,265 95.50%
1971-80	253 3.79%	6,428 96.21%	44 3.34%	1,275 96.66%	209 3.90%	5,153 96.10%
1961-70	114 1.92%	5,839 98.08%	2 0.29%	688 99.71%	112 2.13%	5,151 97.87%
1951-60	66 1.39%	4,696 98.61%	0 0.00%	409 100.00%	66 1.52%	4,287 98.48%
1941-50	18 0.55%	3,244 99.45%	0 0.00%	131 100.00%	18 0.57%	3,113 99.43%
1931-40	6 0.34%	1,766 99.66%	0 0.00%	25 100.00%	6 0.34%	1,741 99.66%
1921-30	4 0.59%	676 99.41%	0 0.00%	12 100.00%	4 0.60%	664 99.40%
1911-20	0 0.00%	115 100.00%	0 n.a.	0 n.a.	0 0.00%	115 100.00%
1905-10	0 0.00%	6 100.00%	0 n.a.	0 n.a.	0 0.00%	6 100.00%

Source: LIFE26

Appendix Table C.15: Migration Decision of Single Fathers and All Other Male Household Heads

Year/Decade	All Male Heads of Household		Single Fathers		All Male Heads of Household	
	Spent Part or All of Year in U.S.	Did Not Spend Year in U.S.	Spent Part or All of Year in U.S.	Did Not Spend Year in U.S.	Spent Part or All of Year in U.S.	Did Not Spend Year in U.S.
Survey Year	906 18.89%	3,889 81.11%	17 21.79%	61 78.21%	889 18.85%	3,828 81.15%
1991-94	525 14.53%	3,089 85.47%	8 11.94%	59 88.06%	517 14.58%	3,030 85.42%
1981-90	7,376 16.73%	36,701 83.27%	230 22.55%	790 77.45%	7,146 16.60%	35,911 83.40%
1971-80	5,813 14.09%	35,441 85.91%	135 15.48%	737 84.52%	5,678 14.06%	34,704 85.94%
1961-70	2,507 8.40%	27,343 91.60%	63 10.19%	555 89.81%	2,444 8.36%	26,788 91.64%
1951-60	1,880 9.87%	17,168 90.13%	44 11.99%	323 88.01%	1,836 9.83%	16,845 90.17%
1941-50	925 8.54%	9,911 91.46%	20 10.87%	164 89.13%	905 8.50%	9,747 91.50%
1931-40	69 1.43%	4,745 98.57%	0 0.00%	58 100.00%	69 1.45%	4,687 98.55%
1921-30	79 5.27%	1,420 94.73%	0 0.00%	5 100.00%	79 5.29%	1,415 94.71%
1911-20	18 6.29%	268 93.71%	0 n.a.	0 n.a.	18 6.29%	268 93.71%
1905-10	3 12.00%	22 88.00%	0 n.a.	0 n.a.	3 12.00%	22 88.00%

Source: LIFE26

Appendix Table C.16: Presence of Friends and Family in U.S. at Time of Interview by Head of Household's Most Recent U.S. Experience

Relative/Friend Present in U.S.?	Total	Most Recent U.S. Migration Experience		
		Within Three-Year Period Prior To Interview	More Than Three Years Prior To Interview	No U.S. Migration Experience
Total	5,482	817	1,688	2,977
% of Total		14.90%	30.79%	54.30%
Any Close Friend or Family Member				
Yes	4,118	749	1,453	1,916
% of Total With Specified Migration Experience	75.12%	91.68%	86.08%	64.36%
% of Total With Specified U.S. Contact	100.00%	18.19%	35.28%	46.53%
No	1,364	68	235	1,061
% of Total With Specified Migration Experience	24.88%	8.32%	13.92%	35.64%
% of Total With Specified U.S. Contact	100.00%	4.99%	17.23%	77.79%
Any Family Member				
Yes	3,919	731	1,409	1,779
% of Total With Specified Migration Experience	71.49%	89.47%	83.47%	59.76%
% of Total With Specified U.S. Contact	100.00%	18.65%	35.95%	45.39%
No	1,563	86	279	1,198
% of Total With Specified Migration Experience	28.51%	10.53%	16.53%	40.24%
% of Total With Specified U.S. Contact	100.00%	5.50%	17.85%	76.65%
Close Friend				
Yes	2,190	477	892	821
% of Total With Specified Migration Experience	39.95%	58.38%	52.84%	27.58%
% of Total With Specified U.S. Contact	100.00%	21.78%	40.73%	37.49%
No	3,292	340	796	2,156
% of Total With Specified Migration Experience	60.05%	41.62%	47.16%	72.42%
% of Total With Specified U.S. Contact	100.00%	10.33%	24.18%	65.49%

Appendix Table C.16 (continued)

Relative/Friend Present in U.S.?	Total	Most Recent U.S. Migration Experience		
		Within Three-Year Period Prior To Interview	More Than Three Years Prior To Interview	No U.S. Migration Experience
Immediate Relatives (1)				
Yes	1,792	480	754	558
% of Total With Specified Migration Experience	32.69%	58.75%	44.67%	18.74%
% of Total With Specified U.S. Contact	100.00%	26.79%	42.08%	31.14%
No	3,690	337	934	2,419
% of Total With Specified Migration Experience	67.31%	41.25%	55.33%	81.26%
% of Total With Specified U.S. Contact	100.00%	9.13%	25.31%	65.56%
Father				
Yes	124	47	52	25
% of Total With Specified Migration Experience	2.27%	5.75%	3.10%	0.84%
% of Total With Specified U.S. Contact	100.00%	37.90%	41.94%	20.16%
No	5,348	770	1,626	2,952
% of Total With Specified Migration Experience	97.73%	94.25%	96.90%	99.16%
% of Total With Specified U.S. Contact	100.00%	14.40%	30.40%	55.20%
Mother				
Yes	103	33	57	13
% of Total With Specified Migration Experience	1.88%	4.04%	3.38%	0.44%
% of Total With Specified U.S. Contact	100.00%	32.04%	55.34%	12.62%
No	5,379	784	1,631	2,964
% of Total With Specified Migration Experience	98.12%	95.96%	96.62%	99.56%
% of Total With Specified U.S. Contact	100.00%	14.58%	30.32%	55.10%

Appendix Table C.16 (continued)

Relative/Friend Present in U.S.?	Total	Most Recent U.S. Migration Experience		
		Within Three-Year Period Prior To Interview	More Than Three Years Prior To Interview	No U.S. Migration Experience
Sibling				
Yes	1,766	474	745	547
% of Total With Specified Migration Experience	32.21%	58.02%	44.14%	18.37%
% of Total With Specified U.S. Contact	100.00%	26.84%	42.19%	30.97%
No	3,716	343	943	2,430
% of Total With Specified Migration Experience	67.79%	41.98%	55.86%	81.63%
% of Total With Specified U.S. Contact	100.00%	9.23%	25.38%	65.39%
Grandparent				
Yes	22	4	9	9
% of Total With Specified Migration Experience	0.40%	0.49%	0.53%	0.30%
% of Total With Specified U.S. Contact	100.00%	18.18%	40.91%	40.91%
No	5,460	813	1,679	2,968
% of Total With Specified Migration Experience	99.60%	99.51%	99.47%	99.70%
% of Total With Specified U.S. Contact	100.00%	14.89%	30.75%	54.36%
Uncle/Aunt				
Yes	1,123	286	433	404
% of Total With Specified Migration Experience	20.49%	35.01%	25.65%	13.57%
% of Total With Specified U.S. Contact	100.00%	25.47%	38.56%	35.98%
No	4,359	531	1,255	2,573
% of Total With Specified Migration Experience	79.51%	64.99%	74.35%	86.43%
% of Total With Specified U.S. Contact	100.00%	12.18%	28.79%	59.03%

Appendix Table C.16 (continued)

Relative/Friend Present in U.S.?	Total	Most Recent U.S. Migration Experience		
		Within Three-Year Period Prior To Interview	More Than Three Years Prior To Interview	No U.S. Migration Experience
Cousin				
Yes	2,193	501	854	838
% of Total With Specified Migration Experience	40.00%	61.32%	50.59%	28.15%
% of Total With Specified U.S. Contact	100.00%	22.85%	38.94%	38.21%
No	3,289	316	834	2,139
% of Total With Specified Migration Experience	60.00%	38.68%	49.41%	71.85%
% of Total With Specified U.S. Contact	100.00%	9.61%	25.36%	65.03%
Nephew/Niece				
Yes	2,214	415	899	900
% of Total With Specified Migration Experience	40.39%	50.80%	53.26%	30.23%
% of Total With Specified U.S. Contact	100.00%	18.74%	40.61%	40.65%
No	3,268	402	789	2,077
% of Total With Specified Migration Experience	59.61%	49.20%	46.74%	69.77%
% of Total With Specified U.S. Contact	100.00%	12.30%	24.14%	63.56%
Brother-/Sister-In-Law				
Yes	1,909	459	769	681
% of Total With Specified Migration Experience	34.82%	56.18%	45.56%	22.88%
% of Total With Specified U.S. Contact	100.00%	24.04%	40.28%	35.67%
No	3,573	358	919	2,296
% of Total With Specified Migration Experience	65.18%	43.82%	54.44%	77.12%
% of Total With Specified U.S. Contact	100.00%	10.02%	25.72%	64.26%

Appendix Table C.16 (continued)

Relative/Friend Present in U.S.?	Total	Most Recent U.S. Migration Experience		
		Within Three-Year Period Prior To Interview	More Than Three Years Prior To Interview	No U.S. Migration Experience
Mother-/Father-In-Law				
Yes	836	170	401	265
% of Total With Specified Migration Experience	15.25%	20.81%	23.76%	8.90%
% of Total With Specified U.S. Contact	100.00%	20.33%	47.97%	31.70%
No	4,646	647	1,287	2,712
% of Total With Specified Migration Experience	84.75%	79.19%	76.24%	91.10%
% of Total With Specified U.S. Contact	100.00%	13.93%	27.70%	58.37%

Source: HOUSFILE

Appendix Table C.17: Presence of Friends and Family in U.S. at Time of Interview by Head of Household's Most Recent U.S. Experience (Males Only)

Relative/Friend Present in U.S.?	Total	Most Recent U.S. Migration Experience		
		Within Three-Year Period Prior To Interview	More Than Three Years Prior To Interview	No U.S. Migration Experience
Total	4,792	780	1,614	2,398
% of Total	100.00%	16.28%	33.68%	50.04%
Any Close Friend or Family Member				
Yes	3,656	715	1,383	1,558
% of Total With Specified Migration Experience	76.29%	91.67%	85.69%	64.97%
% of Total With Specified U.S. Contact	100.00%	19.56%	37.83%	42.61%
No	1,136	65	231	840
% of Total With Specified Migration Experience	23.71%	8.33%	14.31%	35.03%
% of Total With Specified U.S. Contact	100.00%	5.72%	20.33%	73.94%
Any Family Member				
Yes	3,469	697	1,340	1,432
% of Total With Specified Migration Experience	72.39%	89.36%	83.02%	59.72%
% of Total With Specified U.S. Contact	100.00%	20.09%	38.63%	41.28%
No	1,323	83	274	966
% of Total With Specified Migration Experience	27.61%	10.64%	16.98%	40.28%
% of Total With Specified U.S. Contact	100.00%	6.27%	20.71%	73.02%
Close Friend				
Yes	2,062	464	861	737
% of Total With Specified Migration Experience	43.03%	59.49%	53.35%	30.73%
% of Total With Specified U.S. Contact	100.00%	22.50%	41.76%	35.74%
No	2,730	316	753	1,661
% of Total With Specified Migration Experience	56.97%	40.51%	46.65%	69.27%
% of Total With Specified U.S. Contact	100.00%	11.58%	27.58%	60.84%

Appendix Table C.17 (continued)

Relative/Friend Present in U.S.?	Total	Most Recent U.S. Migration Experience		
		Within Three-Year Period Prior To Interview	More Than Three Years Prior To Interview	No U.S. Migration Experience
Immediate Relatives (1)				
Yes	1,631	463	716	452
% of Total With Specified Migration Experience	34.04%	59.36%	44.36%	18.85%
% of Total With Specified U.S. Contact	100.00%	28.39%	43.90%	27.71%
No	3,161	317	898	1,946
% of Total With Specified Migration Experience	65.96%	40.64%	55.64%	81.15%
% of Total With Specified U.S. Contact	100.00%	10.03%	28.41%	61.56%
Father				
Yes	116	46	48	22
% of Total With Specified Migration Experience	2.43%	5.90%	2.99%	0.92%
% of Total With Specified U.S. Contact	100.00%	39.66%	41.38%	18.97%
No	4,666	734	1,556	2,376
% of Total With Specified Migration Experience	97.57%	94.10%	97.01%	99.08%
% of Total With Specified U.S. Contact	100.00%	15.73%	33.35%	50.92%
Mother				
Yes	99	33	55	11
% of Total With Specified Migration Experience	2.07%	4.23%	3.41%	0.46%
% of Total With Specified U.S. Contact	100.00%	33.33%	55.56%	11.11%
No	4,693	747	1,559	2,387
% of Total With Specified Migration Experience	97.93%	95.77%	96.59%	99.54%
% of Total With Specified U.S. Contact	100.00%	15.92%	33.22%	50.86%

Appendix Table C.17 (continued)

Relative/Friend Present in U.S.?	Total	Most Recent U.S. Migration Experience		
		Within Three-Year Period Prior To Interview	More Than Three Years Prior To Interview	No U.S. Migration Experience
Sibling				
Yes	1,606	457	708	441
% of Total With Specified Migration Experience	33.51%	58.59%	43.87%	18.39%
% of Total With Specified U.S. Contact	100.00%	28.46%	44.08%	27.46%
No	3,186	323	906	1,957
% of Total With Specified Migration Experience	66.49%	41.41%	56.13%	81.61%
% of Total With Specified U.S. Contact	100.00%	10.14%	28.44%	61.42%
Grandparent				
Yes	21	4	8	9
% of Total With Specified Migration Experience	0.44%	0.51%	0.50%	0.38%
% of Total With Specified U.S. Contact	100.00%	19.05%	38.10%	42.86%
No	4,771	776	1,606	2,389
% of Total With Specified Migration Experience	99.56%	99.49%	99.50%	99.62%
% of Total With Specified U.S. Contact	100.00%	16.26%	33.66%	50.07%
Uncle/Aunt				
Yes	1,056	284	413	359
% of Total With Specified Migration Experience	22.04%	36.41%	25.59%	14.97%
% of Total With Specified U.S. Contact	100.00%	26.89%	39.11%	34.00%
No	3,736	496	1,201	2,039
% of Total With Specified Migration Experience	77.96%	63.59%	74.41%	85.03%
% of Total With Specified U.S. Contact	100.00%	13.23%	32.15%	54.58%

Appendix Table C.17 (continued)

Relative/Friend Present in U.S.?	Total	Most Recent U.S. Migration Experience		
		Within Three-Year Period Prior To Interview	More Than Three Years Prior To Interview	No U.S. Migration Experience
Cousin				
Yes	1,996	478	821	697
% of Total With Specified Migration Experience	41.65%	61.28%	50.87%	29.07%
% of Total With Specified U.S. Contact	100.00%	23.95%	41.13%	34.92%
No	2,796	302	793	1,701
% of Total With Specified Migration Experience	58.35%	38.72%	49.13%	70.93%
% of Total With Specified U.S. Contact	100.00%	10.80%	28.36%	60.84%
Nephew/Niece				
Yes	1,912	389	846	677
% of Total With Specified Migration Experience	39.90%	49.87%	52.42%	28.23%
% of Total With Specified U.S. Contact	100.00%	20.35%	44.25%	35.41%
No	2,880	391	768	1,721
% of Total With Specified Migration Experience	60.10%	50.13%	47.58%	71.77%
% of Total With Specified U.S. Contact	100.00%	13.58%	26.67%	59.76%
Brother-/Sister-In-Law				
Yes	1,766	450	734	582
% of Total With Specified Migration Experience	36.85%	57.69%	45.48%	24.27%
% of Total With Specified U.S. Contact	100.00%	25.48%	41.56%	32.96%
No	3,026	330	880	1,816
% of Total With Specified Migration Experience	63.15%	42.31%	54.52%	75.73%
% of Total With Specified U.S. Contact	100.00%	10.91%	29.08%	60.01%

Appendix Table C.17 (continued)

Relative/Friend Present in U.S.?	Total	Most Recent U.S. Migration Experience		
		Within Three-Year Period Prior To Interview	More Than Three Years Prior To Interview	No U.S. Migration Experience
Mother-/Father-In-Law				
Yes	696	151	375	170
% of Total With Specified Migration Experience	14.52%	19.36%	23.23%	7.09%
% of Total With Specified U.S. Contact	100.00%	21.70%	53.88%	24.43%
No	4,096	629	1,239	2,228
% of Total With Specified Migration Experience	85.48%	80.64%	76.77%	92.91%
% of Total With Specified U.S. Contact	100.00%	15.36%	30.25%	54.39%

Source: HOUSFILE

Appendix Table C.18: Friends and Family in U.S. at Time of Interview by Head of Household's Most Recent U.S. Experience (Females Only)

Relative/Friend Present in U.S.?	Total	Most Recent U.S. Migration Experience		
		Within Three-Year Period Prior To Interview	More Than Three Years Prior To Interview	No U.S. Migration Experience
Total	690	37	74	579
% of Total	100.00%	5.36%	10.72%	83.91%
Any Close Friend or Family Member				
Yes	462	34	70	358
% of Total With Specified Migration Experience	66.96%	91.89%	94.59%	61.83%
% of Total With Specified U.S. Contact	100.00%	7.36%	15.15%	77.49%
No	228	3	4	221
% of Total With Specified Migration Experience	33.04%	8.11%	5.41%	38.17%
% of Total With Specified U.S. Contact	100.00%	1.32%	1.75%	96.93%
Any Family Member				
Yes	450	34	69	347
% of Total With Specified Migration Experience	65.22%	91.89%	93.24%	59.93%
% of Total With Specified U.S. Contact	100.00%	7.56%	15.33%	77.11%
No	240	3	5	232
% of Total With Specified Migration Experience	34.78%	8.11%	6.76%	40.07%
% of Total With Specified U.S. Contact	100.00%	1.25%	2.08%	96.67%

Appendix Table C.18 (continued)

Relative/Friend Present in U.S.?	Total	Most Recent U.S. Migration Experience		
		Within Three-Year Period Prior To Interview	More Than Three Years Prior To Interview	No U.S. Migration Experience
Close Friend				
Yes	128	13	31	84
% of Total With Specified Migration Experience	18.55%	35.14%	41.89%	14.51%
% of Total With Specified U.S. Contact	100.00%	10.16%	24.22%	65.63%
No	562	24	43	495
% of Total With Specified Migration Experience	81.45%	64.86%	58.11%	85.49%
% of Total With Specified U.S. Contact	100.00%	4.27%	7.65%	88.08%
Immediate Relatives (1)				
Yes	161	17	38	106
% of Total With Specified Migration Experience	23.33%	45.95%	51.35%	18.31%
% of Total With Specified U.S. Contact	100.00%	10.56%	23.60%	65.84%
No	529	20	36	473
% of Total With Specified Migration Experience	76.67%	54.05%	48.65%	81.69%
% of Total With Specified U.S. Contact	100.00%	3.78%	6.81%	89.41%

Appendix Table C.18 (continued)

Relative/Friend Present in U.S.?	Total	Most Recent U.S. Migration Experience		
		Within Three-Year Period Prior To Interview	More Than Three Years Prior To Interview	No U.S. Migration Experience
Father				
Yes	8	1	4	3
% of Total With Specified Migration Experience	1.16%	2.70%	5.41%	0.52%
% of Total With Specified U.S. Contact	100.00%	12.50%	50.00%	37.50%
No	682	36	70	576
% of Total With Specified Migration Experience	98.84%	97.30%	94.59%	99.48%
% of Total With Specified U.S. Contact	100.00%	5.28%	10.26%	84.46%
Mother				
Yes	4	0	2	2
% of Total With Specified Migration Experience	0.58%	0.00%	2.70%	0.35%
% of Total With Specified U.S. Contact	100.00%	0.00%	50.00%	50.00%
No	686	37	72	577
% of Total With Specified Migration Experience	99.42%	100.00%	97.30%	99.65%
% of Total With Specified U.S. Contact	100.00%	5.39%	10.50%	84.11%

Appendix Table C.18 (continued)

Relative/Friend Present in U.S.?	Total	Most Recent U.S. Migration Experience		
		Within Three-Year Period Prior To Interview	More Than Three Years Prior To Interview	No U.S. Migration Experience
Sibling				
Yes	160	17	37	106
% of Total With Specified Migration Experience	23.19%	45.95%	50.00%	18.31%
% of Total With Specified U.S. Contact	100.00%	10.63%	23.13%	66.25%
No	530	20	37	473
% of Total With Specified Migration Experience	76.81%	54.05%	50.00%	81.69%
% of Total With Specified U.S. Contact	100.00%	3.77%	6.98%	89.25%
Grandparent				
Yes	1	0	1	0
% of Total With Specified Migration Experience	0.14%	0.00%	1.35%	0.00%
% of Total With Specified U.S. Contact	100.00%	0.00%	100.00%	0.00%
No	689	37	73	579
% of Total With Specified Migration Experience	99.86%	100.00%	98.65%	100.00%
% of Total With Specified U.S. Contact	100.00%	5.37%	10.60%	84.03%

Appendix Table C.18 (continued)

Relative/Friend Present in U.S.?	Total	Most Recent U.S. Migration Experience		
		Within Three-Year Period Prior To Interview	More Than Three Years Prior To Interview	No U.S. Migration Experience
Uncle/Aunt				
Yes	67	2	20	45
% of Total With Specified Migration Experience	9.71%	5.41%	27.03%	7.77%
% of Total With Specified U.S. Contact	100.00%	2.99%	29.85%	67.16%
No	623	35	54	534
% of Total With Specified Migration Experience	90.29%	94.59%	72.97%	92.23%
% of Total With Specified U.S. Contact	100.00%	5.62%	8.67%	85.71%
Cousin				
Yes	197	23	33	141
% of Total With Specified Migration Experience	28.55%	62.16%	44.59%	24.35%
% of Total With Specified U.S. Contact	100.00%	11.68%	16.75%	71.57%
No	493	14	41	438
% of Total With Specified Migration Experience	71.45%	37.84%	55.41%	75.65%
% of Total With Specified U.S. Contact	100.00%	2.84%	8.32%	88.84%

Appendix Table C.18 (continued)

Relative/Friend Present in U.S.?	Total	Most Recent U.S. Migration Experience		
		Within Three-Year Period Prior To Interview	More Than Three Years Prior To Interview	No U.S. Migration Experience
Nephew/Niece				
Yes	302	26	53	223
% of Total With Specified Migration Experience	43.77%	70.27%	71.62%	38.51%
% of Total With Specified U.S. Contact	100.00%	8.61%	17.55%	73.84%
No	388	11	21	356
% of Total With Specified Migration Experience	56.23%	29.73%	28.38%	61.49%
% of Total With Specified U.S. Contact	100.00%	2.84%	5.41%	91.75%
Brother-/Sister-In-Law				
Yes	143	9	35	99
% of Total With Specified Migration Experience	20.72%	24.32%	47.30%	17.10%
% of Total With Specified U.S. Contact	100.00%	6.29%	24.48%	69.23%
No	547	28	39	480
% of Total With Specified Migration Experience	79.28%	75.68%	52.70%	82.90%
% of Total With Specified U.S. Contact	100.00%	5.12%	7.13%	87.75%
Mother-/Father-In-Law				
Yes	140	19	26	95
% of Total With Specified Migration Experience	20.29%	51.35%	35.14%	16.41%
% of Total With Specified U.S. Contact	100.00%	13.57%	18.57%	67.86%
No	550	18	48	484
% of Total With Specified Migration Experience	79.71%	48.65%	64.86%	83.59%
% of Total With Specified U.S. Contact	100.00%	3.27%	8.73%	88.00%

(1) Immediate relatives are defined to be the head of household's parents, siblings, and grandparents.

Source: HOUSFILE

Appendix Table C.19: Presence of Friends and Relatives in U.S. at Time of Interview by U.S. Migration Experience of Female Heads of Household (26-Community Sample)

Relative/Friend Present in U.S.?	Total	Most Recent U.S. Migration Experience		
		Within Three-Year Period Prior To Interview	More Than Three Years Prior To Interview	No U.S. Migration Experience
Total	690	37	74	579
% of Total	100.00%	5.36%	10.72%	83.91%
Any Close Friend or Family Member				
Yes	462	34	70	358
% of Total With Specified Migration Experience	66.96%	91.89%	94.59%	61.83%
% of Total With Specified U.S. Contact	100.00%	7.36%	15.15%	77.49%
No	228	3	4	221
% of Total With Specified Migration Experience	33.04%	8.11%	5.41%	38.17%
% of Total With Specified U.S. Contact	100.00%	1.32%	1.75%	96.93%
Any Family Member				
Yes	450	34	69	347
% of Total With Specified Migration Experience	65.22%	91.89%	93.24%	59.93%
% of Total With Specified U.S. Contact	100.00%	7.56%	15.33%	77.11%
No	240	3	5	232
% of Total With Specified Migration Experience	34.78%	8.11%	6.76%	40.07%
% of Total With Specified U.S. Contact	100.00%	1.25%	2.08%	96.67%
Close Friend				
Yes	128	13	31	84
% of Total With Specified Migration Experience	18.55%	35.14%	41.89%	14.51%
% of Total With Specified U.S. Contact	100.00%	10.16%	24.22%	65.63%
No	562	24	43	495
% of Total With Specified Migration Experience	81.45%	64.86%	58.11%	85.49%

Appendix Table C.19 (continued)

Relative/Friend Present in U.S.?	Total	Most Recent U.S. Migration Experience		
		Within Three-Year Period Prior To Interview	More Than Three Years Prior To Interview	No U.S. Migration Experience
% of Total With Specified U.S. Contact	100.00%	4.27%	7.65%	88.08%
Immediate Relatives (1)				
Yes	161	17	38	106
% of Total With Specified Migration Experience	23.33%	45.95%	51.35%	18.31%
% of Total With Specified U.S. Contact	100.00%	10.56%	23.60%	65.84%
No	529	20	36	473
% of Total With Specified Migration Experience	76.67%	54.05%	48.65%	81.69%
% of Total With Specified U.S. Contact	100.00%	3.78%	6.81%	89.41%
Father				
Yes	8	1	4	3
% of Total With Specified Migration Experience	1.16%	2.70%	5.41%	0.52%
% of Total With Specified U.S. Contact	100.00%	12.50%	50.00%	37.50%
No	682	36	70	576
% of Total With Specified Migration Experience	98.84%	97.30%	94.59%	99.48%
% of Total With Specified U.S. Contact	100.00%	5.28%	10.26%	84.46%
Mother				
Yes	4	0	2	2
% of Total With Specified Migration Experience	0.58%	0.00%	2.70%	0.35%
% of Total With Specified U.S. Contact	100.00%	0.00%	50.00%	50.00%
No	686	37	72	577
% of Total With Specified Migration Experience	99.42%	100.00%	97.30%	99.65%
% of Total With Specified U.S. Contact	100.00%	5.39%	10.50%	84.11%

Appendix Table C.19 (continued)

Relative/Friend Present in U.S.?	Total	Most Recent U.S. Migration Experience		
		Within Three-Year Period Prior To Interview	More Than Three Years Prior To Interview	No U.S. Migration Experience
Sibling				
Yes	160	17	37	106
% of Total With Specified Migration Experience	23.19%	45.95%	50.00%	18.31%
% of Total With Specified U.S. Contact	100.00%	10.63%	23.13%	66.25%
No	530	20	37	473
% of Total With Specified Migration Experience	76.81%	54.05%	50.00%	81.69%
% of Total With Specified U.S. Contact	100.00%	3.77%	6.98%	89.25%
Grandparent				
Yes	1	0	1	0
% of Total With Specified Migration Experience	0.14%	0.00%	1.35%	0.00%
% of Total With Specified U.S. Contact	100.00%	0.00%	100.00%	0.00%
No	689	37	73	579
% of Total With Specified Migration Experience	99.86%	100.00%	98.65%	100.00%
% of Total With Specified U.S. Contact	100.00%	5.37%	10.60%	84.03%
Uncle/Aunt				
Yes	67	2	20	45
% of Total With Specified Migration Experience	9.71%	5.41%	27.03%	7.77%
% of Total With Specified U.S. Contact	100.00%	2.99%	29.85%	67.16%
No	623	35	54	534
% of Total With Specified Migration Experience	90.29%	94.59%	72.97%	92.23%
% of Total With Specified U.S. Contact	100.00%	5.62%	8.67%	85.71%

Appendix Table C.19 (continued)

Relative/Friend Present in U.S.?	Total	Most Recent U.S. Migration Experience		
		Within Three-Year Period Prior To Interview	More Than Three Years Prior To Interview	No U.S. Migration Experience
Cousin				
Yes	197	23	33	141
% of Total With Specified Migration Experience	28.55%	62.16%	44.59%	24.35%
% of Total With Specified U.S. Contact	100.00%	11.68%	16.75%	71.57%
No	493	14	41	438
% of Total With Specified Migration Experience	71.45%	37.84%	55.41%	75.65%
% of Total With Specified U.S. Contact	100.00%	2.84%	8.32%	88.84%
Nephew/Niece				
Yes	302	26	53	223
% of Total With Specified Migration Experience	43.77%	70.27%	71.62%	38.51%
% of Total With Specified U.S. Contact	100.00%	8.61%	17.55%	73.84%
No	388	11	21	356
% of Total With Specified Migration Experience	56.23%	29.73%	28.38%	61.49%
% of Total With Specified U.S. Contact	100.00%	2.84%	5.41%	91.75%
Brother-/Sister-In-Law				
Yes	143	9	35	99
% of Total With Specified Migration Experience	20.72%	24.32%	47.30%	17.10%
% of Total With Specified U.S. Contact	100.00%	6.29%	24.48%	69.23%
No	547	28	39	480
% of Total With Specified Migration Experience	79.28%	75.68%	52.70%	82.90%
% of Total With Specified U.S. Contact	100.00%	5.12%	7.13%	87.75%

Appendix Table C.19 (continued)

Relative/Friend Present in U.S.?	Total	Most Recent U.S. Migration Experience		
		Within Three-Year Period Prior To Interview	More Than Three Years Prior To Interview	No U.S. Migration Experience
Mother-/Father-In-Law				
Yes	140	19	26	95
% of Total With Specified Migration Experience	20.29%	51.35%	35.14%	16.41%
% of Total With Specified U.S. Contact	100.00%	13.57%	18.57%	67.86%
No	550	18	48	484
% of Total With Specified Migration Experience	79.71%	48.65%	64.86%	83.59%
% of Total With Specified U.S. Contact	100.00%	3.27%	8.73%	88.00%

(1) Immediate relatives are defined to be the head of household's parents, siblings, and grandparents.

Source: HOUSFILE

Supplemental Tables to Chapter 5

Appendix Table D.1: Standardized Parameter Estimates from Participation Models With Four Macroeconomic Variables

Vector/Variable	Gender-Neutral Network Variables		Gender-Specific Network Variables	
	Model 5.1	Model 5.2	Model 5.3	Model 5.4
Individual characteristics				
Age (in years)	0.6931***	0.8048***	0.7129***	0.8156***
Age squared	-1.4816***	-1.6073***	-1.5042***	-1.6178***
Female	-0.2336***	-0.2446***	-0.2333***	-0.2446***
Education (in years)	-0.0369***	-0.0395***	-0.0358***	-0.0371***
College educated	-0.0540***	-0.0551***	-0.0557***	-0.0567***
U.S. interview	0.2228***	0.2175***	0.2238***	0.2182***
U.S. migration experience (in months)	1.1538***	1.2155***	1.1613***	1.2147***
U.S. migration experience squared	-0.5698***	-0.6085***	-0.5746***	-0.6076***
Family responsibilities				
Married	0.0064	0.0143	0.0044	0.0128
Number of minor-age children	0.0112	0.0115	0.0111	0.0116
Single parent	-0.0015	-0.0006	-0.0029	-0.0012
Single mother	0.0435***	0.0446***	0.0417***	0.0446***
Relatives with migration experience				
Grandparent	0.0368***	0.0162***	n.a.	n.a.
Grandfather	n.a.	n.a.	0.0339***	0.0138***
Grandmother	n.a.	n.a.	0.0089	-0.0026
Grandparent (gender not recorded)	n.a.	n.a.	0.0038	0.0062
Father	0.0638***	0.0187***	0.0662***	0.0180***
Mother	-0.0443***	-0.0227***	-0.0406***	-0.0210***

Appendix Table D.1 (continued)

Vector/Variable	Gender-Neutral Network Variables		Gender-Specific Network Variables	
	Model 5.1	Model 5.2	Model 5.3	Model 5.4
Relatives with migration experience (continued)				
Sibling	0.1457***	0.1244***	n.a.	n.a.
Brother	n.a.	n.a.	0.1348***	0.1177***
Sister	n.a.	n.a.	-0.0080	0.0056
Sibling (gender not recorded)	n.a.	n.a.	0.0227***	0.0172***
Relatives with migration experience when household head has not yet migrated				
Grandparent	-0.0461***	n.a.	n.a.	n.a.
Grandfather	n.a.	n.a.	-0.0447***	n.a.
Grandmother	n.a.	n.a.	-0.0193**	n.a.
Grandparent (gender not recorded)	n.a.	n.a.	0.0021	n.a.
Father	-0.1038***	n.a.	-0.1091***	n.a.
Mother	0.0382***	n.a.	0.0349***	n.a.
Sibling	-0.0558***	n.a.	n.a.	n.a.
Brother	n.a.	n.a.	-0.0467***	n.a.
Sister	n.a.	n.a.	0.0257***	n.a.
Sibling (gender not recorded)	n.a.	n.a.	-0.0118	n.a.
Immigration status and policies				
Legal U.S. resident	0.1969***	0.2030***	0.1985***	0.2029***
U.S. citizen	-0.0185***	-0.0182***	-0.0167***	-0.0171***
Bracero Program (1944-64)	0.2206***	0.2242***	0.2211***	0.2237***
Amnesty Program (1988-89)	-0.0160***	-0.0150**	-0.0158**	-0.0151**
Western Hemisphere favored (1968-76)	0.1534***	0.1531***	0.1544***	0.1541***

Appendix Table D.1 (continued)

Vector/Variable	Gender-Neutral Network Variables		Gender-Specific Network Variables	
	Model 5.1	Model 5.2	Model 5.3	Model 5.4
Immigration status and policies (continued)				
Similar treatment of hemispheres (1977-91)	0.1614***	0.1646***	0.1633***	0.1655***
Immigration Act of 1990 (1992-94)	0.0305***	0.0306***	0.0313***	0.0306***
Deportation ratio	0.0462***	0.0479***	0.0465***	0.0479***
Additional income sources				
Number of adult offspring	0.0808***	0.0860***	0.0801***	0.0853***
Agricultural land (in hectares)	-0.1585***	-0.1558***	-0.1573***	-0.1553***
Business ownership	-0.1464***	-0.1488***	-0.1465***	-0.1490***
National economic conditions				
Real per capita GDP in Mexico	0.0403***	0.0398***	0.0415***	0.0409***
Real per capita GDP in U.S.	0.0878***	0.0882***	0.0891***	0.0886***
Real per capita growth in Mexico	0.0211***	0.0204***	0.0210***	0.0203***
Real per capita growth in U.S.	-0.0143**	-0.0156**	-0.0143**	-0.0154**
Log-likelihood (intercept and covariates)	-30,692.05	-30,873.49	-30,699.69	-30,879.07

Results for community dummy variables are not reported.

Results of Wald Chi-squared test on significance of parameter estimate:

***Passes at 99-percent level; **passes at 95-percent level; and *passes at 90-percent level.

Appendix Table D.2: Standardized Parameter Estimates from Participation Models With Three Macroeconomic Variables

Vector/Variable	Gender-Neutral Network Variables		Gender-Specific Network Variables	
	Model 5.5	Model 5.6	Model 5.7	Model 5.8
Individual characteristics				
Age (in years)	0.7014***	0.8130***	0.7212***	0.8236***
Age squared	-1.4831***	-1.6085***	-1.5054***	-1.6186***
Female	-0.2361***	-0.2471***	-0.2359***	-0.2473***
Education (in years)	-0.0294***	-0.0320***	-0.0282***	-0.0295***
College educated	-0.0562***	-0.0573***	-0.0580***	-0.0590***
U.S. interview	0.2235***	0.2183***	0.2244***	0.2189***
U.S. migration experience (in months)	1.1529***	1.2148***	1.1603***	1.2138***
U.S. migration experience squared	-0.5692***	-0.6081***	-0.5739***	-0.6070***
Family responsibilities				
Married	0.0089	0.0167*	0.0070	0.0153*
Number of minor-age children	0.0119	0.0123	0.0119	0.0124
Single parent	-0.0006	0.0004	-0.0018	-0.0002
Single mother	0.0451***	0.0462***	0.0433***	0.0462***
Relatives with migration experience				
Grandparent	0.0372***	0.0166***	n.a.	n.a.
Grandfather	n.a.	n.a.	0.0342***	0.0141***
Grandmother	n.a.	n.a.	0.0091	-0.0024
Grandparent (gender not recorded)	n.a.	n.a.	0.0041	0.0065
Father	0.0646***	0.0196***	0.0669***	0.0188***
Mother	-0.0449***	-0.0232***	-0.0415***	-0.0217***

Appendix Table D.2 (continued)

Vector/Variable	Gender-Neutral Network Variables		Gender-Specific Network Variables	
	Model 5.5	Model 5.6	Model 5.7	Model 5.8
Relatives with migration experience (continued)				
Sibling	0.1477***	0.1263***	n.a.	n.a.
Brother	n.a.	n.a.	0.1364***	0.1193***
Sister	n.a.	n.a.	-0.0067	0.0067
Sibling (gender not recorded)	n.a.	n.a.	0.0228***	0.0174***
Relatives with migration experience when household head has not yet migrated				
Grandparent	-0.0463***	n.a.	n.a.	n.a.
Grandfather	n.a.	n.a.	-0.0447***	n.a.
Grandmother	n.a.	n.a.	-0.0195**	n.a.
Grandparent (gender not recorded)	n.a.	n.a.	0.0021	n.a.
Father	-0.1036***	n.a.	-0.1088***	n.a.
Mother	0.0385***	n.a.	0.0353***	n.a.
Sibling	-0.0561***	n.a.	n.a.	n.a.
Brother	n.a.	n.a.	-0.0468***	n.a.
Sister	n.a.	n.a.	0.0255***	n.a.
Sibling (gender not recorded)	n.a.	n.a.	-0.0118	n.a.
Immigration status and policies				
Legal U.S. resident	0.1972***	0.2033***	0.1988***	0.2032***
U.S. citizen	-0.0189***	-0.0186***	-0.0172***	-0.0175***
Bracero Program (1944-64)	0.2196***	0.2226***	0.2201***	0.2221***
Amnesty Program (1988-89)	-0.0092	-0.0086	-0.0089	-0.0085
Western Hemisphere favored (1968-76)	0.2050***	0.2049***	0.2067***	0.2061***

Appendix Table D.2 (continued)

Vector/Variable	Gender-Neutral Network Variables		Gender-Specific Network Variables	
	Model 5.5	Model 5.6	Model 5.7	Model 5.8
Immigration status and policies (continued)				
Similar treatment of hemispheres (1977-91)	0.2632***	0.2669***	0.2667***	0.2682***
Immigration Act of 1990 (1992-94)	0.0561***	0.0563***	0.0573***	0.0565***
Deportation ratio	0.0390***	0.0406***	0.0392***	0.0405***
Additional income sources				
Number of adult offspring	0.0816***	0.0867***	0.0809***	0.0860***
Agricultural land (in hectares)	-0.1595***	-0.1568***	-0.1585***	-0.1565***
Business ownership	-0.1464***	-0.1488***	-0.1465***	-0.1490***
National economic conditions				
Binational income ratio	-0.0225**	-0.0209**	-0.0233**	-0.0219**
Real per capita growth in Mexico	0.0223***	0.0218***	0.0223***	0.0218***
Real per capita growth in U.S.	-0.0121*	-0.0136**	-0.0121*	-0.0134*
Log-likelihood (intercept and covariates)	-30,709.71	-30,891.42	-30,717.94	-30,897.25

Results for community dummy variables are not reported.

Results of Wald Chi-squared test on significance of parameter estimate:

***Passes at 99-percent level; **passes at 95-percent level; and *passes at 90-percent level.

Variables Used in Chapters 4-6 and Their Sources

Unless otherwise indicated, the variables are drawn from the data set LIFEFILE of the Mexican Migration Project.

Dependent variables:

Migration decision—Dummy variable that equals one if the head of household resided in the United States during any part of year *t* and zero otherwise

Length of Mexican spell—Length of the head of household's Mexican spell of residence, in months

Length of U.S. spell—Length of the head of household's U.S. spell of residence, in months

Independent variables:

Age—Head of household's age in year *t*, in years

Agricultural land—Number of hectares of agricultural land belonging to the household in year *t*

Amnesty Program (1987-88)—Dummy variable that equals one if the year was 1987 or 1988 (the first two years following the enactment of IRCA) and zero otherwise

Bracero—Dummy variable that equals one if the head of household was a Bracero in year *t* and zero otherwise

Bracero Program (1944-64)—Dummy variable that equals one if the Bracero Program was in effect in year *t* and zero otherwise

Business ownership—Dummy variable that equals one if the household owned a business in year *t* and zero otherwise

College educated—Dummy variable that equals one if the head of household has received any education beyond the *preparatoria* (high school); otherwise, the variable equals zero

Community variables—Vector of dummy variables that equal one if head of household is from the specified survey community and zero otherwise (see Table 4.1 for community codes)

Deportation ratio—Ratio of the number of deportable aliens from Mexico apprehended by the INS to Mexico's population in year *t* [number of deportable aliens obtained from INS, *Statistical Yearbook of the Immigration and Naturalization Service*, various issues; population for 1905-49 obtained from Appendix E in Reynolds (1970); population for 1950-94 obtained from *International Financial Statistics*, various issues]

Education—Years of education obtained by the head of household, as of year *t*

Female—Dummy variable that equals one if the head of household is female and zero otherwise

Immigration Act of 1990 (1992-94)—Dummy variable that equals one if the year was greater than or equal to 1992 and less than or equal to 1994; otherwise, the variable equals zero

Legal U.S. resident—Dummy variable that equals one if the head of household possesses the immigration status of legal resident in the United States in year *t* and zero otherwise; legal residency includes U.S. citizenship, the possession of a Green Card or a Silva Card, and amnesty obtained under the provisions of IRCA

Married—Dummy variable that equals one if the head of household was married in year *t* and zero otherwise

Migration networks (family migration experience):

Any relative—Dummy variable that equals one if any person among the head of household's parents, siblings, or grandparents had U.S. migration experience as of year t and zero otherwise

Brother—Dummy variable that equals one if the head of household's brother had U.S. migration experience as of year t and zero otherwise

Father—Dummy variable that equals one if the head of household's father migrated to the United States as of year t and zero otherwise

Grandfather—Dummy variable that equals one if at least one grandfather of the head of household had U.S. migration experience as of year t and zero otherwise

Grandmother—Dummy variable that equals one if at least one grandmother of the head of household had U.S. migration experience as of year t and zero otherwise

Grandparent—Dummy variable that equals one if at least one grandparent of the head of household migrated to the United States as of year t and zero otherwise

Grandparent (gender not recorded)—Dummy variable that equals one if at least one grandparent whose gender was not recorded migrated to the United States as of year t and zero otherwise; this variable cannot equal one when both the variables for grandmother and grandfather equal one

Mother—Dummy variable that equals one if the head of household's mother had U.S. migration experience as of year t and zero otherwise

Sibling—Dummy variable that equals one if at least one sibling of the head of household had U.S. migration experience as of year t and zero otherwise

Sibling (gender not recorded)—Dummy variable that equals one if at least one sibling whose gender was not recorded migrated to the United States as of year t and zero otherwise; this variable cannot equal one when both the variables for brother and sister equal one

Sister—Dummy variable that equals one if at least one sister of the head of household had U.S. migration experience as of year *t* and zero otherwise

Migration networks when head of household has no U.S. experience:

A second set of the network variables listed above was interacted with a dummy variable that equals one if the head of household has no U.S. migration experience and zero otherwise

Number of adult offspring—Number of adult offspring of the head of household, as of year *t*

Number of minor-age children—Number of minor-age children of the head of household as of year *t*

Real per capita GDP in Mexico—Real per capita income of Mexico in year *t* , in U.S. dollars [for 1950-94, calculated using GDP and population figures in IMF, *International Financial Statistics*; various issues; for 1905-49, calculated using GNP data in Pérez López (1967) and population data in Appendix E of Reynolds (1970)]

Real per capita GDP in U.S.—Real per capita income of the United States in year *t* , in U.S. dollars [for 1950-94, calculated using GDP and population figures in IMF, *International Financial Statistics*, various issues; for 1905-49, calculated using GNP data and population figures in Bordo and Jonung (1991)]

Real per capita growth in Mexico—Growth rate of real per capita income of Mexico (as measured in U.S. dollars) in year *t* [for 1950-95, calculated using GDP and population figures in IMF, *International Financial Statistics*, various issues; for 1905-49, calculated using GNP data in Pérez López (1967) and population data in Appendix E of Reynolds (1970)]

Real per capita growth in U.S.—Growth rate of real per capita income of the United States in year *t* [for 1950-94, calculated using GDP and population figures in IMF, *International Financial Statistics*, various issues; for 1905-49, calculated using GNP and population figures in Bordo and Jonung (1991)]

Single mother—Dummy variable that equals one if the head of household was a single mother and zero otherwise; single parenthood is defined as having one or more minor-age children without being married or involved in a common-law relationship

Single parent—Dummy variable that equals one if the head of household was a single parent in year t and zero otherwise; single parenthood is defined as having one or more minor-age children without being married or involved in a common-law relationship

Similar treatment of hemispheres (1977-91)—Dummy variable that equals one if the year was greater than or equal to 1977 and less than or equal to 1991; otherwise, the variable equals zero

U.S. citizen—Dummy variable that equals one if the head of household was a U.S. citizen in year t and zero otherwise

U.S. migration experience—Cumulative total of head of household's U.S. migration experience prior to year t, in months

U.S. interview—Dummy variable that equals one if the interview took place in United States and zero otherwise

Western Hemisphere favored (1968-76)—Dummy variable that equals one if year is greater than or equal to 1968 and less than or equal to 1976; otherwise, the variable equals zero

Variables Used in Chapter 7 and Their Sources

Dependent variables:

Interview location—Dummy variable that equals one if the head of household was interviewed in Mexico and zero otherwise (HOUSFILE)

Monthly earnings—Head of household's monthly earnings, in 1994 Mexican new pesos (HOUSFILE)

Independent variables:

Age—Head of household's age, in years (PERSFILE)

Age at first migration experience—Age at which the head of household first migrated to the United States or, for non-migrants, age at the time of the interview; in years (PERSFILE)

Agricultural land—Number of hectares of agricultural land belonging to the household (HOUSFILE)

Agricultural land and U.S. experience—Number of hectares of agricultural land belonging to households headed by persons with U.S. migration experience; the variable equals zero if the head of household has no such experience (HOUSFILE and PERSFILE)

Business ownership—Dummy variable that equals one if the household owns a business and zero otherwise (HOUSFILE)

Business ownership and U.S. experience—Dummy variable that equals one if the head of household has U.S. migration experience and owns a business; otherwise, the variable equals zero (HOUSFILE and PERSFILE)

College educated—Dummy variable that equals one if the head of household has received any education beyond the *preparatoria* (high school); otherwise, the variable equals zero

Community variables—Vector of dummy variables that equal one if the head of household is from the specified community and zero otherwise (HOUSFILE; see Table 4.1 for community codes)

Education—Years of education obtained by the head of household (PERSFILE)

Education and U.S. experience—Number of years of education obtained by those heads of household with U.S. migration experience; the variable equals zero for heads of household who have never migrated to the United States (PERSFILE)

Father with prior migration experience—Dummy variable that equals one if the individual's father migrated to United States prior to head of household's first U.S. migration experience; otherwise, the variable equals zero (PERSFILE)

Female—Dummy variable that equals one if the head of household is female and zero otherwise (PERSFILE)

Inverse Mills ratio—Inverse of Mills ratio generated by the corresponding probit model

Legal resident of U.S.—Dummy variable that equals one if the head of household possesses the immigration status of legal resident in the United States and zero otherwise; legal residency includes U.S. citizenship, the possession of a Green Card or a Silva Card, and amnesty obtained under the provisions of IRCA (PERSFILE)

Married—Dummy variable that equals one if the head of household is married and zero otherwise (PERSFILE)

Migration network—Dummy variable that equals one if any close friend or relative of the household head lived in the United States at time of interview and zero otherwise; relatives include parents, grandparents, siblings, aunts and uncles, cousins, nephews and nieces, and mothers-, fathers-, brothers-, and sisters-in-law (PERSFILE)

Number of non-workers in household—(HOUSFILE)

Occupational variables:

Agricultural worker—Dummy variable that equals one if the individual works in agriculture and zero otherwise (HOUSFILE)

Industrial owner or supervisor—Dummy variable that equals one if the individual works as an industrial owner or supervisor; otherwise, the variable equals zero (HOUSFILE)

Irregularly employed—Dummy variable that equals one if the individual identified self as a housewife, student, or retiree, looking for work, or incapacitated but still worked outside the home; otherwise, the variable equals zero (HOUSFILE)

Office worker or nonmanual worker—Dummy variable that equals one if the individual works as office worker or in unspecified nonmanual occupation; otherwise, the variable equals zero (HOUSFILE)

Salesperson—Dummy variable that equals one if the individual works as a salesperson and zero otherwise (HOUSFILE)

Service industry—Dummy variable that equals one if the individual works in a service industry or if the occupation is unknown; otherwise, the variable equals zero (HOUSFILE)

Skilled manual worker—Dummy variable that equals one if the individual works as a skilled manual worker and zero otherwise (HOUSFILE)

Technician—Dummy variable that equals one if the individual works as technician and zero otherwise (HOUSFILE)

Unskilled manual worker—Dummy variable that equals one if the individual works as an unskilled manual worker and zero otherwise (HOUSFILE)

Sibling with prior migration experience—Dummy variable that equals one if any of the individual's siblings migrated to the United States prior to the individual's first U.S. migration experience; otherwise, the variable equals zero (PERSFILE)

Spouse works—Dummy variable that equals one if the individual's spouse works outside home and zero otherwise (HOUSFILE)

U.S. migration experience—Total U.S. migration experience of the individual, in years (PERSFILE)

Number of workers in household—(HOUSFILE)

Supplemental Table to Chapter 7

Appendix Table G.1: Results from First Stage of Two-Stage Least-Squares Earnings Regressions

Vector/Variable	Both Genders		Males Only	
	Model 7.1d	Model 7.2d	Model 7.3d	Model 7.4d
Intercept	-18.6490***	-17.5296***	-20.0063***	-19.3327***
Individual Characteristics				
Age	0.8557***	0.9093***	0.9082***	0.9775***
Age squared	-0.0068***	-0.0074***	-0.0076***	-0.0083***
Age at first U.S. migration experience (or age)	-0.3455***	-0.4017***	-0.3265***	-0.3874***
Age at first U.S. experience squared (or age squared)	-0.0012	-0.0006	-0.0016	-0.0010
Female	0.3423	1.0972	n.a.	n.a.
Education (in years)	-0.0056	-0.0739	0.00868	-0.0575
College educated	-0.411	0.1026	-0.7387	-0.2369
Family Responsibilities				
Married	1.1250	1.7254**	1.3475	2.1125**
Number of nonworkers in household	0.0581**	0.0891	0.0716**	0.0956
Additional Income Sources				
Business ownership	0.5179	0.5977*	0.5304	0.5379
Agricultural land (in hectares)	-0.0017	-0.0036	-0.0013	-0.0025
Spouse works	-1.4096***	-1.5869***	-1.3749***	-1.5565***
Number of workers in household	-0.1105**	-0.0596	-0.0940	-0.0266

Appendix Table G.1 (continued)

Vector/Variable	Both Genders		Males Only	
	Model 7.1d	Model 7.2d	Model 7.3d	Model 7.4d
Relative with U.S. experience that predates first U.S. experience of household head				
Father	0.5961**	0.5638*	0.5787*	0.5268*
Any sibling	0.4153*	0.3026	0.4749*	0.3264
Inverse Mills ratio	8.2009***	9.7544***	8.0778***	9.6834***
Occupational Variables				
Irregularly employed	4.1102***	3.6958***	5.0892***	4.6462***
Technician	-1.1086	-0.9093	-1.1250	-0.8946
Office worker or nonmanual worker	0.6238	0.3008	0.7683	0.4020
Salesperson	1.7060**	1.7252**	1.6429**	1.6536**
Industrial owner or supervisor	1.7309	0.8686	1.7892	0.8739
Skilled manual worker	2.0302***	1.9302***	2.0421***	1.9401***
Unskilled manual worker	2.6186***	2.1023***	2.6465***	2.1417***
Agricultural worker	2.8546***	3.0118***=	2.9565***	3.0805***
Service worker or unknown occupation	2.1421***	1.9283***	2.2538***	1.9891***
Scale parameter	4.6318	4.7654	4.6050	4.7531
N	2,767	2,767	2,552	2,552
Log-Likelihood	-3,460.01	-3,499.20	-3,330.66	-3,371.12

Results of Wald Chi-squared test on parameter estimate's significance:

***Passes at 99-percent level; **passes at 95-percent level; and *passes at 90-percent level.

Models 7.1d and 7.3d also include a vector of community dummy variables. The results for these variables are not reported.

Bibliography

Baltagi, Badi H. *Econometric Analysis of Panel Data.* Chichester, England: John Wiley & Sons, 1995.

Bordo, Michael, and Lars Jonung. "The Bretton Woods International Monetary System: An Historical Overview." Paper presented at the University of Colorado at Boulder, 1991.

Borjas, George J. *Friends or Strangers: The Impact of Immigrants on the U.S. Economy.* New York: Basic Books, 1990.

Chiswick, Barry R. "The Effect of Americanization on the Earnings of Foreign-born Men." *Journal of Political Economy,* Vol. 86, No. 5 (1978), pp. 897-921.

Cox, D.R., and D. Oakes. *Analysis of Survival Data.* London: Chapman and Hall, 1984.

García España, Juan Felipe. "Determinants of Internal and International Migration From Rural Areas of Mexico." Ph.D. dissertation, University of Pennsylvania, 1992.

Goldring, Luin. "Diversity and Community in Transnational Migration: A Comparative Study of Two Mexico-U.S. Migrant Circuits." Ph.D. dissertation, Cornell University, 1992.

Graves, Nancy B., and Theodore D. Graves. "Adaptive Strategies in Urban Migration." *Annual Review of Anthropology,* Vol. 3 (1974), pp. 117-151.

Graves, Philip E., and Thomas A. Knapp. "A Theory of International Migration Flows: United States Immigration From Mexico." *The Review of Regional Studies,* Vol. 14, No. 1 (Winter 1984), pp. 1-7.

Greene, William H. *Econometric Analysis.* Second Edition. New York: MacMillan Publishing Company, 1993.

Greenwood, Michael J. "An Analysis of the Determinants of Geographic Labor Mobility in the United States." *The Review of Economics and Statistics*, Vol. 51, No. 2 (May 1969), pp. 189-194.

————. "Lagged Response in the Decision to Migrate." *Journal of Regional Science*, Vol. 10, No. 3 (1970), pp. 375-384.

Hirabayashi, Lane Ryo. *Cultural Capital: Mountain Zapotec Migrant Associations in Mexico City*. Tucson: The University of Arizona Press, 1993.

Immigration and Naturalization Service (INS). *Statistical Yearbook of the Immigration and Naturalization Service*, various issues.

Kalbfleisch, J.D., and R.L. Prentice. *The Statistical Analysis of Failure Time Data*. New York: John Wiley and Sons, 1980.

Kiefer, Nicholas. "Economic Duration Data and Hazard Functions." *Journal of Economic Literature*, Vol. XXVI (June 1988), pp. 646-679.

Killingsworth, Mark R. *Labor Supply*. New York: Cambridge University Press, 1983.

Kossoudji, Sherrie A. "Playing Cat and Mouse at the U.S.-Mexican Border." *Demography*, Vol. 29, No. 2 (May 1992), pp. 159-180.

Lee, Elisa T. *Statistical Methods for Survival Data Analysis*. Second edition. New York: John Wiley and Sons, 1992.

MacDonald, John S., and Leatrice D. MacDonald. "Chain Migration, Ethnic Neighborhood Formation, and Social Networks." In Charles Tilly (ed.), *An Urban World*, (Boston: Little, Brown, 1974).

Martin, Philip L. *Trade and Migration: NAFTA and Agriculture*. Policy Analyses in International Economics, No. 38. Washington: Institute for International Economics, October 1993.

Massey, Douglas S. "Social Structure, Household Strategies, and the Cumulative Causation of Migration." *Population Index*, Vol. 56, No. 1 (Spring 1990), pp. 3-26.

Massey, Douglas S., Rafael Alarcón, Jorge Durand, and Humberto González. *Return to Aztlan: The Social Process of International Migration from Western Mexico*. Berkeley: University of California Press, 1987.

Massey, Douglas S., Joaquín Arango, Graeme Hugo, Ali Kouaouci, Adela Pellegrino, and J. Edward Taylor. "Theories of International Migration: A Review and Appraisal." *Population and Development Review*, Vol. 19, No. 3 (September 1993), pp. 431-466.

Massey, Douglas S., Joaquín Arango, Graeme Hugo, Ali Kouaouci, Adela Pellegrino, and J. Edward Taylor. "An Evaluation of International

Migration Theory: The North American Case." *Population and Development Review*, Vol. 20, No. 4 (December 1994), pp. 699-750.

Massey, Douglas S., and Felipe García España. "The Social Process of International Migration." *Science*, Vol. 237 (14 August 1987), pp. 733-738.

Massey, Douglas S., and Kristin Espinosa. "What's Driving Mexico-U.S. Migration?" *American Journal of Sociology*, Vol. 102, No. 4 (January 1997), pp. 939-999.

Massey, Douglas S., Luin Goldring, and Jorge Durand. "Continuities in Transnational Migration: An Analysis of Nineteen Mexican Communities." *American Journal of Sociology*, Vol. 99, No. 6 (May 1994), pp. 1492-1533.

Massey, Douglas S., and Emilio Parrado. "Migradollars: The Remittances and Savings of Mexican Migrants to the USA." *Population Research and Policy Review*, Vol. 13 (1994), pp. 3-30.

Mátyás, László, and Patrick Sevestre (eds.). *The Econometrics of Panel Data: Handbook of Theory and Applications*. Dordrecht: Kluwer Academic Publishers, 1992.

Nelson, Phillip. "Migration, Real Income, and Information." *Journal of Regional Science*, Vol. 1, No. 2 (Spring 1959), pp. 43-74.

Olea, Héctor Alonso. "The Economics of Undocumented Immigration: Mexican Participation in the U.S. Labor Market." Ph.D. dissertation, Rice University, 1988.

Pérez López, Enrique. "The National Product of Mexico: 1895 to 1964." In Pérez López, et al., *Mexico's Recent Economic Growth: The Mexican View* (Austin: The University of Texas Press, 1967), pp. 23-44.

Reynolds, Clark W. *The Mexican Economy: Twentieth-Century Structure and Growth.* New Haven: Yale University Press, 1970.

Secretaría de Relaciones Exteriores (SRE). "Programa Para Las Comunidades Mexicanas en el Extranjero." México, D.F.: SRE, October 1995.

Sjaastad, Larry A. "The Costs and Returns of Human Migration." *Journal of Political Economy*, Supplement, Vol. 70, No. 5, Part 2 (October 1962), pp. 80-93.

Sprouse, Terry Wayne. "Household Labor Decisions and Migration in San Luís Potosí, Mexico." Master's thesis, University of Arizona, 1991.

Taylor, J. Edward. "Undocumented Mexico-U.S. Migration and the Returns to Households in Rural Mexico." *American Journal of Agricultural Economics*, Vol. 69, No. 3 (August 1987), pp. 626-638.

————. "Migration Networks and Risk in Household Labor Decisions: A Study of Migration from Two Mexican Villages." Ph.D. dissertation, University of California, Berkeley, 1984.

Tilly, Charles, and C.H. Brown. "On Uprooting, Kinship, and the Auspices of Migration." *International Journal of Comparative Sociology*, Vol. 8 (1967), pp. 139-164.

Todaro, Michael P. "A Model of Labor Migration and Urban Unemployment in Less Developed Countries." *American Economic Review*, Vol. 59, No. 1 (March 1969), pp. 138-148.

United Nations. *World Population Prospects, The 1992 Revision*. New York: United Nations, 1993.

Verbeek, Marno, and Theo Nijman. "Incomplete Panels and Selection Bias." In László Mátyás and Patrick Sevestre (eds.), *The Econometrics of Panel Data: Handbook of Theory and Applications* (Dordrecht: Kluwer Academic Publishers, 1992), pp. 262-302.

Weintraub, Sidney. "Nafta Benefits Flow Back and Forth Across the Rio Grande." *Wall Street Journal*, 10 May 1996, p. A11.

White, Michael J., Frank D. Bean, and Thomas J. Espenshade. "The U.S. 1986 Immigration Reform and Control Act and Undocumented Migration to the United States." *Population Research and Policy Review*, Vol. 9 (1990), pp. 93-116.

Index

abuse of migrants, 16
accumulation of human capital:
  See human capital
adult offspring:
  absence of variable from
    earnings model, 128
  and head of household's
    migration decision, 74, 79, 92
  and head of household's
    migration spells, 111, 115-
    116, 122
  See also workers in household
AIDS, 94-96
age:
  of earliest economic decision
    making, 39-40
  of first migration:
    as predictor of total U.S.
      experience, 141
  of head of household:
    distribution in sample, 49
    lack of returns in San Ramon
      labor market, 148n. 1
    and Mexican earnings, 129,
      138, 144
    and migration decision, 75,
      77-78, 91, 97-98, 99, 151

and migration spells, 110,
    113-115
  as predictor of interview
    location, 132
  as proxy for work experience,
    129, 138, 144
agricultural land:
  and head of household's
    Mexican earnings, 131, 138-
    139, 145
  and head of household's
    migration decision, 72, 77, 90
  and head of household's
    migration spells, 111, 113,
    115-116, 122
  interaction term with U.S.
    experience, 131, 132, 138-
    139, 145
alcoholism, 16-17, Table 3.2, 29
Amnesty Program:
  See Immigration Reform and
    Control Act of 1986
aunts (of head of household):
  presence in U.S., 46, Table 4.3
border enforcement, 149
  and migration spells, 14, 155
  See also deportation ratio

Border Patrol, 81
borrowing money, 10, 28
Bracero Program, 149, 150
    and definition of legal
        residency, 41
    and formation of migration
        networks, 96, 150
    and head of household's
        migration decision, 80, 92, 97
    and head of household's
        migration spells, 111-112,
        113-115, 116, 122
"brain drain," 4
brothers (of head of household):
    and head of household's
        migration decision, 72, 83,
        96-97, 98-99, 150-151
business ownership:
    and head of household's
        Mexican earnings, 131, 135,
        138-139, 145, 148
    and head of household's
        migration decision, 74, 79, 92
    and head of household's
        migration spells, 111, 115-
        116, 122
    interaction term with U.S.
        experience, 131, 132, 135,
        138-139, 145
    as predictor of interview
        location, 135
cabecera, 36, 68n. 1
citizenship, U.S.:
    distribution in sample, 41
    and migration decision, 50, 80,
        92
college education:

and head of household's
    Mexican earnings, 135, 138
and head of household's
    migration decision, 78
community variables:
    and head of household's
        Mexican earnings, 132, 139-
        140
    and head of household's
        migration decision, 93
    as predictor of interview
        location, 135
communities:
    See survey communities
conclusions:
    duration model, 121-122
    earnings model, 145-148
    final, 149-156
    participation model, 98-99, 150-
        151, 152
coyotes:
    absence of variable in duration
        models, 108
    as cost of migration, 4, 10, 74,
        81, 156
    definition of, 4
Cristero Rebellion, 50
data sets:
    HOUSFILE, 36, 42, 43, 46, 49,
        54, 127
    LIFE26, 39, 40-41, 42, 43, 46-
        49, 49-54, 68, 72, 75, 84, 116
    LIFEFILE, 35, 39, 42, 43, 72,
        83, 84, 101-102
    PERSFILE, 36, 127
    survey communities in, 15-16,
        36-39, 40, 46
dependents:

See marital status, minor-age
children, non-workers in
household
deportation ratio:
and head of household's
migration decision, 81, 93
deportations, 10, 81
absence of variable from
duration models, 108
of legal residents, 80
duplicate interviews, 28
Durand, Jorge, 5, 15, 36, 46
duration model:
conclusions, 121-122
distributions, 103-104, Table
6.1, 113
econometric specification, 104-
108
explanatory variables, 103, 108-
113
hypotheses, 108-113
overview, 7
previous research, 108
results, 113-121
See also migration spells
earnings model:
conclusions, 145-148
econometric specification, 127
endogeneity of Mexican
earnings and U.S. experience,
126, 141, 145, 148
explanatory variables, 128-132
hypotheses, 128-132
measurement of Mexican
earnings, 126
Mills ratio, 125-126, 127, 131,
139, 140

ordinary least squares (OLS),
135-141, 144, 145
overview, 8
probit model, 127, 128, 132-
135, 140
results, 132, 135-148
selection bias, 8, 125-126, 126-
127, 131, 139, 140
tobit model, 141-144, 145
two-stage least squares (2SLS),
126, 141-145, Table 7.6
education:
distribution in sample, 49
and head of household's
Mexican earnings, 131, 138-
139, 145
and head of household's
migration spells, 110, 115
and head of household's
migration decision, 75, 78,
91-92
interaction term with U.S.
experience, 131, 132, 138-
139, 145
See also college education;
educational system, Mexican
educational system, Mexican, 40
ejidos, 13, 19n. 8
endogeneity of Mexican earnings
and U.S. experience:
See earnings model
entrepreneurs:
See business owners
experience:
See age, family migration
experience, migration
experience
family:

and migration, 10-11, 50-51
See also adult offspring, family
   migration experience, family
   reunification, marital status,
   migration experience, minor-
   age children, migration
   networks, non-workers in
   household
family migration experience:
   distribution in sample, **43-49**,
      151-152
   and head of household's first
      migration, 72, 82, 83, 93, 94,
      96, 98, 116-117, 121, 150
   and head of household's
      migration decision, 51-67,
      71-72, 81-83, 91, 93-97, 98-
      99, 150, 151
   and head of household's
      migration spells, 103, 112-
      113, 116-122, 150
   and head of household's repeat
      migration, 72, 82, 83, 93, 94,
      96, 98-99, 116-117, 121, 150
   measurement of, **42-43**, 72, 82-
      83, 91, 103, 112-113, 128,
      151
   as predictor of head of
      household's total U.S.
      experience, 141-143
   as predictor of interview
      location, 128, 135
   See also aunts, brothers, father,
      grandparents, mother,
      siblings, sisters, uncles,
      migration networks
family reunification, 155
farmland:

See agricultural land
father:
   of head of household:
      distribution of migration
         experience, 43, Table 4.2,
         46
      and head of household's
         migration decision, 51-54,
         Table 4.5, 68, 72, 82, 83,
         93-94, 96, 98, 117, 150-
         151
      and head of household's
         migration spells, 103, 113,
         117-121
      as predictor of head of
         household's total U.S.
         experience, 141-144
   See also single parents
female heads of household, **41-42**,
   77, 110, 126, 129, 138
   See also gender
fieldwork:
   in San Ramon, 5, 15, **21-29**, 32,
      33
   in U.S., **29-33**
first migration:
   and migration networks, 7, 72,
      82, 83, 93, 96, 98, 150
   and head of household's
      migration spells, 112-113,
      116-118, 121
   See also age of first migration
free labor agreement (proposed),
   122
friends:
   and migration, 10-11, 117
   See also migration experience
      of friends

gender:
distribution in sample, 41-42
and head of household's
Mexican earnings, 126, 129,
138, 140-141
and head of household's
migration decision, 49, 51,
68, 75, 77, 91, 97-98
and head of household's
migration spells, 110, 115,
117, 122
and Mexican Migration Project,
18, 33-34, 41-42
and migration networks, 46, 68,
96-97, 150-151
See also female heads of
household
grandparents (of head of
household):
distribution of migration
experience, 43, Table 4.2
and head of household's
migration decision, 51-54,
Table 4.8, 72, 82, 83, 93-94,
96, 98, 150
and head of household's
migration spells, 103, 113,
117-121
Greenwood, Michael J., 5, 12
guestworker program (proposed),
122, 123n. 5, 153
Hemispheres, Eastern and
Western:
differentiated treatment by U.S.
immigration law:
and head of household's
migration decision, 80-81,
92-93

HOUSFILE data set, 36, 42-43,
46, 49, 54, 127
housing census, 21-22
human capital, 3-4
accumulation during migration,
3-4, 125, 129, 135-138, 145,
156
definition of, 3
hypotheses:
duration model, 108-113
earnings model, 128-132
participation model, 75-84
Immigration Act of 1990, 155
Immigration and Naturalization
Service (INS), 10, 14, 30, 36,
43, 50, 81
immigration laws:
See border enforcement;
Bracero Program; family
reunification; Hemispheres,
Eastern and Western;
Immigration Act of 1990;
Immigration Reform and
Control Act of 1986
Immigration Reform and Control
Act of 1986 (IRCA), 149,
153, 155
and head of household's
migration decision, 80, 93
and head of household's
migration spells, 112, 116
immigration status:
See Bracero Program;
citizenship, U.S.; legal
residency in U.S.
interaction terms:

agricultural land and U.S.
experience, 131, 132, 138-
139, 145
business ownership and U.S.
experience, 131, 132, 135,
138-139, 145
education and U.S. experience,
131, 132, 138-139, 145
internal migration, 13
interview location (country):
distribution in sample, 41
and head of household's
migration decision, 75, 97
and head of household's
migration spells, 110, 115
interviews:
belligerent respondents, 29
duplicates, 28
elderly respondents, 27-28
frightened respondents, 29
hospitality of respondents, 27,
31
refusals, 22, 23, 24, Tables 3.2
to 3.3, 30, 31
in San Ramon, 6, **22-29**, 33
survey instrument, 26-27, 29, 30
in U.S., 6, **29-33**
See also interview location,
methodology
job contacts, 10-11
Kossoudji, Sherrie A., 14, 108,
155
land:
See agricultural land
Las Vegas, Nevada, 6, 16, 29, 30,
32
legal residency in U.S.:
definition of, 41

distribution in sample, 41, 49
and head of household's
migration decision, 50, 68,
80, 81, 92, 97, 99, 151
and head of household's
migration spells, 111, 116,
117, 122
and Immigration Reform and
Control Act of 1986, 155
as predictor of interview
location, 135
legalization dependents, 155
LIFE26 data set, **39**, 40-41, 42, 43,
46-49, 49-54, 68, 72, 75, 84,
116
LIFEFILE data set, **35**, 39, 42, 43,
72, 83, 84, 101-102
logit model, 7, 14, 74-75
See also multinomial logit
model, participation model
Los Angeles, California, 6, 11, 16,
29, 30, 32
macroeconomic conditions:
See national economic
conditions
marital status:
distribution in sample, 49
and head of household's
Mexican earnings, 129-131,
138
and head of household's
migration decision, 78-79, 99
and head of household's
migration spells, 110-111,
115
as predictor of interview
location, 132

Massey, Douglas S., 5, 11, 12, 14, 15, 36, 46, 68n. 2, 71, 72, 77, 79, 82, 92
methodology, **21-26, 29-30**, 103
  housing census, 21-22
  random sampling, 22, 29-30, 32
  selection bias, 29-30
  "snowball" sampling, 30, 32, 132
  strengths, 32, 33, 34
  survey instrument, 26-27, 29, 30, **Appendices A to B**
  weaknesses, 18, 32, 33, 34
  See also interviews
Mexican experience:
  See age
Mexican interviews:
  See interviews
Mexican Migration Project:
  data sets of, **35-36**, 39, 40-41, 42, 43, 72, 83, 84, 101-102, 126, 127
  and gender, **18, 33-34, 41**
  leadership of, 5, 36
  methodology of, **21-26, 29-30**, 103
  origins of, 36-39, 68n. 2
  research support of, 5, 12-13
  survey communities of, 15-16, **36-39**, 40, 46
  survey instrument of, 26, 33, **Appendix A**
Mexican Revolution, 50
Mexican spells:
  See duration model, migration spells
migration:

  See family migration experience, internal migration, migration decision, migration experience, migration networks, migration prevalence ratio, migration spells, motives for migration, "psychic costs" of migration
migration decision:
  distribution in sample, 49-54
  economic model of, 73-74
  and migration networks, **13-14, 51-68**
  See also motives for migration, participation model
migration experience, U.S.:
  of friends:
    distribution in sample, 46, Table 4.3, Table 4.9
    and head of household's migration decision, 54, Table 4.9, 68
    as predictor of interview location, 128, 135
  of head of household:
    distribution in sample, 49-68
    endogeneity with Mexican earnings, 126, 141, 145, 148
    and Mexican earnings, 8, 125, 129, 135, 140, 144-145, 148
    and migration decision, 49-68, 75, 78, 91, 97, 98, 99, 151
    and migration spells, 115, 122

See also aunts, brothers, father,
  grandparents, mother,
  siblings, sisters, uncles,
  family migration experience,
  migration networks,
  interaction terms
migration networks, **3-4, 9-13,**
  149-150
  "bad" migration networks, 16-
  17
  definition of, 3-4, 9
  distribution in sample, 43-49
  econometric evidence of, 13-14
  examples of, 3-4, 9
  and head of household's first
    migration, 7, 72, 82, 83, 93,
    94, 96, 98
  and head of household's
    migration decision, 7, 13, 51-
    68, 71-72, 81-83, 91, 93-97,
    98-99, 150, 151
  and head of household's
    migration spells, 7, 103, 112-
    113, 116-122, 150
  and head of household's repeat
    migration, 7, 72, 82, 83, 93,
    94, 96, 98-99
  functions of, 3-4, 9-11, 17-18,
    81-82, 117, 156
  gender differentiation of, 46, 68,
    96-97, 150-151
  and immigration laws, 155
  measurement of, 10, **15-17, 42-**
    43, 72, 82-83, 91, 103, 112-
    113, 128, 151
  and migration costs, 81-82, 156
  origins of concept, 12

as predictor of head of
  household's total U.S.
  experience, 141-144
as predictor of interview
  location, 128, 135
See also family migration
  experience
migration prevalence ratio, 15, 46
migration spells:
  and border enforcement, 14, 155
  measurement of, 39, 101-103
Mills ratio:
  See earnings model
minor-age children:
  absence of variable from
    earnings model, 128
  distribution in sample, 41, 42,
    49
  and head of household's
    migration decision, 50-51, 68,
    74, 78-79, 92, 99
  and head of household's
    migration spells, 110-111,
    115
  possible miscounting of, 39
  See also non-workers in
    household
mother:
  of head of household:
    distribution of migration
      experience, 43, Table 4.2,
      46
    and head of household's
      migration decision, 51-54,
      Table 4.6, 68, 72, 82, 83,
      96, 98, 99, 100, 101, 152-
      153

and head of household's
migration spells, 103, 113,
117-121
See also single parents
motives for migration:
accumulation of human capital,
125, 129, 135-138, 145, 156
adventure, 156
dependent children, 51
economic model, 73-74
finding a mate, 156
underemployment, 84
unemployment, 84
work, 84, 156
multinomial logit model, 13
municipios, 34n. 2, 36, 68n. 1
NAFTA, 28, 152-153
national economic conditions:
and head of household's
migration decision, 83-84, 97,
98, 99, 152, 153
non-workers in household:
and head of household's
Mexican earnings, 129-131,
138
as predictor of interview
location, 128, 132
North American Free Trade
Agreement (NAFTA), 28,
152-153
occupations, Mexican:
and Mexican earnings, 131-132,
139, 141
ordinary least squares (OLS):
See earnings model
paisanos, 9, 11, 16
parents:
of head of household:

distribution of migration
experience, 43, Table 4.2,
46
and head of household's
migration decision, 51-54,
Table 4.5 to 4.6, 68, 72, 83,
93-94, 96, 98, 150-151
and head of household's
migration spells, 103, 113,
117-121
See also single parents
participation model:
conclusions, 98-99, 150-151,
152
econometric specification, 74-
75
explanatory variables, 75-84
hypotheses, 75-84
logit model, 7, 74-75
overview, 7
previous research, 77, 78-79,
82, 91-92
results, 84-99, 150-151
theoretical model, 73-74
PERSFILE data set, 36, 127
"Peso Crisis" of 1994, 28, 153
polleros:
See coyotes
population growth, Mexican:
and migration, 151-152
prestamistas, 28, 34n. 5
prevalence ratio:
See migration prevalence ratio
primaria, 40
probit model, 13, 14
See also earnings model
Proposition 187, 28
"psychic costs" of migration, 11

random sampling, 22, 29-30, 32
refusals, 22, 23, 24, Tables 3.2 to
    3.4, 30, 31
rejections:
    See refusals
relative deprivation, 14
remittances, 9, 14, 17, 26-27
repeat migration:
    and head of household's
        migration spells, 112, 116-
        117, 121
    and migration networks, 7, 72,
        82, 83, 93-94, 96, 98-99, 150
research questions, 6-7
return migrants:
    Mexican earnings of, 125, 131,
        135, 139, 140, 144-148, 156
    See also earnings model,
        interaction terms
Salinas de Gortari, Carlos, 28-29
San Ramon, Colima, **5-6**
    buildings in, 22, 23, 28
    businesses in, 139
    characteristics of, 5-6, 33, 34n.
        2
    economic base of, 5-6
    fieldwork in, 5-6, 15, **21-29**, 33
    hospitality of its people, 27
    and internal migration, 13
    lack of returns to Mexican
        experience, 148n. 1
    life in, 28, 31, 33
    limited contact among siblings,
        15
    impressions of U.S., 24, 27, 28,
        94-96
    and Mexican earnings, 139-140

occupations of poorer
    respondents, 139
participation in migration, 93
    as predictor of interview
        location, 135
schooling:
    See education; educational
        system, Mexican
secundaria, 40
selection bias, 29-30, 125-126,
    126-127, 131, 139, 140
siblings:
    of head of household:
        distribution of migration
            experience, 43, Table 4.2,
            46
        and head of household's
            migration decision, 51-54,
            Table 4.7, 72, 82, 83, 93-
            94, 96-97, 98-99, 150-151
        and head of household's
            migration spells, 103, 113,
            117, 121, 150
        as predictor of head of
            household's total U.S.
            experience, 141-144
        limited contact among, 15
    See also brothers, sisters
single parents:
    distribution in sample, 42
    and migration decision, 51, 78-
        79, 92
    and migration spells, 110-111,
        113, 115
sisters (of head of household):
    and head of household's
        migration decision, 72, 83,
        96, 97, 150-151

See also siblings

"snowball" sampling, 30, 32, 132

spells of residence:
See duration model, migration spells

spousal employment:
and head of household's Mexican earnings, 131, 135, 138
as predictor of interview location, 128, 135

Sprouse, Terry Wayne, 13, 17, 77, 79, 91, 92

survey communities, 15-16, **36-39**, 40, 46

survey instrument:
addendum to basic instrument, 26-27, 29, 30, 33, **Appendix B**
of Mexican Migration Project, 26, 33, **Appendix A**

Taylor, J. Edward, 13, 14, 17, 77, 79, 91, 92, 126

tobit model:
See earnings model

two-stage least squares (2SLS):
See earnings model

uncles (of head of household):
job contacts, 10
presence in U.S., 46, Table 4.3

undocumented workers, 16

United States of America:
Mexican impressions of, 24, 27, 28, 94-96, 150

U.S. citizenship:
See citizenship, U.S.

U.S. interviews:
See interviews

U.S. migration spells:
See duration model, migration spells

welfare, 156

workers (in household):
and head of household's Mexican earnings, 131
as predictor of interview location, 128